T0031783

ONE
DAY
NEARER

STEVE MILLER

HARVEST PROPHECY
An Imprint of Harvest House Publishers

Unless otherwise indicated, all Scripture verses are taken from the ESV® Bible (The Holy Bible, English Standard Version®), copyright © 2001 by Crossway, a publishing ministry of Good News Publishers. Used by permission. All rights reserved.

Verses marked NASB are taken from the (NASB®) New American Standard Bible®, Copyright © 1960, 1971, 1977, 1995, 2020 by The Lockman Foundation. Used by permission. All rights reserved. www.lockman.org.

Verses marked NIV are taken from the Holy Bible, New International Version®, NIV®. Copyright © 1973, 1978, 1984, 2011 by Biblica, Inc.™ Used by permission of Zondervan. All rights reserved worldwide. www.zondervan.com. The "NIV" and "New International Version" are trademarks registered in the United States Patent and Trademark Office by Biblica, Inc.™

Verses marked NKJV are taken from the New King James Version®. Copyright © 1982 by Thomas Nelson. Used by permission. All rights reserved.

Scripture verses marked NLT are taken from the Holy Bible, New Living Translation, copyright © 1996, 2004, 2015 by Tyndale House Foundation. Used by permission of Tyndale House Publishers, Inc., Carol Stream, Illinois 60188. All rights reserved.

All italics in Scripture verses are author's emphasis.

Cover design by Bryce Williamson

Cover photos © Kykyshka / Getty Images; Evgeniya Litovchenko / Shutterstock

Interior design by KUHN Design Group

For bulk, special sales, or ministry purchases, please call 1-800-547-8979.
Email: Customerservice@hhpbooks.com

This logo is a federally registered trademark of the Hawkins Children's LLC. Harvest House Publishers, Inc., is the exclusive licensee of this trademark.

One Day Nearer
Copyright © 2023 by Steve Miller
Published by Harvest House Publishers
Eugene, Oregon 97408
www.harvesthousepublishers.com

ISBN 978-0-7369-8485-0 (pbk)
ISBN 978-0-7369-8486-7 (eBook)

Library of Congress Control Number: 2023934163

All rights reserved. No part of this publication may be reproduced, stored in a retrieval system, or transmitted in any form or by any means—electronic, mechanical, digital, photocopy, recording, or any other—except for brief quotations in printed reviews, without the prior permission of the publisher.

Printed in the United States of America

23 24 25 26 27 28 29 30 31 / LB / 10 9 8 7 6 5 4 3 2 1

The grace of God has appeared, bringing salvation for all people, training us to renounce ungodliness and worldly passions, and to live self-controlled, upright, and godly lives in the present age, waiting for our blessed hope, the appearing of the glory of our great God and Savior Jesus Christ.

TITUS 2:11-13

ACKNOWLEDGMENTS

With a grateful heart to...
   my mom, who chose to give me life and gave her all.
   my sister, God's ideal choice of a sibling.
   Debby Stone, whom God used providentially to point me
      to a lifetime in Christian publishing.
         We're one day nearer to that great reunion in heaven.

At Harvest House Publishers, with thanks to...
   Bob Hawkins for his passion for truth, integrity,
      and Bible prophecy.
   Nate Miller for his excellent editorial work.
   Kim Moore for her oversight of the editorial process.
   Georgia Varozza, Rosalie Krusemark, and Cindi McMenamin
      for their great proofing skills.

And...
   to my wife, who said yes.
   to my three sons, their wives, and three grandchildren
      for bringing me such great joy.
   to the Lord for His infinite greatness in all who He is.

CONTENTS

> The end times are rapidly approaching. Our Lord has called us to be watchful and faithful, using our time well and making our lives count for eternity. The better we know God's purposes for the future, the more we are able to live wisely today.

> The best way to get a clear understanding of the future is to know God's grand purposes for all time. We were created to fellowship with God and live eternally. Yet on that fateful day when sin entered the Garden of Eden, we were separated from God and destined for eternity apart from Him. From that moment onward, God revealed, through many prophecies, His plans for rescuing us and restoring His creation. As we see Bible prophecy unfold from Genesis to Revelation, we come to realize how great God is, how much He loves us, and how wonderful of a future He has in store for us.

GROWING IN OUR LOVE
FOR CHRIST AND HIS RETURN

With every rising and setting of the sun, we draw one day nearer to the return of our Lord Jesus Christ. Every believer should look forward to His triumphant coming with eagerness because of what it means to this world and to all who love the Lord. On that day, all the imperfect kingdoms of mankind will be swept aside and replaced by His perfect kingdom. At long last, the government will rightfully be on the shoulders of the one who created and owns this universe, and He will rule over all with perfect wisdom and righteousness and love. As the King of kings and Lord of lords, He will bring about a global kingdom that is heaven on earth. For the first time since Adam and Eve fell into sin, true peace will exist because He is the Prince of Peace.

No longer will Satan be the "ruler of this world" (John 12:31). No longer will evil and its effects plague us. Scripture tells us that during Christ's earthly kingdom, "the earth will be filled with the knowledge of the glory of the LORD" (Habakkuk 2:14). People will know "gladness and joy, and sorrow and sighing shall flee away" (Isaiah 35:10). Even all the animals will know harmony at last—the lamb will lie down with the lion (Isaiah 11:6).

With Christ on His throne in Jerusalem, we will experience our first taste of life as God meant for it to be. Our existence will no longer be defined by struggles with sin, trials, pain, and mortality. Instead, it will be defined by light, love, and the joy of serving alongside the Lord as He rules. Life under Christ's reign will be far greater and more fulfilling than we anticipate.

An even brighter future awaits us as we make the transition from Christ's millennial kingdom to the new heavens and earth. The final chapters of the book of Revelation describe the glories of paradise restored—of eternity in God's presence, and every tear wiped away from our eyes. Life in heaven will be more heavenly than we can imagine.

As Christians, we are children of a king whose kingdom is not yet here. The devotions in this book have been written with the hope that, with each day that goes by, our love for Christ and our eagerness for His return will magnify. As we grow in our knowledge of the Lord and His plans for our future, may our desires for the things of earth diminish and be replaced by increasingly fervent longings for the things of heaven.

—*Steve Miller*

PART 1:

LIVING WISELY IN THESE LAST DAYS

THE PURPOSES OF BIBLE PROPHECY #1: TO GIVE HOPE

The Lord himself will descend from heaven with a cry of command...Then we...will be caught up...in the clouds to meet the Lord in the air...Therefore encourage one another with these words (1 Thessalonians 4:16-18).

I magine the Bible with no prophecies in it. Suppose God had decided not to tell us anything about the second coming, ultimate victory over evil, and our future home in heaven and eternity. If God had left prophecies out of His Word, we would have no idea of what the future holds. Instead, all we would know is that the world we live in is descending deeper and deeper into darkness, evil, and hopelessness.

With no knowledge of what is to come, life would be bleak. We would have nothing to look forward to. We would go from day to day filled with dread and uncertainty.

But because God chose to provide us with glimpses of the glorious future that awaits us, we can live with hope. That is a major reason God filled the Bible with so many prophecies about what is to come: to give us hope.

What we know about the *future* helps to influence our thoughts and actions in the *present*. Because we know the ultimate outcome of the battle now being waged on earth, we can live with anticipation rather than angst. Bible prophecy helps us to have an eternal focus—it reminds us that no matter how bad things get, good and righteousness *will* prevail. Victory *is* certain.

That is why, in 1 Thessalonians 4, Paul wrote at length about the promised rapture that will deliver us from this world and take us to heaven. He concluded with the exhortation that we "encourage one another with these words" (verse 18). The more we remind each other of God's prophetic promises, the more we give one another hope.

THE PURPOSES OF BIBLE PROPHECY #2: TO GIVE US AN ETERNAL FOCUS

The sufferings of this present time are not worth comparing with the glory that is to be revealed to us (Romans 8:18).

Because we live in a fallen world, life is filled with struggles. Romans 5:12 says that "sin came into the world through one man, and so death spread to all men because all sinned." No one can avoid sin and its devastating consequences. Even "creation [is] subjected to futility"— all of nature is in "bondage to corruption." It groans in anticipation of the day when we are freed from our decaying mortal bodies and given new, immortal bodies (Romans 8:19-23).

Sin is the reason that life is filled with pain and trials. And after we receive salvation in Christ, we enter a new kind of battle. Because we have turned away from sin to walk in the light, we are now at odds with the darkness around us. Jesus warned the disciples—and us, by extension—that "in the world you will have tribulation" (John 16:33).

But notice Jesus' very next words: "Take heart; I have overcome the world." In our times of suffering, we can find hope in the Lord's promises of future redemption and victory. Even when life becomes so unbearable we don't know how we can possibly go on, we are reminded that "the sufferings of this present time are not worth comparing with the glory that is to be revealed to us."

God's promises about the future are meant to help us look beyond the present and develop an eternal focus. As we learn what it means to live with our minds and hearts set on eternity, we are more able to persevere through the difficulties we face now. Every prophecy about the future is designed to keep us looking up and ahead at the glory that awaits us.

THE PURPOSES OF BIBLE PROPHECY #3: TO MOTIVATE US TO PURITY

We know that when [Christ] appears we shall be
like him…And everyone who thus hopes in him
purifies himself as he is pure (1 John 3:2-3).

One of the most amazing truths in Scripture is that someday, we will be fully transformed into the likeness of Christ.

Because we dwell in imperfect bodies in a fallen world, we are not able to fully grasp what we will become. As the apostle Paul wrote, "for now we see in a mirror dimly" (1 Corinthians 13:12). There is coming a day when we will see clearly—when "the perishable puts on the imperishable, and the mortal puts on immortality" (1 Corinthians 15:54). At long last, we will be conformed to the image of God's Son (Romans 8:29).

We eagerly look forward to that day, don't we? We tire of succumbing to temptation and stumbling into sin. We become increasingly frustrated as we fight the same spiritual battles over and over. With Paul, we say, "I have the desire to do what is right, but not the ability to carry it out…I do not do the good I want" (Romans 7:18-19).

When we struggle with sin, the prophetic promise that we will someday have glorified bodies and be like Christ is uplifting. This hope not only keeps us going, it also motivates us to personal purity. As 1 John 3:3 says, "Everyone who thus hopes in him purifies himself as he is pure."

As we fix our hope on the promise that we will be transformed to Christlikeness in the future, the result is that we will want to be more like Him in the present. In this way, Bible prophecy has a powerful and sanctifying effect on our lives.

THE PURPOSES OF BIBLE PROPHECY #4: TO SPUR US TO SHARE THE GOSPEL

We must work the works of him who sent me while it is day;
night is coming, when no one can work (John 9:4).

Time is running out. Each day that we draw nearer to Christ's second coming, we draw closer to when it will be too late for unbelievers to receive Jesus as their Savior. When the King of kings and Lord of lords descends from heaven to reclaim the earth, He will wield "a sharp sword with which to strike down the nations" (Revelation 19:15). On that day, every unbeliever on earth will have their eternal fate sealed.

Now, it is true that after Christ raptures all believers to heaven, the seven-year tribulation will offer more time for unbelievers to come to salvation. We might think, *If my loved one or friend doesn't become a Christian before the rapture, they will still have opportunities during the tribulation.*

But consider the dismal survival rates of those who end up being on earth during the tribulation. In Revelation 6:7-8, we are told that one-fourth of the world's population will die during the fourth seal judgment. Then in Revelation 9:15-18, we read about four angels who will "kill a third of mankind." Between those two events alone, nearly half the people on earth will die. Also, many people will be so hardhearted that even when they recognize God as the source of the tribulation judgments, they will call for the rocks and mountains to fall upon them rather than turn from their sin (Revelation 6:15-17).

When it comes to sharing the gospel, sooner is better than later. The fact we don't know the time of Christ's coming should fill us with a sense of urgency. God's desire is that Bible prophecy will spur us to proclaim the message of salvation before it's too late.

THE PURPOSES OF BIBLE PROPHECY #5: TO CONFIRM THAT GOD IS GOD

*I am God, and there is no other; I am God, and there is
none like me, declaring the end from the beginning and
from ancient times things not yet done (Isaiah 46:9-10).*

Only God is able to declare "the end from the beginning." And not
only does He *know* the future, He *plans* it. In the above passage
from Isaiah, He goes on to say, "I will accomplish all my purpose...I
will bring it to pass; I have purposed, and I will do it" (Isaiah 46:10-11).

Those aren't just empty words. Up to this point in time, every one of
God's declarations about the future—in the form of Bible prophecies—
has come to pass with precision. This helps us to realize that prophecies
are not merely guesses or predictions; rather, they reveal exactly what
God will do. Prophecy is history written in advance.

The abundance of fulfilled prophecies serves as powerful confirmation that God truly is God. His sovereignty is total; nothing can alter
what He says will happen. He who created and sustains the universe
guides the course of human history and our individual lives. As chaos
swirls seemingly out of control here on earth, all is calm in God's throne
room. As surely as Jesus silenced the storm and the waves, God has all
world events in His hands.

Because every single prophecy about Christ's first coming was fulfilled literally with 100 percent accuracy, we can rest confident the same
will be true with every single prophecy about Christ's second coming.
There is coming a day when every wrong in this world will be righted—
for all eternity. Nothing can keep that from happening, because God
is God. Because His sovereignty is total, our heavenly future is secure.

A COMPLETE PANORAMA
OF BIBLE PROPHECY

Christ, having been offered once...
will appear a second time (Hebrews 9:28).

If we were to summarize the big picture of Bible prophecy from Genesis to Revelation, what would it look like? Here's a brief panoramic outline that takes us from Eden to eternity:

Christ will come to save the lost. As soon as Adam and Eve sinned, God promised that someday, a Savior would come who would bruise Satan's head. Satan won in Eden, but he would be defeated by Christ's death and resurrection, which makes our salvation possible.

The church will spread the gospel. Christ entrusted the disciples to proclaim the gospel and take it far and wide. The church will grow, yet also face persecution.

Israel will be reborn. God promised that before Christ's second coming, Israel will be reborn. This was necessary because Israel is the stage on which the end times will play out.

The church will be taken up in the rapture. Jesus promised that someday, He will come to take His own to be with Him in the Father's house (John 14:1-3). We will be delivered from the wrath to come (1 Thessalonians 1:10) and dwell with our Savior in heaven.

During the tribulation, God will bring judgment upon the world. In the end times, God will pour out His wrath. In mercy, He will also have the gospel proclaimed everywhere.

Christ will come again to establish His kingdom. When Christ returns, He will destroy His enemies and set up His millennial kingdom, in which we will live peacefully.

Christ will defeat Satan one last time before eternity. After 1,000 years, Satan will rebel one last time. Christ will crush Satan, cast him into the lake of fire, and judge all unbelievers.

God will bring forth the new heavens and new earth. This will usher in eternity, and we will dwell with God forever in perfect, peaceful bliss.

FOREVER FAITHFUL

O LORD God of hosts, who is mighty as you are, O LORD,
with your faithfulness all around you? (Psalm 89:8).

God always does what He says He will do. He is forever faithful, never forgetting a promise. The hundreds of prophecies in Scripture that have been fulfilled through the ages stand as a powerful testimony to His perfect faithfulness.

From our limited human perspective, we may have times when we feel as if God has forgotten us. As we face trials that appear to have no solution, we may find ourselves wrongly concluding that God isn't answering our prayers. When we wonder why God seems unresponsive, we can lean on the following truths and rest assured of God's faithfulness to us:

God's love and mercies are never-ending. Lamentations 3:22-23 says, "The steadfast love of the LORD never ceases; his mercies never come to an end; they are new every morning; great is your faithfulness." Every day begins with a new supply of God's goodness. Even when we cannot see how He is sustaining us, we have the promise that He is.

God's presence with you is constant. At all times, God is with you. It's impossible to escape His presence (Psalm 139:7-10). Nothing can remove us from His hand (John 10:28-29). In Matthew 28:20, Christ said, "I am with you always, to the end of the age."

God's promises will never fail. In 1 Kings 8:56, we read that of all God's promises to Israel, "not one word has failed." Because God's character is constant and unchanging, this truth applies to believers as well. God will keep every promise He has made to us. He is able to do so because He is fully sovereign over all things.

Though we can never be certain about life, we can always be certain about God. As Psalm 89:8 says, His faithfulness surrounds Him. And it surrounds you too.

THE OLD TESTAMENT'S
VALUE TO US TODAY

*Whatever was written in former days was written for our
instruction, that through endurance and through the encouragement
of the Scriptures we might have hope (Romans 15:4).*

Everything that God has communicated to us in the Old Testament—
including hundreds of Bible prophecies about the future—has great
value to us today. Here are three ways we are helped:

We gain knowledge about God and what He desires of us. The Old Testament was "written for our instruction" so that we would know how to live. As we see how God worked in the lives of His people and the ways they responded, we can grow in wisdom and maturity.

We learn the value of patience. It is "through endurance" that we learn to persevere. This is especially true about the Old Testament prophecies regarding God's plans for our future. We are told, "Be patient...until the coming of the Lord. See how the farmer waits for the precious fruit of the earth, being patient about it...You also be patient. Establish your hearts, for the coming of the Lord is at hand" (James 5:7-8). In this present day, we are constantly bombarded by trials and evil. When Christ returns, all that will change. Until then, we're to be patient.

We are encouraged and given hope. It is "through the encouragement of the Scriptures" that we "have hope." God's Word promises a bright future for us, and every reminder of that future helps to carry us through the hardships we face today. The psalmist wrote, "I hope for your salvation, O Lord" (Psalm 119:166). Scripture is filled with assurances of that coming great day when we will be delivered from all the effects of sin. Among the sad accounts of human failure in the Old Testament, we are given many prophetic infusions of hope.

The revelations God provided in the Old Testament were recorded for our benefit today. They edify us, teach us to endure, and remind us to await our glorious future with hope.

GOD'S PROPHETIC INVOLVEMENT IN YOUR LIFE

In your book were written, every one of them, the days that were
formed for me, when as yet there was none of them (Psalm 139:16).

A re you aware that God has prophetically planned out your entire life, from the time of your conception to the day of your death? That's what Psalm 139:16 says—your days "were written, every one of them" long before you existed. God wrote you into the master script of His plans for all things, and you have your special place, for purposes in accord with His will.

You might not feel like there is anything special about your life. But the very fact God ordained all your days so far in advance and determined when and where you would live is a clear indicator that He wanted you in certain places at certain times for certain reasons.

You might never get a clear sense of God's purposes for you, but to know that an all-wise and all-loving God cared about you to this extent should give you a confidence that you do have a special place in His plans. He desires to use you where He has placed you.

Perhaps you face circumstances that cause you to question God's design for your life. But even when you struggle with doubt or uncertainty about where you fit in God's purposes, a right response to Him will always be to lean not on your understanding, but to trust and submit to Him (Proverbs 3:5-6).

Ephesians 1:4-10 says that God thought of you even before the foundation of the world. He chose you to be His own so you could enjoy a redemption that is eternal. Not only did God prophetically determine your days on earth, but more importantly, He chose to lavish His grace on you so you could be with Him for all of eternity! He has plans for you here on earth, and greater plans for you in heaven. A love so great is worthy of every praise you can lift to Him.

EQUIPPED FOR EVERY GOOD WORK

All Scripture is given by inspiration of God, and is profitable
for doctrine, for reproof, for correction, for instruction in
righteousness, that the man of God may be complete, thoroughly
equipped for every good work (2 Timothy 3:16-17 NKJV).

More than one-fourth of Scripture is prophetic in nature. And because prophecy is part of "all Scripture," it is also profitable for doctrine, correction, and instruction. It's not just the instructive portions of God's Word that help thoroughly equip us, but the prophecies as well.

How so? Within Bible prophecies, we learn doctrines relating to God's character and promises. Prophetic shadows in the Old Testament reveal details about the coming sacrificial Lamb and His conquest of sin, informing us about salvation, redemption, and glorification.

Prophecies have also been given to help us discern truth from error. The same prophecies that prove Jesus is the Messiah also help us to reject all imposters. Some prophetic passages were given to alert us to false or incorrect teachings about the future.

Because prophecy exhorts us to be ready constantly for the rapture, we're motivated to righteous living. "Everyone who has this hope in Him purifies himself" (1 John 3:3).

Prophecy contributes to making us complete. In a world careening deeper into darkness, imagine not knowing what the future holds. We would live in fear rather than with confidence. We wouldn't know that in the end, sin will be crushed and righteousness will prevail.

Prophecy helps to equip us for every good work. When we live with our eyes on the future, we recognize the importance of living as salt and light and of building up one another as we see the day approaching. Prophecy also spurs us to share the gospel with unbelievers because we know the days are short—this is the greatest good work that Scripture equips us to do.

WALKING WISELY

Look carefully then how you walk, not as unwise but as wise, making the best use of the time, because the days are evil (Ephesians 5:15-16).

Scripture calls us to live the Christian life in a constant state of alertness. That's because the world we live in is a spiritual battlefield littered with landmines. If we're not careful, we can easily give in to temptations that weaken us or render us ineffective.

That is why we're admonished to "look carefully then how you walk." To "look carefully" is to be observant, to pay attention continually. We cannot afford to let down our guard even for a moment because we have an adversary who never rests. The urgency of this command becomes even more evident when we read that we are to be "making the best use of the time."

The word the apostle Paul used for "time" is not the Greek term *chronos*, which has to do with time measured in minutes or hours. Rather, it's *kairos*, which speaks of a fixed season or an allocated amount of time. God has predetermined our lifespan, which means a boundary has been set on the time we have for walking wisely. Once that time is gone, it's gone.

"How you walk" refers to our manner of life. Everything about us— our thoughts, our words, our actions—is part of our walk, or how we live. To walk wisely means to use our time well, for we have limited opportunity and great opposition.

The closer we are to our Lord's return and the worse evil becomes, the greater the urgency of the command to walk wisely. As we go through each day and seek to use our time well, we need to ask: *Am I walking wisely as I do this?* When we are diligent to exercise wisdom with each step we take, we will make the best use of the time God has given us.

REDEEMING THE TIME

See then that you walk circumspectly...redeeming the
time, because the days are evil (Ephesians 5:15-16 NKJV).

For the Christian, time is a precious commodity. God calls us to use it to prepare for eternity. The ways that we use our time reveal how much or little we care about eternity.

Let's look at Ephesians 5:15-16 again—this time in the New King James version, which uses the phrase "*redeeming* the time." Here, the Greek term *exagorazo* is translated "redeeming," which captures for us the literal meaning of "buying up" time. The use of "redeeming" here provides us with a wonderful picture of what it means to make the best use of our time.

Embedded in the term *exagorazo* is the word *agora*, which means "the marketplace." In the ancient world, marketplaces were open for only a limited amount of time. In rural areas, they were set up one day a week. Merchants would bring their goods for people to buy, and due to limited transportation capabilities, these goods were available in small quantities. The cooler hours of the morning were best for perishables, and it was not feasible to be open at night.

Because marketplace hours were so limited, buyers knew that good deals would not last long. Once a merchant ran out of goods, the opportunity to purchase them was gone. This made it necessary for people to buy what they could while it was available. This required thoughtful planning and preparation. If you missed out, you would have to wait another week for the marketplace to open again. In those days, that was a high price to pay.

Even Jesus recognized the need to redeem His time. In John 9:4, He said, "I must work the works of Him who sent Me while it is day; the night is coming when no one can work."

Time is limited. The more committed we are to walking wisely and using time well, the more we can make it count for eternity.

HOW TO REDEEM THE TIME

*Be constantly taking heed therefore how accurately you are
conducting yourselves, not as unwise ones but as wise ones,
buying up for yourselves the opportune time, because the days
are pernicious (Wuest's translation of Ephesians 5:15-16).*

Greek scholar Kenneth Wuest provides us with great insight for what it means to redeem the time. He defines this as "making a wise and sacred use of every opportunity for doing good."[1]

Wuest's use of the word *sacred* helps to sharpen our thinking. Ultimately, the time we have been given here on earth can be used in two ways: sacred, or not. For God's purposes, or earthly. We can make our time count for eternity or waste it on the temporal.

The Puritan Thomas Brooke put it this way: "Time is a jewel [of] more worth than a world. Time is not yours to dispose of as you please; it is a glorious talent that men must be accountable for as well as any other talent."

Brooke then said we "have much work to do in a short time: your souls to save, a God to honour, a Christ to exalt, a hell to escape, a race to run, a crown to win, temptations to withstand, corruptions to conquer, afflictions to bear, mercies to improve, and your generation to serve."[2] Here, Brooke lists nearly a dozen responsibilities related to redeeming our time well—every one of them sacred. With careful thought, we can add more to his list.

How wisely are you using the time God has entrusted to you? If you were to examine the motives and goals behind all you do, would they reveal you are living with a Godward focus that ensures your time is used well? Even the secular responsibilities and tasks we engage in each day can take on eternal significance when they are done with the intent to honor and glorify God.

MAKING CHRIST ATTRACTIVE
TO A WATCHING WORLD

*Show yourself in all respects to be a model of good works, and
in your teaching show integrity, dignity, and sound speech
that cannot be condemned, so that an opponent may be put to
shame, having nothing evil to say about us (Titus 2:7-8).*

Scripture calls us to live as positive witnesses in a negative world. We're to conduct ourselves with an awareness that people's perceptions of God are strongly influenced by our attitudes, words, and actions.

In Titus chapter 2, Paul provides instructions for specific groups of people in the church: young and older men, young and older women, and slaves. Yet many of the principles directed at the groups listed in Titus 2 can be found elsewhere in the Bible for *all* believers. So we can rightly say that the exhortations found in Titus 2:7-8, which were aimed at young men, are relevant to all Christians.

A key purpose of godly living is to prevent unbelievers from finding any reason to criticize God. When those who oppose us are unable to legitimately speak wrongly about us, we disarm them from opportunities to speak wrongly about God.

What about when people bring false accusations against us? We shouldn't let those distract us. All we should care about is what God knows to be true about us. Even those who falsely speak evil against us know deep within that they are being untruthful.

As Christians, our conduct will either draw people to God or away from Him. We should want nothing in our lives to detract others from seeing Jesus and the gospel clearly. Because we bear Christ's name and profess to be His followers, we should care about how we represent Him to a watching world.

ADORNING YOUR LIFE WITH DOCTRINE

Teach what accords with sound doctrine...so that in everything
[you] may adorn the doctrine of God our Savior (Titus 2:1, 10).

In today's ungodly culture, it's becoming more and more of a challenge to know how to live as a godly witness. Titus 2 is rich with wisdom about how we, as believers, can make Christ attractive to unbelievers.

Paul opens by urging Titus to "teach what accords with sound doctrine" (verse 1). Here, he is not talking about the teaching of sound doctrine itself, but the character qualities that line up with or result from living in God's truth. In the verses that follow, Paul then lists the biblical attitudes and behaviors that are the fruit of living according to biblical doctrine.

The more we inform ourselves of God's truth and allow it to fill our minds and hearts, the more we allow His truth to shape our thoughts. This, in turn, shapes our attitudes and actions. There is a definite connection between sound doctrine and sound living. The fruit of right doctrine is right living.

After Paul lists the character qualities that ought to mark our lives, he explains why they are important: "so that in everything [you] may adorn the doctrine of God our Savior" (verse 9). The word "adorn" comes from a Greek term that gives us the word *cosmetics*, which refers to external attractiveness. The term is used to speak of arranging jewels together in a way that best displays their beauty.

When we exhibit attitudes and behaviors that are the fruit of right doctrine, we put the beauty of God's truth on display for others. That's what it means to "adorn the doctrine of God our Savior." This is why the pursuit of sound doctrine and truth is so important. This is a vital part of being a light that shines in a dark world.

OUR REAL CITIZENSHIP

Our citizenship is in heaven, from which we also eagerly
wait for a Savior (Philippians 3:20 NASB).

At the moment of salvation, when by faith we receive Christ as our Savior, we are made citizens of heaven. On this side of heaven, our citizenship is spiritual because we have invited the King of kings and Lord of lords to reign in our hearts. But there is coming a day when our citizenship will be physical as well—when we live in Christ's physical kingdom on earth, then in heaven and eternity.

As citizens of heaven, we have both responsibilities and privileges. As those who have chosen to live under Christ's authority, we are responsible to submit to His commands. We are obliged to yield to His kingship even though we are still on earth. Our conduct on earth should reflect that we are a heavenly people.

And the privileges? They are many. In Christ, we have been blessed "with every spiritual blessing in the heavenly places" (Ephesians 1:3). Love, peace, joy, forgiveness, a personal relationship with God, and eternal life are among the benefits of our heavenly citizenship. We have "an inheritance that is imperishable, undefiled, and unfading" (1 Peter 1:4).

Above all, note that when Philippians 3:20 calls us citizens of heaven, we are described as a people who "eagerly wait for a Savior." As those who belong in heaven, we cannot wait to live there. In our hearts, we possess an intense yearning for our Lord to call us home. Living with this kind of anticipation will cause us to think, speak, and act in the light of eternity.

Living with the awareness that we are citizens of heaven will have a positive effect on our lives here on earth. Colossians 3:2 exhorts us to "set [our] minds on things that are above, not on things that are on earth." A mind focused on heaven will result in heavenly living.

OUR FUTURE HOME

*In my Father's house are many rooms...I am going there
to prepare a place for you (John 14:2 NASB).*

O ne of the more amazing promises about the future is that Jesus
Himself is the one who is preparing our heavenly dwelling place.

The truth that Jesus is building our future home is made all the more
awe-inspiring as we remember what Colossians 1:16 tells us: "By [Christ]
all things were created, in heaven and on earth, visible and invisible...
all things were created through him and for him." The very one who
spoke the universe into existence and sustains it is the one who is preparing our eternal abode right now.

It is humbling to consider that the master artist whose infinite cre-
ativity is on display all throughout creation is the architect who is building our future residence. That is enough to tell us our dwelling place
will be beyond spectacular.

Jesus' words "I am going there to prepare a place for *you*" are lovingly personal. Remember the setting: Jesus is with the disciples observing Passover. In a matter of hours, He will be arrested, put on trial, and
crucified. When He tells them He is about to leave them, they become
distressed. In fear, Peter asks, "Lord, where are you going?" (John 13:36).

Jesus assures them, "Let not your hearts be troubled" (John 14:1).
Then He says He is going to His Father's house. Why? To prepare a place
for them, "that where I am you may be also" (verse 3).

Jesus' whole purpose for coming to earth and dying on the cross was
so we could be in heaven with Him. That's how much He desires our
fellowship. That's how much He loves us. So we can be certain it is with
great joy that He is preparing our future home!

TRUE COMPASSION SPEAKS THE TRUTH

Speaking the truth in love…(Ephesians 4:15).

In today's culture, many of us as Christians are torn about taking a stand for biblical values because we do not want to be viewed as judgmental. Rather than risk the consequences of offending someone for their ungodly beliefs or behavior, we wonder if we should stay silent. There are some who say it is better that we not voice our convictions, no matter how graciously we try to do so. They reason, "If we can show people just how loving we are, maybe they'll become more attracted to the Christian faith."

But is that line of reasoning valid? When we attempt to please people rather than God, we end up letting culture influence the church rather than being a church that influences culture. To do this is to exhibit worldly compromise rather than godly compassion. It is to allow the world to redefine love on its own terms rather than on biblical terms.

Worldly love says we should not disagree with another person's views and behaviors no matter what. This kind of love indulges a person's sinful views and desires and does not line up with God's definition of love. Scripture says God's kind of love cannot be separated from what is true. First Corinthians 13:6 says that love "*rejoices* with the truth." Ephesians 4:15 says we're to speak the truth in love. It is entirely possible for us to be truthful and loving at the same time.

Imagine Jesus failing to tell people that their sins would lead to eternal condemnation. That wouldn't have been compassionate. The most loving thing we can do as believers is to direct people away from error and toward truth because their eternal destiny is at stake. That requires addressing their sin, and it *can* be done in love—godly love.

To be loving, we must be truthful. And when we speak the truth, we must do so with the right balance of grace and conviction. That's the nature of true and godly compassion.

THE POWER OF ONE FAITHFUL PERSON

*I am not ashamed of the gospel, for it is the power of God
for salvation to everyone who believes (Romans 1:16).*

Charles Haddon Spurgeon, a preacher in nineteenth-century England, continues to have a strong ministry impact on today's world. Many of his books are still in print. It's estimated that by his death in 1892, some 50 million copies of his sermons had been sold in more than 20 languages. His church was the largest in London, able to seat 5,000 people with standing room for another 1,000.

Spurgeon's fame contrasts sharply with the humble beginnings of his faith. One Sunday morning while still a youth, as he headed to church, a severe snowstorm prevented him from reaching his destination. He turned down a side street and found refuge in a tiny chapel with about a dozen people. The regular minister had not shown up, so a clearly uneducated man stood to preach. He gave a simple, short sermon—unable to pronounce some of the words correctly—and Spurgeon found Christ as his Savior.

Afterward, as Spurgeon's fame grew, several men claimed to be the preacher who spoke that eventful morning, but none looked or sounded like him. Spurgeon never did find him. While his identity remains unknown, this we do know: Though he was poorly equipped, he was a faithful instrument of the gospel. It was not his eloquence that led to Spurgeon's conversion, but the power of the gospel itself. The man was merely a vessel, and God did the transforming work.

May we be found equally faithful. We may think God cannot possibly use us, but He can use anyone who is a willing instrument. It's not our personal or professional skills that make us useful, but our commitment to abiding in Christ so we can bear spiritual fruit. All God calls us to do is to be available. He will do the rest.

WAITING WITH ANTICIPATION, NOT DREAD

Come, Lord Jesus! (Revelation 22:20).

As we see the world collapsing all around us, it's easy to become discouraged. We find ourselves feeling overwhelmed as evil runs rampant and truth is being trampled underfoot. The spiritual darkness that surrounds us can have a depressing effect.

And yet we know this is what we should expect. Jesus Himself said that in the end times, "lawlessness will be increased, the love of many will grow cold" (Matthew 24:12). His words describe the culture we live in today. People have become calloused and flagrant about sinful behavior. They are so self-focused that they no longer care about others and even hate them. According to what Scripture tells us, we know everything is destined to get worse, and all hell will break loose during the tribulation.

The seven-year period during which God will vent His wrath against evil will be unlike any other experienced by mankind. It is frightening to read about the extent to which wickedness will prevail and the gravity of the judgments God will pour out upon the world. Even though we know that all believers will be snatched up to heaven before the tribulation, still, just knowing what is to come can fill us with foreboding and trepidation.

And yet we have no reason to dread this seemingly inescapable downward spiral. We know what awaits us: the Father's house, our heavenly rewards, the marriage supper of the Lamb, the millennial kingdom, and eternity. We will live in absolute, perfect bliss forever, in God's presence.

As we endure the darkness of this present age, we can live with joyful anticipation for the age to come. This world is temporary and will be replaced by a kingdom that is eternal. It is with that perspective that we can joyfully proclaim, "Come, Lord Jesus!"

HIS LOVE NEVER LETS YOU GO

*I am sure that neither death nor life, nor angels nor rulers, nor
things present nor things to come, nor powers, nor height nor depth,
nor anything else in all creation, will be able to separate us from
the love of God in Christ Jesus our Lord (Romans 8:38-39).*

If you are a Christian, God's love for you is so permanent, so indestructible, so everlasting that nothing—*absolutely nothing!*—can separate you from Him. This promise in Romans 8:38-39 is so all-encompassing that it has no exceptions whatsoever.

In the times when you feel unworthy of God's love, remember that He deliberately and knowingly reached out to you in love even while you were at your worst as His enemy (Romans 5:8-10). He did not withhold His love until you got your act together and made yourself more worthy. No, He loved you first—with a love so great that even when you were a child of wrath who was dead in sin, He made you alive in Christ (Ephesians 2:3-5). His love for you goes back to before the foundation of the world! (Ephesians 1:4-5).

Consider God's love this way: The gift of salvation and eternal life is free and cannot be earned. Because there is nothing you can do to earn God's love, there is nothing you can do to lose it. God saved you even with His full knowledge of all you did wrong in the past and all you will do wrong in the future. Your salvation is secure because you possess Christ's righteousness, not your own. There is "no condemnation for those who are in Christ Jesus" (Romans 8:1). That your salvation is permanent is confirmation that God's love is permanent. The absolute security of your salvation serves as evidence of the absolute security of God's love for you.

It is because of God's infinite love for you that you can joyfully proclaim, "Give thanks to the God of heaven, for his steadfast love endures forever" (Psalm 136:26).

OUR TWO CONSTANT COMPANIONS

Surely goodness and mercy shall follow me all the days of my life,
and I shall dwell in the house of the LORD forever (Psalm 23:6).

On every single day of our journey toward heaven, we have two constant companions: God's goodness and His mercy.

It is because of God's goodness—His generosity toward us—that James could write, "Every good gift and every perfect gift is from above, coming down from the Father of lights, with whom there is no variation or shadow due to change" (James 1:17). And it is because of God's mercy that Paul could declare, "There is therefore now no condemnation for those who are in Christ Jesus" (Romans 8:1).

God provides for our every need—that is His goodness. And He forgives all our sins and gifts us with eternal life—that is His mercy. He is our sustainer and our sanctifier.

The fact God pours out His goodness and mercy "all the days" of our lives speaks of His constant watchfulness over us. Not a moment goes by that He is inattentive. We are assured of our Lord's uninterrupted presence in our lives by His promise, "Behold, I am with you always" (Matthew 28:20).

So secure are we in God's goodness and mercy that we can say, with certainty, "I shall dwell in the house of the LORD forever" (Psalm 23:6). Nothing can deprive us of our future with God. Scripture affirms that truth when it speaks of our "inheritance...*reserved* in heaven." Our place in heaven is reserved because we are "*kept* by the power of God" (1 Peter 1:4-5 NKJV).

Because God's goodness and mercy never cease, we can rest in the peace that comes from knowing our eternal destiny is sure. Our security as believers is anchored to the bedrock of God's unchanging faithfulness.

SEVEN TRUTHS TO REMEMBER
AS THE WORLD FALLS APART

I wait for the LORD…and in his word I put my hope (Psalm 130:5 NIV).

The world around us is collapsing. Bad news bombards us from every direction, and evil is getting worse. As those who love God, we can't help but wonder: *How much longer can this continue? Is the tribulation almost here? How can we possibly have a positive influence in such a negative world?*

For more reasons than ever before, the future looks bleak. People are on edge. Fear is in the air. So much is trending in the wrong direction that we seem to have gone beyond the point of no return. This world is truly falling apart.

We shouldn't be surprised. Ultimately, the world is suffering because of humanity's rejection of God and enslavement to sin. Scripture warns how bad conditions will get as we draw closer to the end times. Jesus Himself said it will become "as the days of Noah were" (Matthew 24:37). Genesis 6:5 describes those days for us: "The wickedness of man was great in the earth, and…every intention of the thoughts of his heart was only evil continually."

With so much going wrong, we may think it's impossible for us, as believers, to have a positive effect anymore. But as long as the rapture hasn't happened yet, we're here to be salt and light. We're here to offer people the hope found in God's Word alone.

In the next several devotions, we're going to look at seven truths that serve as reminders that no matter how bad things get, God can use us. These truths can help us to persevere and not become discouraged.

Anytime we are overwhelmed by the chaos and evil in our world, the solution is to wait on the Lord and find our hope in His Word. The truths in Scripture are a bedrock of certainty in a world filled with uncertainty. As we fill our minds with these truths, our hearts will know peace.

TRUTH #1: GOD IS STILL IN CONTROL

Our God is in the heavens; he does all that he pleases (Psalm 115:3).

In the days of Noah, all of humanity hit rock bottom. Evil was everywhere, just as it is today. But we know that God was still in control because He brought an end to that world. He poured out His judgment and prevailed over evil. This will happen again in the end times. When the world is at its worst, Christ will return and will replace man's reign of evil with His reign of righteousness.

Another very dark moment in history was when Jesus died on the cross. At the time, Satan seemed to have won. But then, Jesus rose from the grave—and He conquered Satan, sin, and death. What looked like a victory for the enemy became God's victory.

God's sovereignty has no boundaries. The universe, world events, spiritual powers, and all people and creatures are in His hands. All are inescapably accountable to Him alone.

Isaiah 14:24 declares, "The LORD of hosts has sworn: As I have planned, so shall it be, and as I have purposed, so shall it stand." Psalm 135:6 says, "Whatever the LORD pleases, he does, in heaven and on earth, in the seas and all deeps." Daniel 4:35 reveals there are no constraints whatsoever on God's sovereignty: "All the inhabitants of the earth are accounted as nothing, and he does according to his will among the host of heaven and among the inhabitants of the earth; and none can stay his hand or say to him, 'What have you done?'"

No matter how greatly evil appears to triumph, God is still in control. So infinitely sovereign is He that evil cannot and will never be able to oppose His authority. God has demonstrated the totality of His power over all things many times in the past and will continue to do so in the future. Scripture tells us there is coming a day when He will say, "Enough!" and His sovereignty will never be challenged again. What a glorious day that will be!

TRUTH #2: OUR VICTORY HAS BEEN WON

If God is for us, who can be against us? (Romans 8:31).

We can fully expect that in this world, we will have times when we feel defeated. Evil will appear to be winning. We will find ourselves weighed down by one difficult circumstance after another. Or spiritual warfare will leave us frustrated and fatigued. Or the uncertainties we face about the future will be so constant that we wonder if we'll ever get beyond them.

In all these ways, it's easy for us to be robbed of our hopes. But no matter what happens in this life, an important truth that helps to put everything into perspective is that our eternal destiny is secure. Nothing can take away our salvation or the promise of eternal life in heaven. That's because Jesus already determined the outcome at the cross. He has forever defeated Satan, sin, and death—and all the problems they cause in our lives.

First Corinthians 15 says that someday, our mortal bodies will become immortal. The corruptible will become incorruptible, for death is swallowed up in victory (verses 52-54). The passage then climaxes with these words: "Thanks be to God, who gives us the victory through our Lord Jesus Christ."

Because of the victory Christ secured for us, a new day is coming. Revelation 21:4 describes it this way: "[God] will wipe away every tear from our eyes, and death shall be no more, neither shall there be mourning, nor crying, nor pain anymore, for the former things have passed away."

No matter how bad this world becomes, our victory has already been won. Nothing will change the outcome. We may feel as though we have no victory in life now, but because Christ has already won, we have total assurance that we will too. A day is coming when sin will forever be banished from our presence and Christ will rule the world, and we will reign alongside Him.

TRUTH #3: THE CHURCH WILL PREVAIL

I will build my church (Matthew 16:18).

In Matthew 16:18, Jesus said, "On this rock I will build my church, and the gates of hell shall not prevail against it." It's been 2,000 years since Jesus said that. The church had a small beginning. Where is it today? It's worldwide. Jesus is still building His church. Through the ages, He has sustained it and protected it. And when the rapture happens, He will remove it.

The powers of evil are not able to stop the church. They will work fiercely to hinder it, and there will be times when the battle gets intense. Jesus warned that "in the world you will have tribulation" (John 16:33). We as Christians can expect to be criticized, vilified, and persecuted—and some of us, even killed. From a human perspective, it will seem the church is losing ground, but because it is the all-powerful Christ who is building the church, we can be certain it will continue to grow. The gospel will be proclaimed and draw new people to Christ. The faith will move onward.

Back when the church was first born, it faced severe persecution. Some of the Roman emperors of that day were determined to wipe it out. Many other persecutions of Christians have taken place since. But Christianity continues to spread. It's all because Christ promised He would build His church. No matter how great the opposition, the church will advance.

Before Jesus went to the cross, He prayed to the Father for every believer who would become part of His church: "I do not ask that you take them out of the world, but that you keep them from the evil one" (John 17:15). Paul wrote, "The Lord is faithful. He will establish you and guard you against the evil one" (2 Thessalonians 3:3). We can have every confidence that no matter how hard the battle, God will use us—in ways we might not see or understand—to further His kingdom and His glory.

TRUTH #4: OUR MISSION HAS NOT CHANGED

Shine as lights in the world (Philippians 2:15).

Even though the world all around is constantly changing, the struggles of the human heart have never changed. God made people to know fulfillment, joy, and peace, but their bondage to sin makes that impossible. Apart from God, they will always struggle with dissatisfaction and hopelessness. They will forever be restless, unable to answer the deeper questions of life: *Why am I here? What is my purpose? Where can I find meaning?* Because sin has separated them from God, they've also been separated from the answers to those questions.

God wired people for fellowship with Him. He also created them to live eternally. Because of sin, every person has a God-sized void within them, and everyone fears death. Their wiring tells them something is wrong, but they're not sure what. They try to fill the void with whatever they think will satisfy, but their efforts will always be futile. Only God can fill that void. And our purpose, as Christians, is to point people to Jesus as the answer to every human need. That is our mission.

Matthew 5:13-14 calls us to be salt and light. We're to have a godly influence on those around us. Second Corinthians 5:20 says, "Now, then, we are ambassadors for Christ." First Peter 2:9 states our purpose this way: "You are…a people for [God's] own possession, that you may proclaim the excellencies of him who called you out of darkness into his marvelous light."

Those verses were written long ago but remain true today. Because the problem of sin hasn't changed, neither has our special assignment. No matter what we do for a living, no matter what our age, no matter what our background, we as believers all have the same mission: to be salt and light, to be ambassadors for Christ, and to proclaim the one who called us out of darkness into light.

TRUTH #5: EVERY CHRISTIAN COUNTS, INCLUDING YOU

You are the body of Christ and individually
members of it (1 Corinthians 12:27).

In the previous devotion, we looked at how our mission has not changed. That is true for every believer. The command to live as salt and light and to be an ambassador for Christ applies to all. Every saved person is a called person, commissioned to carry on the work Jesus began.

But maybe you feel like you don't have anything to contribute. You may be thinking, *I'm not good at talking about Christianity*, or *My realm of influence is small*. Perhaps most of your time is spent at home with very young children, or your life or work situation exposes you to very few people. Because your mission field is small, you might assume it is unimportant. But it's not the size of your mission field that matters, it's whether you are using it to influence lives.

God has planted you where you are for a reason. That's where your ability to be a godly influence is most needed. No one else has the same realm of influence you do.

To God, having an influence on even just one person is important. In the parable of the lost sheep in Matthew 18, the man who had 100 sheep left the 99 to search for the one that went astray. When he found it, he rejoiced more over that one than over the 99 that never left. In Luke 15:10, we're told that the angels of God rejoice "over one sinner who repents." The salvation of even just one person brings great joy to God and all of heaven!

The truth that every Christian counts applies to church life as well. In Hebrews 10:24-25, we are told that as we see Christ's return drawing near, we are not to neglect our fellow believers, but to "consider how to stir up one another to love and good works." Just as we need other believers to uphold and encourage us, they need us to do the same for them.

Your influence matters. As you allow God to work through you, He will accomplish His purposes. As you avail yourself for His use, you'll become a channel of blessing to others.

TRUTH #6: GOD WILL EMPOWER US

To him who is able to do far more abundantly than all that we ask or think, according to the power at work within us (Ephesians 3:20-21).

The best part of our calling to shine as light, be an ambassador, and encourage fellow believers is that God does not expect us to do all these things in our own power. He promises to supply us with His power!

In Acts 1:8, before Jesus told His disciples, "You will be my witnesses...to the end of the earth," He said, "You will receive power when the Holy Spirit has come upon you." He would gift the Spirit first; then they would go out. Because the Holy Spirit indwells every believer, you have this power.

Second Peter 1:3 tells us the Lord's "divine power has granted to us all things that pertain to life and godliness." God's power resides in us and enables us for every work pertaining to life and godliness—including sharing the gospel with the lost and building up fellow believers.

Ephesians 3:20-21 says God "is able to do far more abundantly than all we ask or think, according to the power at work within us." Backing up to verse 19, we're told where this starts: We must be "filled with all the fullness of God." This means yielding ourselves completely to Him—including being filled with His Spirit (Ephesians 5:18) and letting His Word dwell in us richly (Colossians 3:16). Being filled with the fullness of God, yielding wholly to the Spirit, and letting His Word dwell in us richly unleashes God's power. But when we allow sin to gain a foothold in our lives, we hinder God's work, "for the desires of the flesh are against the Spirit...to keep you from doing the things you want to do" (Galatians 5:17).

God would never call us to do a divine work without providing us with His divine power. Our part is to empty ourselves of whatever would impede His power from working through us.

TRUTH #7: HEAVEN IS OUR HOME

We seek the city that is to come (Hebrews 13:14).

Does your heart ache for heaven? As new creations in Christ, we can expect to feel unsettled in this sin-plagued world. It is no longer our home; we are citizens of heaven (Philippians 3:20).

Hebrews 11:13 describes us as strangers and exiles here on earth—we are pilgrims. Hebrews 13:14 says, "Here we have no lasting city, but we seek the city that is to come."

All of creation groans because it has been subjected to the futility that has resulted from sin. Likewise, "we ourselves, who have the first-fruits of the Spirit, groan inwardly as we wait eagerly for...the redemption of our bodies" (Romans 8:23). This is why we feel so out of place here on earth and we eagerly anticipate life in heaven.

Living with an awareness of our future home and glory is what sustains us and enables us to persevere when we become distracted and discouraged by this world. As we keep our eyes on the finish line, we train ourselves to have an eternal perspective that fills us with hope. A great way to cultivate that focus is to hold fast to the scriptural truths that remind us of the following:

- God is still in control.
- Our victory has been won.
- The church will prevail.
- Our mission has not changed.
- Every Christian counts, including you.
- God will empower us.
- Heaven is our home.

As we hold fast to God's promises of Christ's return and our home in heaven, we will gain the strength and determination we need to run the race all the way to the finish line.

THE DISTINCTION BETWEEN SALVATION AND REWARDS

If anyone's work is burned up, he will suffer loss, though
he himself will be saved (1 Corinthians 3:15).

Many Christians wonder whether it's possible to lose their salvation if their behavior or works aren't pleasing enough to God. They fear that somehow, they might mess up in ways that will cause God to change His mind about their admission into heaven.

While faith and works both have important roles in the Christian life, it's vital that we keep a proper distinction between them. Ephesians 2:8-9 clearly states, "By grace you have been saved through faith. And this is not your own doing; it is the gift of God, not a result of works, so that no one may boast." Salvation is given to us totally apart from works. Then verse 10 adds, "We are his workmanship, created in Christ Jesus for good works." While good works do not *bring* salvation, they will *follow* it. We are saved *by* faith, and we are saved *to* do good works.

And what if your works aren't so great? As 1 Corinthians 3:15 says above, even if a person's works are "burned up...he himself will be saved." No matter what the verdict about your works, your salvation is secure. Here's another way of looking at it: It's your *belief* that determines your salvation, and it's your *behavior* that determines the rewards you'll receive.

Second Corinthians 5:10 lovingly alerts us there is coming a day when "we must all appear before the judgment seat of Christ, so that each one may receive what is due for what he has done." This is not a judgment of our faith or our salvation, but of our works. Christ has already paid sin's penalty on our behalf, which makes us righteous before God.

Our appreciation for the gift of eternal life should inspire us to be eager to serve our Lord well. When we take care to serve Christ in ways that honor Him, we will have nothing to fear when it comes time for our works to be judged.

LABORS THAT COUNT

Be steadfast, immovable, always abounding in the work of the Lord,
knowing that in the Lord your labor is not in vain (1 Corinthians 15:58).

Paul urges us to always abound in our service to the Lord, for such efforts are never in vain. This informs us there are two kinds of labor: that with lasting value, and that without.

Read 1 Corinthians 15:58 again, and this time, ponder its words with this in mind: Inevitably, all of us will die (or be raptured). One of the starkest realities of death is that we cannot take anything with us. Even so, the way we live our life here on earth does have a bearing on the rewards we will receive in eternity. We cannot take earthly treasures with us, but we can have heavenly treasures awaiting us upon our arrival.

When we talk about laboring for the Lord, this doesn't mean only ministry-related work has value. Rather, as 1 Corinthians 10:31 says, "Whatever you do, do all to the glory of God." What counts is making sure we do things in ways that bring honor to God.

Though our service to the Lord might be done quietly or might be quickly forgotten by others, such labor is never done in vain. God remembers every good deed. As Ephesians 6:8 says, "Whatever good anyone does, this he will receive back from the Lord."

Our time on earth is but a dot on a line that stretches through all of eternity. At the start of each day, we ought to look ahead and ask, *Is there some way my activities can bring honor to God? How can I make that happen?* This will help us to live in ways that count.

The challenge for all of us is this: So many labors can be done quickly without any thought of God. That's why we need to be "steadfast, immovable," as 1 Corinthians 15:58 says. Carefully choosing to do our labors with an eternal perspective takes discipline—but the fulfillment we gain will last forever.

GOD DELIGHTS IN REWARDING US

Well done, good and faithful servant (Matthew 25:21, 23).

The parable of the talents is one of Jesus' most famous teachings. In this story, a man trusted three of his servants with his money, then left on a journey. Two of the servants used their master's funds well and earned more. The third hid the money and did nothing with it.

When the master returned, the first two servants gave back his money, with substantial gain. The master said to each, "Well done, good and faithful servant." He then gave them generous rewards. But the third servant, who had done nothing, was punished.

For Christians, the application is clear: As we wait for Jesus to return, we're to be good stewards of what He has entrusted to us. We've been given spiritual gifts, skills, and opportunities to bear fruit for Him. Jesus said, "Engage in business till I come" (Luke 19:13). Faithful servants will be rewarded and entrusted with more. The fact this will happen *after* He returns seems to show our reward will include responsibilities in Jesus' millennial kingdom.

There are other helpful life lessons in this parable. First, it appears the good servants were genuinely eager to please their master. They didn't serve merely out of duty, but out of love. As we serve Christ, may we do so not for duty's sake, but because we love Him so much.

Second, the master gave generous rewards to the good servants. This reflects God's generosity to His children. He delights in giving to us! The greatest example of the extent of His love and generosity is what He did for us at the cross.

Third, we know the master took great joy in rewarding his servants. He said, "Enter into the joy of your master" (Matthew 25:21, 23) and gave generous gifts to them.

In the same way that *you* will feel great delight as you hear your Lord say, "Well done, good and faithful servant," *He* will take great delight in saying those words to you!

RESPONDING TO HOSTILITY

Overcome evil with good (Romans 12:21).

It is a challenge to live in a last-days culture that has become increasingly hostile to believers. When we are criticized, rejected, treated unjustly, or wrongly accused, our natural human reaction is vengeance. We want to treat our enemies the way they treated us.

Yet because we are ambassadors for Christ, we're called to restraint. The apostle Paul had a lot to say about this in Romans 12. Let's break down his instructions.

"Bless those who persecute you; bless and do not curse them" (verse 14). This means to do good to our enemies and treat them as friends.

"Repay no one evil for evil, but give thought to do what is honorable in the sight of all" (verse 17). For believers, there is no place for vengeance. Instead, we're to do what is honorable. This means doing what is right and beneficial to our enemy, knowing that others are watching.

"Live peaceably with all" (verse 18). Even when another person is combative or unkind to us, we're to be peaceful in response. This means showing kindness and setting aside anger.

"Never avenge yourselves, but leave it to the wrath of God, for it is written, 'Vengeance is mine, I will repay, says the Lord'" (verse 19). No matter how serious the wrong done against us, we're to leave payback to God. He will ensure justice is done—in His timing and His way.

Romans 12 ends with this great counsel: "Do not be overcome by evil, but overcome evil with good" (verse 21). We should not allow evil to overwhelm us. And if we want to overcome evil—yes, *overcome* it— the best way to do so is by doing good.

It's hard to imagine that good can overcome evil. But it's when we do good that God can work through us. Vengeance accomplishes nothing because our enemy will only see *us* rather than *Christ in us*. It's when we respond with good that Christ in us becomes visible.

IN CHRIST, YOU ARE A NEW PERSON

If anyone is in Christ, he is a new creation (2 Corinthians 5:17).

To be "in Christ" means to be in relationship with Him. This happens when you repent of your sins and receive Him as your Savior and Lord. In the moment that this transformation takes place, you truly do become a new creation.

When you are "in Christ," you are...

- granted eternal life, which begins at the moment of salvation (Ephesians 2:8-9)
- clothed with His righteousness (2 Corinthians 5:21)
- sealed by the Spirit (Ephesians 1:13-14)
- forgiven and without condemnation (Ephesians 1:7; Romans 8:1)
- complete in Him (Colossians 2:9-10)
- chosen by God, holy and beloved (Colossians 3:12)
- a child of light (Ephesians 5:8)
- blessed with every spiritual blessing (Ephesians 1:3)
- lacking nothing (Philippians 4:19)
- more than a conqueror (Romans 8:37)
- able to access the throne of grace in time of need (Hebrews 4:16)
- an ambassador for Him (2 Corinthians 5:20)
- a citizen of heaven (Philippians 3:20)

In Christ, you become a new person in the most remarkable ways. What Christ has done in you is miraculous. There is so much He has done—and continues to do—on your behalf that you will never run out of ways to marvel over His goodness!

IN CHRIST, YOU HAVE A NEW FUTURE

Christ in you, the hope of glory (Colossians 1:27).

While you are here on earth, you'll experience many benefits from being "in Christ." And there are many additional blessings that await you in the future, in heaven—blessings that will never cease:

- You have "an inheritance that is imperishable, undefiled, and unfading" (1 Peter 1:4).
- You will experience "an eternal glory that far outweighs" your momentary afflictions (2 Corinthians 4:17-18 NIV).
- You will never again cry, mourn, or experience pain, "and death shall be no more" (Revelation 21:4).
- Having been justified, you will also be glorified (Romans 8:30).
- You will "be changed" and "put on the imperishable, and... put on immortality" (1 Corinthians 15:51-53).
- You will be recognized for your service to the Lord—He will "reward each one as his work deserves" (Revelation 22:12).
- You will reign on the earth with Christ during the millennium (Revelation 20:6).
- You will dwell in "a new heaven and a new earth" (Revelation 21:1).
- You will "have the right to the tree of life" (Revelation 22:14).
- You will live in God's presence forever (Revelation 21:3).

This is the future that awaits every believer—"Christ in you, the hope of glory" (Colossians 1:27). When Christ is in us, we have the promise of heaven and the guarantee of eternal bliss.

A SURE DELIVERANCE

God has not destined us for wrath, but to obtain salvation
through our Lord Jesus Christ (1 Thessalonians 5:9).

In 1 Thessalonians 5:2, Paul wrote about the day of the Lord, a time during which God will pour out judgment against sin. Eventually the day of man will end, and the day of the Lord will begin. At the start of the tribulation, God will once again intervene in human affairs and supernaturally exercise His direct ruling authority over the earth. This includes both a phase of wrath during the tribulation and a phase of restoration during the millennium and eternity.

With that as our context, we read here, a few verses later, that "God has not destined us for wrath." Because our sin penalty has been paid for, and because we are clothed in Christ's righteousness, there is no reason for us to face God's tribulation-era wrath. The teaching that a pretribulation rapture will remove us to heaven before God's judgment is poured out upon the wicked is in agreement with the blessed truth in Romans 8:1 that "there is...no condemnation for those who are in Christ Jesus."

If we are not destined for wrath, then we are destined for the rapture. That word "destined" tells us God has already sovereignly determined for this to happen. It's stunning to realize God planned this outcome long before we were born: "He chose us in him before the foundation of the world, that we should be holy and blameless before him" (Ephesians 1:4). Saying we are destined is like saying, "God has decided, and this is a done deal."

Instead of wrath, we are appointed to "salvation through our Lord Jesus Christ." This speaks of the *future* aspect of our salvation—our glorification. Through Christ, we will not face judgment, but glory. On the calendar of our lives, God has already reserved our appointment to be taken up to heaven before the day of the Lord. Our coming deliverance is sure!

THE POWER OF THE WORD *FROM*

Because you have kept my word about patient
endurance, I will keep you from the hour of trial that
is coming on the whole world (Revelation 3:10).

Some people believe that Christians will remain here on the earth when God pours out His judgments during the tribulation. Others say we will be raptured before the end times. Still others contend that we will be taken up to heaven at the midpoint of that seven-year period of wrath.

The proponents of all three views use various Bible passages to support their arguments. However, there is a tiny Greek word in the New Testament that provides a powerful affirmation in support of the pretribulation view—the view that Christ will remove all believers from earth *before* God's wrath is poured out. That Greek word is *ek*, which translates to "from." It appears in these two key passages:

- *1 Thessalonians 1:9-10*—"How you…wait for his Son from heaven, whom he raised from the dead, Jesus who delivers us *from* the wrath to come."

- *Revelation 3:10*—"Because you have kept my word about patient endurance, I will keep you *from* the hour of trial that is coming on the whole world."

God has promised we will be kept *from* His tribulation-era wrath, not go *through* it. In the same way that the Lord protected Noah's family in the ark during the global judgment of the flood, He will take us, His church, up to heaven prior to the global judgments of the tribulation. Also, it does not make sense for believers to face God's wrath, for Christ already did that for us.

The assurance that we will be raptured before God pours out His end-time wrath is a great source of comfort for believers. But it should also be a great source of discomfort that compels us, out of love, to urge unbelievers to come to Christ before it is too late.

WHY CHRIST DIED

[Christ] died for us so that...we might live
with him (1 Thessalonians 5:10).

First Thessalonians chapter 5 opens with 11 verses about the coming day of the Lord. Paul packs several important truths about the end times in this passage. And as he draws near to his conclusion, he proclaims the comforting message that we are not destined for wrath, but we will be taken up to heaven before the tribulation begins.

Deep within this passage is a short and profound statement that is easy to miss. In our enthusiasm to learn all we can about the rapture, God's wrath, and the day of the Lord, we're prone to overlook these seemingly ordinary words that declare one of the most amazing truths in the Bible: "[Christ] died for us so that...we might live with him" (verse 10).

To get the full impact of these words, let's rephrase them this way: Why did Christ die for us? So we could live *with* Him.

We are the reason Christ went to the cross. That's how much He desired our presence with Him in heaven. That's how precious we are to Him.

Yet another amazing truth conveyed in 1 Thessalonians 5:10 is this: So sufficient is what Christ did on the cross that He has irrevocably secured our place in heaven. Our future destiny is locked in. Nothing can overrule what Christ has done on our behalf.

Notice this incredible statement comes immediately after Paul's assurance that we are not destined for wrath. That highlights even more the greatness of Christ's love for us, doesn't it? It doesn't make sense that so great a love would ask us to go through the tribulation, as some people think.

Paul then closed by saying, "Therefore encourage one another." The fact Christ died for us so we could be with Him has to be one of the greatest encouragements a believer could have!

ENCOURAGE ONE ANOTHER

God has not destined us for wrath... Therefore encourage one another and
build one another up, just as you are doing (1 Thessalonians 5:9, 11).

In 1 Thessalonians 4, after Paul provided the Christians in Thessalonica with a clearer understanding of the rapture, he wrote, "Encourage one another with these words" (verse 18). Then a few verses later, after he explained that we are not appointed to the wrath of the tribulation but to glory in heaven, he again said, "Encourage one another."

This double exhortation to "encourage one another" is no accident. God has very intentionally placed prophecy-related promises in the Bible to give us comfort, assurance, and especially hope. In our interactions with fellow believers, we are to remind one another of these promises because they help to fill us with needed encouragement.

God knows that the never-ending challenges of living in a fallen world can discourage us and leave us weary. In our hearts we desire to love and pursue Him, but our human flesh is all too prone to be lured by temptation and sin. Today's culture constantly bombards and pressures us in the direction of compromise. We are citizens of heaven living on an earthly spiritual battlefield that lies in the power of the evil one.

Bible prophecy is God's way of urging us to keep our eyes on the future in the middle of all the struggles and distresses around us. He is telling us that better days are ahead—days that will have no end! And we can help one another to persevere and run the race well by reminding each other of the hope before us. As we talk about God's prophetic promises together, we build up one another.

The more we take God's prophetic promises to heart, the more we'll be ready to offer the very kind of encouragement that helps our fellow believers live with an eternal perspective.

THE RESURRECTION OF
NEW TESTAMENT BELIEVERS

The dead in Christ will rise first. Then we who are alive…will
be caught up together with them (1 Thessalonians 4:16-17).

At the moment of death, our spirit is taken into Christ's presence immediately. When Stephen, the first Christian martyr, was stoned to death, he cried out, "Lord Jesus, receive my spirit" (Acts 7:59). Spiritually, Stephen entered Christ's presence instantly. This is true of the Old Testament saints as well. In Luke 20:38, while speaking about Abraham, Isaac, and Jacob, Jesus said that God "is not God of the dead, but of the living, for all live to him."

The resurrection of our *physical* bodies, however, is a separate event. When will this happen? Some are surprised to learn that the Old Testament and New Testament saints will be physically raised up on two separate occasions, as we'll see in today's and tomorrow's devotions.

The bodily resurrection of every New Testament saint is taught in 1 Thessalonians 4:16-17, a passage that is also about the rapture: "The Lord himself will descend from heaven with a cry of command, with the voice of an archangel, and with the sound of the trumpet of God. And the *dead in Christ* will rise first. Then we *who are alive, who are left, will be caught up together* with them in the clouds to meet the Lord in the air."

Notice that "the dead in Christ will rise first." Then "we who are alive…will be caught up." This is the order in which we will be raised. This applies to every New Testament saint—everyone who has received Christ as Savior from the beginning of the church age to the end.

Our future physical resurrection is guaranteed. Because Christ rose from the dead, we will too. His power over death means death no longer has any power over us. When we die, our spirit immediately enters the Lord's presence. And at the rapture, our physical bodies will be restored and join our spirits. For believers, death leads directly to Christ, then heavenly glory.

THE RESURRECTION OF OLD TESTAMENT BELIEVERS

Those who sleep in the dust of the earth shall
awake, some to everlasting life (Daniel 12:2).

If only the New Testament saints will be physically resurrected at the rapture, what about the Old Testament saints? When will they be raised physically?

Daniel 12:1-2 reveals the answer: "There shall be a time of trouble, such as never has been…at that time your people shall be delivered, everyone whose name shall be found written in the book. And many of those who sleep in the dust of the earth shall awake, *some to everlasting life*, and some to shame and everlasting contempt."

"A time of trouble, such as never has been" points to the worst time ever in human history. This is a clear reference to the tribulation. "At that time your people shall be delivered, everyone whose name shall be found written in the book" tells us a remnant of Daniel's people—the Jews—will be saved prior to Christ's second coming. Their names are "in the book"—that is, the book of life. We also see this Jewish repentance in Zechariah 12:10 and Romans 11:26.

Then we read that "those who sleep in the dust of the earth shall awake, some to everlasting life, and some to shame and everlasting contempt." The literal Hebrew text indicates two resurrections separated by time—those risen to life will rise after the tribulation, and those risen to shame will rise after the millennial kingdom.[3] Daniel 12:3 then says that those who are raised "to everlasting life"—including Old Testament believers—will shine "like the stars." Chronologically, this pictures their glorified existence in the millennial kingdom. This means the resurrection in Daniel 12:2 must happen at the end of the tribulation, before the millennium.

Taken together, the clues in Daniel 12:1-3 tell us the Old Testament saints will be raised when Christ returns. Imagine the great joy they will express upon meeting their Savior!

THE RESURRECTION OF TRIBULATION-ERA BELIEVERS

I saw the souls of those who had been beheaded for the
testimony of Jesus... They came to life and reigned with
Christ for a thousand years (Revelation 20:4).

The bodily resurrection of New Testament believers will take place at the rapture, prior to the tribulation. And the physical raising up of Old Testament believers will occur at the end of the tribulation, prior to the millennium.

That leaves us with one last group of believers unaccounted for. When will those who become Christians during the tribulation—and then are put to death for their faith—rise up?

We see these saints in Revelation 20:4, which takes place after Christ's return and before the millennial kingdom: "I saw the souls of those who had been beheaded for the testimony of Jesus and for the word of God, and those who had not worshiped the beast or its image... *They came to life and reigned with Christ* for a thousand years." Because they will rule in the millennial kingdom, their resurrection will happen at the same time as that of the Old Testament saints—when Christ returns.

The New Testament saints will be resurrected at the rapture, and the Old Testament and martyred tribulation saints will be raised up before the millennium. Together, we'll have the joy of entering Christ's kingdom in our glorified bodies! The exception is believers on earth who survive the tribulation—they will enter the millennial kingdom in their unglorified state. It is they who will give birth to new people who will populate the world during the millennium.

For believers, the promise of a future physical resurrection is sure. Christ "will transform our lowly body to be like his glorious body" (Philippians 3:21). Never again will we grow old. Never again will we die. Our transformation will be total and forever!

RESPONDING AS CHRIST
DID TO PERSECUTION

Father, forgive them (Luke 23:34).

E ven when Jesus was in great agony on the cross, He prayed for those who had crucified Him: "Father, forgive them, for they know not what they do." Surely the apostle Peter had this in mind when he wrote, "To this you have been called, because Christ also suffered for you, leaving you an example, so that you might follow in his steps" (1 Peter 2:21).

Christ's call to follow Him assumes we are willing to die for Him. "If anyone would come after me, let him deny himself and take up his cross and follow me" (Matthew 16:24). When the disciples heard these words, they did not miss their meaning. They knew that to carry one's cross meant to head toward one's crucifixion. This spoke of total surrender, even to the point of a violent physical death. That's how serious the call to follow Jesus is.

Among the most difficult commands Jesus gave are these: "Love your enemies, do good to those who hate you, bless those who curse you, pray for those who abuse you" (Luke 6:27-28). No matter how badly we are treated, we are to respond in love—even though we would rather pull out our swords and slash away, as Peter did in the Garden of Gethsemane.

Jesus was clear about the consequences of identifying with Him. "If they persecuted me, they will also persecute you" (John 15:20). Similarly, Paul wrote, "All who desire to live a godly life in Christ Jesus will be persecuted" (2 Timothy 3:12).

Godly living is a magnet for persecution.

Jesus said in Luke 6:22, "*Blessed are you* when people hate you and when they exclude you and revile you and spurn your name as evil, on account of the Son of Man!"

Hated. Excluded. Reviled. Spurned. As painful as it is to be persecuted, remember that it will all be temporary. The blessings you receive for persevering will be eternal.

THE BENEFITS OF PERSECUTION

Blessed are those who are persecuted for
righteousness' sake (Matthew 5:10).

From a human perspective, it's hard to see how persecution is beneficial. We can quickly think of many reasons we would rather *not* suffer just because we identify with Christ.

But from a spiritual perspective, when we are reviled for our faith, it's to our gain. Here are some important ways we benefit:

Christ's example in persecution instills us with the strength to persevere. Hebrews 12:3 says, "Consider him who endured from sinners such hostility against himself, so that you may not grow weary or fainthearted." As we look to Christ's example, we're inspired to keep going and not give up.

Persecution brings inner joy. Matthew 5:10 says, "Blessed are those who are persecuted for righteousness' sake." Here, "blessed" means to experience a divinely bestowed sense of bliss and fulfillment. It's a deeply satisfying inner happiness that cannot be taken away from us.

Persecution produces endurance, character, and hope. Romans 5:3-4 says, "We rejoice in our sufferings, knowing that suffering produces endurance, and endurance produces character, and character produces hope." The heat and pressure brought against us in persecution help to refine and shape us. They prepare us to persevere, motivate us to have a right heart and attitudes, and help us to focus on the hope that lies before us at the finish line.

When we realize the good that can come from suffering for Christ's sake, we'll find our anxieties replaced by determination and gratitude. In the same way that Jesus was able to go to the cross with joy because He knew what lay on the other side, we can endure persecution with joy because we know the positive results God can produce as we keep moving onward.

OUR SOURCE OF STABILITY

I bless the LORD who gives me counsel; in the night also my heart instructs me. I have set the LORD always before me; because he is at my right hand, I shall not be shaken (Psalm 16:7-8).

God is our source of wisdom. He provides counsel freely: "If any of you lacks wisdom, let him ask of God, who gives generously" (James 1:5). Because He knows our needs better than we do, and because He has special purposes for us, we could not ask for a better counselor. He prepares the way before us; we need only to trust Him.

When we take God's guidance to heart, it stays with us and can inform us even during the night. As we meditate upon His instructions and promises during the quiet hours, we can find ourselves comforted, encouraged, or strengthened. So it makes sense to enter our sleep time with prayer and some moments of meditation upon Scripture. In these ways, we can set the direction our minds take during the evening.

The psalmist was intentional about his focus both day and night: "I have set the LORD always before me." He sought God at all times in all places. His mind and heart were fixed so he would not lose sight of the Lord no matter what he was doing.

When we make a deliberate effort to focus on God and His counsel, our lives become more stable. And with Him at our right hand, we have access to all the protection and aid we need. We cannot be shaken, for He is steadfast and unmovable.

No matter how fierce our enemies or life's storms, the wisdom and stability offered to us by God enables us to say, "I have no reason to be afraid." This is especially relevant in our day of increasing wickedness and so many unknowns about the future. Thankfully, we have the assurance that when we "set the LORD always" before us, we will not be shaken.

WAITING WELL

They themselves report…how you…wait for his
Son from heaven (1 Thessalonians 1:9-10).

The believers in Thessalonica had a reputation: They were known for eagerly awaiting Jesus' coming. Their zeal was so great that Paul heard about it some 350 miles away in Corinth, where he penned this letter.

The word "wait" might give the impression these believers were passively biding their time, standing by for Jesus to call them to heaven. The opposite was true. In the preceding verses, Paul praised them for being "an example to all…in Macedonia and Achaia" (1 Thessalonians 1:7). They kept busy in ministry to the point of being "imitators of [Paul] and of the Lord" (verse 6). Paul wrote that "the word of the Lord has sounded forth" from them (verse 8), meaning they were actively proclaiming the gospel. Theirs was a busy kind of waiting!

The knowledge that our Lord could call us home at any time should motivate us to live in a state of preparedness. That is one aspect of the discipline of waiting: making sure our lives are in order. And because our Lord commanded us to "engage in business until I come" (Luke 19:13), we don't want to waste time. That's another aspect of the discipline of waiting: staying active in our service to the Lord.

Active ministry and expectant waiting are both commanded of us. As we do both wholeheartedly, we will become like the good servants in Jesus' parable of the talents, who practiced the wise stewardship of their master's resources in anticipation of his eventual return. It was they who heard the words, "Well done, good and faithful servant" (Matthew 25:21).

As we wait for the rapture, we are called to a busy kind of waiting. We're to continually watch for ways we can give our best to our Lord while we are still here on earth.

IT'S ALL BY GRACE

At the present time there is a remnant, chosen by grace (Romans 11:5).

There are many foreshadows and prophecies of Christ in the Old Testament. That means any eyewitnesses who paid attention to His words and actions and compared them to the prophecies in the Old Testament could come to only one reasonable conclusion: this was the Messiah promised from God the Father and spoken of by the prophets. What's more, many of the prophecies meant to help God's people identify their Messiah were given to Abraham, Moses, and David. In these three, we have Israel's greatest forefather, greatest deliverer, and greatest king. All three were still highly revered by the people of Israel at the time of Christ's first coming.

But what happened when Jesus arrived? "He came to his own, and his own people did not receive him" (John 1:11). Even though the prophecies about Messiah had been recorded and handed down through the ages, and even though they originated with some of Israel's greatest heroes—Abraham, Moses, and David—a major disconnect took place. Many rejected Jesus. Their spiritual blindness prevented them from correctly identifying Christ.

A few people were alert and understood—the shepherds in Bethlehem, Simeon, Anna, the magi, John the Baptist, and others. God has always had a remnant of true seekers. In Acts 2:41 and 4:4, thousands of Jews came to faith in Christ. In Romans 11:5, Paul wrote, "So too at the present time there is a remnant, chosen by grace."

Chosen by grace. Many Jews were trusting their heritage (descendants of Abraham) and their works (adherence to the law) to save them. They hadn't realized salvation had always been by grace alone, even for their forefather, Abraham (Genesis 15:6). God showed grace to Adam and Eve, Noah, Abraham, all through the Old Testament and the New, and still does today. When we realize we have nothing to offer to God, we will see grace everywhere in the Bible.

SLOW TO ANGER

The LORD is merciful and gracious, slow to anger and
abounding in steadfast love. He will not always chide, nor
will he keep his anger forever (Psalm 103:8-9).

When Scripture says the Lord is slow to anger, it is saying He is incredibly patient. Even when His righteous anger has been aroused, He remains controlled and is slow to punish.

When God judged the world in Noah's day, He said, "My Spirit shall not abide in man forever...his days shall be 120 years" (Genesis 6:3). Though God had already determined to destroy all of mankind, He would wait 120 years before sending the flood.

For centuries, the Jewish people rebelled against God, and prophet after prophet warned of coming judgment. The northern kingdom was taken captive about 722 BC, and God waited nearly another 100 years before sending the southern kingdom into exile. That's patience!

Even as wicked people shake their fists at God, He is slow to anger. Why? Second Peter 3:9 says He "is patient...not wishing that any should perish, but that all should reach repentance." God's mercy and grace are expressions of His unrelenting love, which does not give up on us.

In contrast, how often have we wished we could bring swift judgment against those who offend or harm us? Because we are called to "be imitators of God" (Ephesians 5:1), we are to "put on...compassionate hearts, kindness, humility...and patience" (Colossians 3:12).

God is longsuffering with the wicked, and we should be patient with them as well. God *will* bring judgment—in *His* time. Until that happens, we should be slow to anger and love our enemies, praying that they might receive Christ as their Savior.

THE COMMAND TO PRAY
FOR THOSE IN AUTHORITY

I exhort first of all that supplications, prayers, intercessions,
and giving of thanks be made for all men, for kings and
all who are in authority (1 Timothy 2:1-2 NKJV).

Scripture commands us to pray for our government officials. Notice that the apostle Paul did not include any exceptions or qualifiers about such prayer. He didn't say, "Pray for all authorities as long as they fulfill their duties honorably and well."

In response, you may find yourself saying, "How can I pray for such-and-such leaders? They say and do things that are unbiblical. They are morally and spiritually corrupt. Why should I pray for those who are enemies of what I stand for?"

But we can't use disagreement with governing leaders as an excuse to not pray for them. God has that base covered in Matthew 5:44. There, He commands us to love our enemies and pray for them.

It's helpful for us to remember that the New Testament was written when much of the known world was ruled by Roman dictators, including some who brutally persecuted Christians. Anyone who didn't abide by Rome's laws could lose their job, be rejected in their community, go to jail, or face execution. Even so, believers were exhorted to pray for their leaders.

The fact we are to pray for all authorities—without exception—confirms this command is relevant to us no matter what kind of government we're under—a democracy or a dictatorship.

Why pray for our leaders? God "desires all people to be saved and to come to the knowledge of the truth" (1 Timothy 2:4). To God, heart change is a higher priority than political change. Earthly kingdoms are temporary, stained by sin, and irredeemable. As ambassadors for Christ, our time is best spent not on political warfare, but on praying for leaders to be drawn to a kingdom that is eternal, and to a King who is able to accomplish what no earthly king can.

THE BENEFITS OF PRAYING
FOR THOSE IN AUTHORITY, PART 1

I urge that supplications, prayers…be made for all people…This is good,
and it is pleasing in the sight of God our Savior (1 Timothy 2:1, 3).

I t's not easy to pray for leaders we disagree with. But there is good that comes out of such prayer, no matter how opposed we are to the views and policies of those who rule over us.

When we pray for government officials, we are reminded that ultimately, it is God who is sovereign—no matter how powerful the human leader. Romans 13:1 says, "There is no authority except from God, and those that exist have been instituted by God." To make sure we didn't miss the point, Paul stated it twice in this one verse: It is God who appoints leaders their places!

Jesus Himself affirmed this truth. When Pilate said, "Do you not know that I have authority to release you and authority to crucify you?," Jesus answered, "You would have no authority over me at all unless it had been given you from above" (John 19:10-11).

No matter how mighty the nation or leader, ultimately, it is God who is in control. Every human king and kingdom that rises will fall; God reigns over all and His power will prevail.

When we pray for government authorities, we are reminded that they answer to an even higher authority: God. He alone has control over all outcomes. While we may struggle mightily with why God allows certain leaders to get into power, or why He allows certain laws to pass, we can take confidence in the truths that He rules over all, and no one can overrule Him.

No matter what happens in this world, it was permitted by God's authority. In our finite minds, we will not understand why. What we do know is that God is all-wise and all-knowing. Rather than question Him, we need to trust Him. He has purposes we don't know about, and He has the power and ability to fulfill those purposes in ways that He knows are best.

Anytime we pray for our leaders, we are blessed as we remember God's sovereignty.

THE BENEFITS OF PRAYING FOR THOSE IN AUTHORITY, PART 2

*I urge that supplications, prayers, intercessions, and
thanksgiving be made for all people, for kings and all who
are in high positions, that we may lead a peaceful and quiet
life, godly and dignified in every way (1 Timothy 2:1-2).*

As citizens of heaven who have chosen allegiance to the God who rules the universe, we will often find it challenging to submit to human governing authorities. That's because we recognize their sin nature and tendency to legislate in ways that are morally and spiritually deficient.

This brings us to additional reasons it is beneficial for us to pray for government leaders.

It teaches us to release our anxieties and trust God. Scripture commands that when we pray, we yield our concerns to God and place them in His hands (Philippians 4:6). Anytime we find ourselves agitated by government or politics, it's time to pray—and to surrender our frustrations. When we do so, the peace of God will guard our hearts and minds (verse 7).

It reminds us to pray for God's guidance for leaders. As we pray for those in authority, we're to pray that they would rule in such a way that we can "lead a peaceful and quiet life, godly and dignified in every way" (1 Timothy 2:2). Yet even when they don't, we still need to remember that we represent Christ. If we're going to find ourselves at odds with our government, let it be because of our righteous convictions, and not because we have broken laws or done wrong.

The practice of praying for our leaders is good because it puts us in a position of being completely dependent upon God when we're in circumstances that are beyond our control. Prayer also helps to posture our hearts so that we are more likely to respond in God-honoring ways to those over us even when they are unjust or do wrong to us.

THE BENEFITS OF PRAYING
FOR THOSE IN AUTHORITY, PART 3

*If any of you lacks wisdom, let him ask of God, who gives to all liberally
and without reproach, and it will be given to him (James 1:5 NKJV).*

In the times when we're unsure of how to pray for governing authorities, we can appeal to Scripture's promise that God will give wisdom to those who ask for it.

Frequently when it comes to government and politics, we find ourselves uncertain of what to do. We don't want to become so politically focused or strident to the point that we compromise our spiritual priorities and our example to unbelievers. And we don't want to be so cautious that we fail to take a stand for what is right when it is necessary to do so.

During election season, these struggles are magnified. We may be uncertain about which candidate to choose, or how to vote on certain issues. Sometimes we're not comfortable with any of the choices before us.

On all matters related to government, it is always wise to pray and seek God's wisdom. Coming before God in prayer has a way of reminding us that in all things, we are to "seek first the kingdom of God and his righteousness" (Matthew 6:33). As we are deliberately mindful of our heavenly citizenship, we become more sensitive to our need to live as earthly citizens who conduct ourselves in a Christlike manner. In the times when we're unsure of what choices to make in relation to government and politics, it is vital that we represent the Lord honorably before a watching world. Our accountability to God's authority should inform us on how we live out our accountability to human authorities.

We benefit when we pray for our leaders. We are reminded that God is sovereign, that we are to yield our anxieties to the Lord, that we are to live quiet and godly lives, that we are to seek wisdom from God, and that we're to care about the salvation of those over us.

GODLY CITIZENS, GODLY BEHAVIOR

Remind them to be submissive to rulers and authorities…and
to show perfect courtesy toward all people (Titus 3:1-2).

D isagreements over political issues can do a lot of damage—not only between believers and unbelievers, but between believers as well. How can we engage with others on issues we care about without contributing to the political strife around us?

In Titus 3:1-2, Paul wrote, "Remind them to be submissive to rulers and authorities." Note what he said next: We are "to be obedient, to be ready for every good work, to speak evil of no one, to avoid quarreling, to be gentle, and to show perfect courtesy toward all people." In those few words, he packed six commands about our speech and actions toward those who rule over us and others around us. When it comes to our conduct as citizens, God sets the bar high.

With the call to good citizenship comes a call to good behavior. God ties the two together. There's a clear message here: In all our interactions—including those involving the government and politics—we need to be careful about what we say and do.

This doesn't mean we can't feel strongly about political issues. God isn't telling us to tamp down our spiritual and moral convictions for the sake of getting along. Rather, when it comes to disagreement, we're to be gracious. Ephesians 4:15 guides us toward the perfect balance when it says to "speak the truth in love." We should never abandon the truth nor our convictions, but we should speak the truth and our convictions with love.

In this fallen world, how we conduct ourselves will shape the way people perceive God and Christianity. If we end up in conflict with governing authorities or those around us, let it be because of where we stand spiritually and morally, and not because we're being combative or strident.

UNASHAMED

I am not ashamed of the gospel of Christ, for it is the
power of God to salvation (Romans 1:16 NKJV).

A growing number of people in today's culture say there is no objective truth. Rather, truth is whatever a person determines it to be, based on their personal experiences. And to tell them otherwise is said to be unloving.

For this reason, it has become increasingly difficult for us as Christians to tell others that God's Word is the only source of truth in this world. Often, the response is that we're being judgmental and oppressive by imposing our views on others.

When people reject the idea that objective truth exists, they also reject the sole means of distinguishing right from wrong. Absolute truth gives us indisputable reference points that make it possible to determine what is good and what isn't. But if truth is whatever any person wants it to be, then it becomes impossible to arrive at universal standards of right and wrong. In such a world, the concept of sin becomes meaningless. This is what unbelievers want.

This puts us in a difficult place when it comes to sharing the gospel. Because we don't want to be accused of intolerance, rather than point out that sin condemns a person to eternal separation from God, we find ourselves tempted to stay silent. Yet as culture makes it more costly for us to speak the truth, we must ask: Which is more loving—to speak up or stay silent?

Romans 1:16 makes it clear it is the gospel alone that is "the power of God to salvation." The lost may think they are happy in their own truth, but they'll never know real happiness apart from *the* truth. From a human perspective we'll be told that speaking biblical truth is unloving. But from God's perspective, it is the most loving thing we can do. That's what it means to be unashamed of the gospel—to love others to the point we're willing to speak and face rejection.

WHO ARE WE TRUSTING AS OUR AUTHORITY FOR TRUTH?

While Paul was waiting for them at Athens, his spirit was provoked within him as he saw that the city was full of idols. So he reasoned in the synagogue with the Jews and the devout persons, and in the marketplace every day with those who happened to be there (Acts 17:16-17).

While in Athens, Paul grieved when he saw the many idols around him. They were evidence of the many worldviews people held to. Note Paul's response: He took the initiative to reason with others about their beliefs. He created open doors and built bridges so he could speak about Jesus.

As Paul did this, he wisely sought to earn himself a hearing. This is evident by the fact a group of philosophers invited him to share what he had to say: "May we know what this new teaching is that you are presenting?" (Acts 17:19).

What Paul did next is worth paying attention to. He said, "Men of Athens, I perceive that in every way you are very religious" (verse 22). He made sure to connect by first understanding where they came from. Paul noted their altars and their objects of worship (verse 23). He took the time to acknowledge their views and beliefs. He showed interest in them and care for them.

Then Paul made this transition: "The God who made the world and everything in it, being Lord of heaven and earth…he himself gives to all mankind life and breath and everything" (verses 24-25). Paul didn't say, "You have your truth; here is mine." Instead, he said, "Let me point you to the God whose truth is for everyone." He appealed to an external, higher authority. And we should do the same. This helps others to realize that different views ultimately come down to this: Who are we trusting as our authority for truth? This helps to frame the discussion as one between them and God. Some may be willing to listen to you, and others won't. But what counts is that you've lovingly let them know that ultimately, they answer to God.

UNITY A HIGH PRIORITY

*Standing firm in one spirit, with one mind striving side
by side for the faith of the gospel (Philippians 1:27).*

When it comes to cultural issues, sometimes Christians will find themselves on opposing sides. When that happens, we are in danger of letting disagreements damage our unity in Christ.

This calls for great discernment. We must ask ourselves: Is this issue a matter of choosing between truth and error? Or is it about personal preferences? Is any aspect of the issue at odds with a core teaching of Scripture? Or is there legitimate room for disagreement?

When truth or biblical teachings are at stake, it's essential to draw a line. When Jesus wrote His letters to the seven churches in Revelation 2–3, He made it clear He did not want sin or false teachings to be tolerated among His own. He desires a church that is "cleansed…by the washing of water with the word…without spot or wrinkle or any such thing, that she might be holy and without blemish" (Ephesians 5:26-27). But when it comes to matters that aren't detrimental to a person's salvation or the church's biblical integrity and purity, we should set aside our differences so that they don't hinder our ability to minister to one another and to draw unbelievers to Christ.

Among believers, unity should be a high priority. God calls us to have the same mind, the same love, and to be humble (Philippians 2:2-3). We're to "love one another with brotherly affection," and to "live in harmony with one another" (Romans 12:10, 16).

A winsome church is more likely to attract people to Christ. A gospel message backed by unity is a powerful witness. That's why Paul wrote, "Let your manner of life be worthy of the gospel of Christ, so that… I may hear of you that you are standing firm in one spirit, with one mind striving side by side for the faith of the gospel" (Philippians 1:27).

QUESTIONS TO ASK WHEN YOU STUDY BIBLE PROPHECY

Do your best to present yourself to God as one approved...
rightly handling the word of truth (2 Timothy 2:15).

Because "all Scripture is...profitable...for training in righteousness" (2 Timothy 3:16), it is good for us to study Bible prophecy. But one key challenge to understanding the prophetic passages of Scripture is that there are many people who have abused and sensationalized them. That's why it's so important to let the biblical text speak for itself. As we seek to gain a clear understanding of the prophecies in God's Word, here are some helpful questions we can ask:

What is the context of this prophecy? Look at the immediate context—the paragraph, chapter, and book. Contextual clues can tell us a lot about what a prophecy is saying and is *not* saying.

What is this prophecy about? Based strictly on the words that appear in the passage and the context, discern the main points without appealing to outside ideas.

What can I learn from parallel passages or key words? If there are parallel passages, or if key words within the passage are used in similar ways elsewhere, look those up. Carefully comparing like passages and key words can help enlarge your understanding of a prophecy.

Are there historical or cultural insights given in the context of the prophecy that can help interpret it clearly? Historical and cultural facts can sometimes help provide clarity.

What can the fulfilled prophecies about the past teach me about the unfulfilled prophecies about the future? Fulfilled prophecies are often the clearest ones to understand and can offer important principles or patterns that equip us to rightly interpret passages about the future.

Because the Bible is God's own Word to us, it's vital that we handle it carefully. The above questions can help serve as guardrails to ensure we stay within the boundaries of what God says. As we handle prophetic truth correctly, we bring honor to God and blessing to ourselves.

QUESTIONS TO ASK WHEN YOU APPLY BIBLE PROPHECY

Be doers of the word, and not hearers only (James 1:22).

All of Scripture is useful for spiritual wisdom and growth. This includes the portions that are so often overlooked by today's Christians—the Old Testament and the prophetic passages.

At first glance, Bible prophecies may seem to be little more than information about the past or the future, with minimal value for practical application today. But if we think carefully and ask ourselves the right questions, we can find even the prophetic passages of Scripture helpful toward transforming our minds and influencing our lives. As Paul correctly wrote, "Whatever was written in former days was written for our instruction" (Romans 15:4).

With that in mind, let's turn our attention to some questions we can ask when it comes to searching for practical applications in Bible prophecies. These can help us to glean useful wisdom and life lessons that serve us well in our everyday living:

What do I learn about God or Christ in this prophecy? Through Bible prophecy, we can learn wonderful truths about God and Christ's nature, character, and attributes. They include insights about God's sovereignty, wisdom, or justice. Or about Christ's deity, mercy, and authority. Every prophecy is an opportunity to better know God the Father or God the Son.

What wisdom can I gain from this prophecy? Even prophecies that are primarily informational can contribute to our spiritual wisdom. Ask: Why does God want me to read this?

Does this prophecy include any life lessons? Both the fulfilled prophecies of the past and the unfulfilled prophecies of the future can offer valuable applications for us. For example, they can teach us the importance of trusting God, exercising patience, using our time well, and more.

Bible prophecies can have a valuable place in our growth as believers. Searching for wisdom and life lessons in past and future prophecies can help us to live better in the present.

THE SUPERSIGN OF THE END TIMES

I will gather them from all the countries to which I drove them in my anger and my wrath and in great indignation. I will bring them back to this place, and I will make them dwell in safety (Jeremiah 32:27).

One of God's greatest modern-day miracles is the rebirth of the nation of Israel. Because the Jewish people are back in their homeland, it is now possible for the Bible's prophecies about the end times to be fulfilled. Without Israel in the land, none of these prophecies could take place. Scripture makes it clear that Israel is the stage on which the last days will play out.

That is why the rebirth of Israel is called the supersign of the end times. This is the reason we can be confident that we are nearer than ever to our Lord's return.

What's especially remarkable is that the Jewish people were scattered around the world for 2,000 years before being restored as a nation. Never has a people survived and come back together again after such a long exile.

Also amazing is how this took place in the face of overwhelming opposition. Prior to Israel's rebirth, proposals for the creation of a Jewish state were fiercely rejected by the surrounding Arab nations. They did not want a Jewish country in their midst. In fact, less than 24 hours after Israel declared her independence on May 14, 1948, five Arab armies attacked with the goal of total annihilation. Against unbelievable odds, Israel prevailed, and today is among the most powerful and prosperous nations in the world.

Only God could have brought about Israel's rebirth. The regathering of the Jewish people is confirmation that God's prophetic plans continue to march forward—and that we are drawing closer to Christ's second coming. We are seeing God at work!

A KEY PURPOSE FOR THE TRIBULATION

*It is a time of distress for Jacob; yet he shall
be saved out of it (Jeremiah 30:7).*

All through the ages, God has been and continues to work through every person and every event to accomplish His plans. We may struggle with such a sweeping statement when it comes to evil, yet the Bible affirms that God can use people's wickedness to achieve His perfect purposes. This is true of even the greatest crime and injustice ever committed in history: the crucifixion.

In Acts 2:23, just weeks after the resurrection, Peter proclaimed to a crowd, "This Jesus [was] delivered up according to the definite plan and foreknowledge of God, you crucified and killed." At the cross, Satan attempted to forever shut down Christ's plan to redeem mankind. Yet everyone who put Jesus to death was unknowingly part of carrying out God's "definite plan." If God could work through this greatest evil ever, He can work through all others.

That is true of the tribulation as well. During that time, evil will be unleashed as never before. As God responds in judgment, He will accomplish His will. The prophet Jeremiah said about the tribulation, "Alas! That day is so great there is none like it; it is a time of distress for Jacob; yet he shall be saved out of it" (Jeremiah 30:7). Here, Jacob refers to Israel. Jeremiah was saying that Israel "shall be saved" in this time of trouble.

Through the tribulation, God will chastise His people Israel so they are driven to receive the Messiah they rejected. Looking to the last days, Zechariah prophesied that God "will pour out on the house of David… a spirit of grace and pleas for mercy, so that, when they look on me, on him whom they have pierced, they shall mourn for him" (12:10). Though Satan will be at his worst during the tribulation, determined to turn people away from God, the Lord will still draw countless more souls to Him, including from wayward Israel. Though the tribulation will be a time of great evil, it will also be a time of great salvation—including for God's chosen people.

THE SEVERITY OF THE TRIBULATION

That day is so great there is none like it (Jeremiah 30:7).

The tribulation will be a time like no other. It will be unparalleled in intensity. Evil will peak as never before, and God's judgments will be correspondingly severe.

This raises a big question: Is it possible that for some people, God's wrath will be excessive? After all, the "least" of sinners will face the same judgments as the worst.

Two truths in God's Word help provide perspective on this.

First, sin is far more sinful than we will ever understand. In the darkness of our fallen state, we cannot comprehend the enormity of the gulf between our sinfulness and God's holiness. Sin makes us complete enemies of God (Romans 5:8, 10). By nature, we are sons of disobedience and children of wrath (Ephesians 2:2-3). "Out of the heart come evil thoughts, murder, adultery, sexual immorality, theft, false witness, slander" (Matthew 15:19). Though we do not all commit the same sins, we all have the same fallen heart, capable of giving birth to any sin. Apart from Christ, we are entirely unrighteous (Romans 3:10, 23).

Second, God is a God of mercy. From the moment sin first raised its ugly head in Eden, God promised He would send a Savior who would defeat sin and Satan (Genesis 3:15). From then onward, we see God's patience, love, and mercy toward a rebellious mankind leap out from every page of Scripture. Repeatedly, He warns people before He sends His wrath. He "is longsuffering toward us, not willing that any should perish but that all should come to repentance" (2 Peter 3:9 NKJV). Through Christ, God offers a way back to Him. More amazingly, the gift of salvation is free (Romans 6:23). Those who reject this gift do so at their own peril.

The wretchedness of sin requires that it be punished. At the same time, God is merciful—incredibly so. In these two truths, we can know that God is entirely just and entirely loving.

AMAZING LOVE, AMAZING GRACE

He first loved us (1 John 4:19).

Before we receive Christ as Savior, we are slaves to sin. So powerful is our bondage that we cannot escape it. So destitute are we that Ephesians 2:1 describes us as "dead in trespasses and sin." That word "dead" means exactly that—we have no ability at all to go from dead to alive. The only way we can possibly be freed from sin's grip is with the help of an outside power.

When it comes to receiving salvation through Christ, you may have heard the illustration that unbelievers are like people who are drowning in rough seas, calling out to rescuers for a life ring. But because we are spiritually dead, it's more accurate to say we're at the bottom of the ocean. Unable to make our way to the surface, our only hope is for someone to come down and pull us up.

That's exactly what God did.

First John 4:19 says, "He first loved us." Romans 5:8 echoes this, saying, "God shows his love for us in that while we were still sinners, Christ died for us." When we were helplessly dead in sin, God took the initiative and reached down. He had to because our spiritual deadness made it impossible for us to reach up.

This demonstrates the greatness of God's love for us. He made salvation possible for us even when we were dead in sin and had nothing to offer Him. We didn't even desire Him. As Romans 3:10-11 puts it, "None is righteous, no, not one; no one understands; no one seeks for God." Paul's five negatives show just how bad our situation was.

So when we read that before the world was created, God Himself "chose us...In love he predestined us for adoption" (Ephesians 1:4-5), we should be filled with gratitude. *That's* amazing love. *That's* amazing grace. May our gratefulness never cease.

A RIGHT VIEW OF SIN AND JUDGMENT

That you may be…blameless in your judgment (Psalm 51:4).

The extent to which sin can blind us is made clear in the story of David and Bathsheba. After David committed adultery with her, she became pregnant. He plotted to hide his guilt by calling Bathsheba's husband, Uriah, home from battle. He hoped Uriah would have relations with his wife, but Uriah refused, saying he couldn't possibly do that while his fellow soldiers were still at war (2 Samuel 11:11).

When David saw that Plan A had failed, he turned to Plan B. He ordered that Uriah be sent into the heat of battle, then abandoned so that he would be killed. David's wickedness is astounding, considering he was a man after God's own heart (Acts 13:22). Sin does that.

After the prophet Nathan confronted David, the king made a stunning confession that, amazingly, stated a correct view of human sin and God's judgment. First, he said to the Lord, "Against you, you only, have I sinned and done what is evil in your sight" (Psalm 51:4). He had sinned not only against others around him, but ultimately, God Himself. Note especially what he said next: "So that you may be justified in your words and blameless in your judgment."

When we sin, God is perfectly justified in punishing us. Our unrighteousness provokes His righteous response. Our wrong deserves His judgment. Before Him, we have no excuse.

What can we learn from David's example and confession? Succumbing to one sin can lead to others. That's the danger of allowing it a foothold in our lives. Also, the seriousness of sin affirms the justness of God's justice. If ever we wonder whether the judgments people will face during the tribulation or in hell will be too harsh, the answer is no. As Romans 3:19 says, when the lost stand before God, they will recognize their guilt. They will know they have no defense. They will say to Him, "You are blameless in Your judgment."

PRAYER: A MIGHTY PURSUIT

*First of all, then, I urge that supplications, prayers...be made for all
people, for kings and all who are in high positions...This is good, and
it is pleasing in the sight of God our Savior, who desires all people to be
saved and to come to the knowledge of the truth" (1 Timothy 2:1-4).*

Prayer can easily seem to be one of the more ordinary duties of a
Christian. But it's not. When we pray, we have the opportunity
to call upon God to do His work in the hearts of people everywhere,
including those in the highest places. This makes prayer a mighty pursuit.

1. *The priority of prayer*—"First of all, then." Paul begins by urging us to pray. This should be a primary passion for us because
it helps us to keep a Godward focus.

2. *The extent of prayer*—We should pray for all people, even
"kings and all who are in high positions." Paul wrote those
words in a pagan world ruled by cruel, godless dictators. We
should pray for "people to be saved," and that those "in high
positions" will rule in a way that allows believers to "lead a
peaceable and quiet life" (1 Timothy 2:2).

3. *The spirit of prayer*—As hard as it can be to pray for ungodly
people and leaders, we should do so willingly, not grudgingly.
Inherent in this command to pray for everyone is God's desire
that we show love to them. What better way can we love others
than by praying for them? When we find ourselves reluctant
to pray for those who hurt us or do evil, we should remember that "many are the plans in the mind of a man, but it is
the purpose of the LORD that will stand" (Proverbs 19:21).

4. *The reward of prayer*—For us to pray for all people, including
governing authorities, is "pleasing in the sight of God." Even
when our external circumstances are difficult, we'll know inner
peace because we're doing what God has asked of us.

PRAYING IN A TIME OF CRISIS

*Father, if you are willing, remove this cup from me. Nevertheless,
not my will, but yours, be done (Luke 22:42).*

There is much we can learn from Jesus' simple prayer shortly before
His death on the cross.

Our Lord knew what would soon happen. Humanly, the agony He
felt caused His sweat to become "like great drops of blood" (Luke 22:44).
He knew the pain that lay ahead would be excruciating. It's understandable that He would say to His Father, "If you are willing, remove this
cup from me."

Yet in His very next words, He said, "Not my will, but yours, be
done." Divinely, He knew God's end purpose—a purpose that would
make the horrors of the cross worth it all.

Because we live in a fallen world, suffering, pain, and hurt are certain. We can most definitely pray for deliverance—we find many such
prayers in the Psalms. But there are times when God has a purpose that
requires a great price from His own—as with martyrs in ages past, or
with persecuted believers today, and yes, as might happen to us.

Jesus' example teaches us that in times of severe crisis, we should gladly
yield to God's will rather than cling to self-preservation. That was our
Lord's outlook all through His life. It's why He was able to make it all
the way to the end of His ministry and say to the Father, "I glorified you
on earth, having accomplished the work you gave me to do" (John 17:4).

As we prayerfully seek God's help in times of great duress, our foremost desire should be that His will be done. This doesn't mean that we
passively give up, but rather, that we actively participate in whatever
work God is accomplishing. This takes trust and submission.

Though we may not see it, we can be confident God will always do
what is right and best, even in the worst trials. The result of Christ's
work on the cross is the supreme example of that.

GOD'S WORK ON DISPLAY IN US

It was not that this man sinned, or his parents, but that the
works of God might be displayed in him (John 9:3).

When Jesus and the disciples crossed paths with a blind man, the disciples asked, "Rabbi, who sinned, this man or his parents, that he was born blind?" (John 9:2). Jesus responded, "It was not that this man sinned, or his parents, but that the works of God might be displayed in him." After this exchange, Jesus healed the blind man.

We are not given the age of the man, but because he was blind from birth, we can safely assume he had been blind for perhaps a couple decades or more. When the disciples asked who was at fault for his condition, they resorted to a common assumption of that day: that a person's infirmities were due to sin. But Jesus refuted that and said God had purposed for the man to be born blind so His work could be made evident to others. What the disciples had wrongly attributed to human sin, Jesus attributed to divine purpose.

As our lives unfold day by day, that which appears unexpected to us is expected by God. That which seems to be coincidence to us is God working out His plan. God's every action is determined in advance and has a purpose. He is never random; He always acts with fixed goals. Whatever He has ordained to happen will come to pass. The future has already been settled. With God, nothing is accidental; everything is intentional. God's sovereignty is truly absolute.

God said in Isaiah 55:11, "So shall my word be that goes out from my mouth; it shall not return to me empty, but it shall accomplish that which I purpose." God's divine purposes undergird everything. This assurance applies to Bible prophecy. And gratefully, it applies to us as well. God is at work in us. We might never realize His intent. But we can be confident that in every aspect of our lives, God desires to put His divine purpose on display through us.

THE BIBLE: GOD SPEAKING TO YOU

No prophecy of Scripture comes from someone's own interpretation. For no prophecy was ever produced by the will of man, but men spoke from God as they were carried along by the Holy Spirit (2 Peter 1:20-21).

B ecause the entire Bible originated from God, its message is supernatural. Every revelation recorded came down from heaven to messengers specially chosen by the Lord Himself. In 2 Peter 1:20-21, here is what we are told about the source and nature of the Bible:

Every prophecy comes from God alone. "No prophecy was ever produced by the will of man." As Paul said to Timothy, "All Scripture is breathed out by God" (2 Timothy 3:16). Every word is of divine origin. And because God can be trusted, we can trust His Word.

Every prophecy was revealed by God to His messengers. "Men spoke from God." Those who wrote the Bible were God's mouthpieces. What they spoke was revealed from above. Implied in the phrase "men spoke from God" is that God chose the human vessels who proclaimed and wrote His Word.

Every messenger was guided by the Holy Spirit. "They were carried along"—the Spirit inspired and superintended them to pen what was to be written.

The Bible is entirely authored by God, recorded by messengers chosen by God, who were guided by God the Spirit, for the purpose of proclaiming God's message to all people.

Every single word in Scripture is God speaking to us. Presently, it is the most direct means by which He is able to personally communicate His thoughts to us and His love for us. He has given us this treasure so that we may know His heart and His ways. In light of this, may we respond to His Word just as reverently as we would respond to God Himself while standing before His throne in heaven.

BIBLE VERSES TO REMEMBER AS EVIL GROWS WORSE

The LORD preserves all who love him, but all the
wicked he will destroy (Psalm 145:20).

In Matthew 24:12, when Jesus described the signs of the end times, He said that lawlessness will increase, and the love of many will grow cold. That's exactly what we see happening today. For us to witness unrestrained evil can be discouraging. We wish things would get better, but they won't. Bible prophecy warns that our world's descent into spiritual darkness will get worse. With this in mind, let's look at three important truths and verses we can look to for comfort.

God is aware of what's happening. Proverbs 15:3 says, "The eyes of the LORD are in every place, keeping watch on the evil and the good." God sees everything. Nothing escapes His attention. This passage is a warning to the wicked and an encouragement to the good.

God will protect the righteous and punish the wicked. Psalm 145:20 says, "The LORD preserves all who love him, but all the wicked he will destroy." God shields His children and will avenge those who do evil. Justice will prevail. We can trust God to help us navigate our way through a hostile world.

Because of God's protection, we can live with courage instead of fear. Psalm 27:1 says, "The LORD is my light and my salvation; whom shall I fear? The LORD is the stronghold of my life; of whom shall I be afraid?" At the cross, God secured our salvation and eternal destiny. And as our stronghold, He is greater than even the greatest enemy we face.

When we're surrounded by evil, we have no reason to be afraid. The God who sees all will never let us out of His sight. He is our refuge and will keep us secure in His hands. And we can rejoice in Scripture's many promises that ultimately, righteousness will prevail—for all eternity.

WRITTEN FOR A REASON

These are written so that you may believe that Jesus
is the Christ, the Son of God, and that by believing
you may have life in his name (John 20:31).

The Gospel of John ends with this mind-boggling statement: "There are many other things that Jesus did. Were every one of them to be written, I suppose that the world itself could not contain the books that would be written" (John 21:25). When Matthew, Mark, Luke, and John wrote their Gospels, they had to be selective. Still, they compiled far more than enough evidence to help anyone realize that Jesus is the Messiah and that they "may have life in his name."

The New Testament writers pointed their audiences to these key sources of evidence:

The fulfillment of Old Testament prophecies. Within the four Gospels, we see many instances of Jesus doing exactly what the prophets said He would do. In just the last 24 hours of His life on earth, Jesus fulfilled 33 specific prophecies.

Their eyewitness testimony. John wrote, "That which...we have seen with our eyes, which we looked upon and have touched with our hands, concerning the word of life—the life was made manifest, and we have seen it, and testify to it and proclaim to you the eternal life" (1 John 1:1-2). What the disciples had written was credible because they were firsthand eyewitnesses. *All* of them could vouch for what had happened. Their words could be trusted.

The resurrection. Soon after Christ arose, Peter taught a large crowd, "This Jesus God raised up, and of that we are all witnesses...Let all the house of Israel therefore know for certain that God has made Him both Lord and Christ" (Acts 2:32, 36).

Our faith in Christ is not based on mere feelings or wishful thinking. The Bible is filled with facts "written so that you may believe." The proofs are abundant and rock solid. So it is with full confidence that we can share this evidence and invite others to embrace Christ.

LIVING IN ANTICIPATION OF HEAVEN

We are waiting for new heavens and a new earth, in
which righteousness dwells (2 Peter 3:13).

Our future home—heaven—is mentioned frequently in the Bible. The word *heaven* appears in the very first verse: "In the beginning, God created the heavens and the earth" (Genesis 1:1). And the final two chapters of the book of Revelation are all about the new heavens and new earth.

More than 50 of the 66 books of the Bible refer to heaven. Because Bible translations vary in how they handle the Hebrew, Aramaic, and Greek texts, there is no single count of how many times the word *heaven* appears, but the range runs from roughly 450 times to more than 600. In the book of Matthew alone, the phrase "kingdom of heaven" appears more than 30 times.

For many, a favorite verse about what life will be like in heaven is Revelation 21:4: "He will wipe away every tear from their eyes, and death shall be no more, neither shall there be mourning, nor crying, nor pain anymore, for the former things have passed away." Merely reading those words is enough to make us wish we could leave this sin-scarred world right now! All of us have experienced the sorrows that come from trials and suffering and spiritual warfare.

Jesus said much about heaven, and gave this wonderful promise in John 14:2-3: "In my Father's house are many rooms. If it were not so, would I have told you that I go to prepare a place for you? And if I go and prepare a place for you, I will come again and will take you to myself, that where I am you may be also." Here, we are given these reasons to find heaven appealing and endearing: Christ Himself is preparing a place for us, He promises to come again to take us home, and we will live with Him there forever. For these reasons and more, our hearts should long deeply for heaven. Every time we read about heaven in the Bible, our anticipation for our eternal home should increase!

THE CROSS: OUR BRIDGE TO HEAVEN

*Between us and you a great chasm has been fixed, in order
that those who would pass from here to you may not be
able, and none may cross from there to us (Luke 16:26).*

If there is any one reason for an unbeliever to fear death, it is this: Once he or she dies, their eternal destiny is final. There is no going back to change their mind. It's impossible because there is a great chasm fixed between Hades and heaven. There is no way to cross from one place to the other. There is no second chance. Hebrews 9:27 is clear on this: "It is appointed for man to die once, and after that comes judgment."

No amount of human pleading or ingenuity can change the outcome once a person has passed beyond death's veil. In that moment, whatever decision a person has made about Christ—to repent and receive Him or to refuse and reject Him—takes on a fearsome finality. Judgment is permanent.

The converse is true as well. We who are believers have the assurance we will dwell in heaven forever. Once our mortal bodies put on immortality, sin and death will be no more. In fact, our reservations for heaven are locked in at the moment of salvation. When we believe, we are "sealed with the promised Holy Spirit, who is the guarantee of our inheritance until we acquire possession of it" (Ephesians 1:13-14). Our future in heaven is guaranteed!

Anytime we find ourselves looking forward to heaven, we should thank God for the cross. We have a wonderful future ahead of us because of a great exchange that took place there long ago. What happened at the cross is the heart of the gospel: "For our sake he made him to be sin who knew no sin, so that in him we might become the righteousness of God" (2 Corinthians 5:21). The cross made access to heaven possible, and for it we should be forever grateful.

GOD'S PROVISIONS IN
SPIRITUAL WARFARE

We do not wrestle against flesh and blood, but against...the
spiritual forces of evil in the heavenly places (Ephesians 6:12).

B ecause of the presence of sin and evil in this world, spiritual warfare is inevitable. We are surrounded by enemies eager to defeat us.
First John 2:16 lists three perpetual sources of temptation for us: "the
desires of the flesh and the desires of the eyes and pride of life."

Our ultimate foe, of course, is Satan himself. First Peter 5:8 warns,
"Be sober-minded, be watchful. Your adversary the devil prowls around
like a roaring lion, seeking someone to devour." He is tireless in this effort.
Revelation 12:10 says he accuses us "day and night before our God." As
long as we live in this world, we will have no rest from spiritual warfare.

Yet God has given us effective ways to protect ourselves. He has given
us prayer, through which we can place our concerns into His hands (Philippians 4:6-7). He has equipped us with spiritual armor that enables
us to "be strong in the Lord and in the strength of his might" (Ephesians 6:10-18). With this armor, we are able to "withstand in the evil day"
and "extinguish all the flaming darts of the evil one." But we cannot be
passive about this armor—we must "put on" what God has given, and
"keep alert with all perseverance." Diligence is essential.

God has also given us the promise that when we submit to Him, we
will be able to "resist the devil, and he will flee" (James 4:7).

Above all, God has given us Christ, who has "disarmed the rulers and
authorities" of darkness "by triumphing over them" (Colossians 2:15).
John 15:5 promises that when we abide in Christ, we will bear much
fruit. Philippians 4:13 says we can "do all things through him."

With the helps of prayer, our spiritual armor, our submission to
God, and our abiding in Christ, victory is possible in spiritual warfare.
In these, we find shelter and safety.

EAGER ANTICIPATION FOR CHRIST'S FIRST COMING

Concerning this salvation, the prophets who prophesied about
the grace that was to be yours searched and inquired carefully...
things into which angels long to look (1 Peter 1:10, 12).

I magine the Old Testament prophets and angels standing on their tip-toes in anticipation of Christ's first coming. With great curiosity they looked into the future, eager to see the fulfillment of God's grand plan to bring salvation to mankind.

Through the ages, God gradually revealed more details about this Savior who would rescue the lost. With each successive prophecy, the prophets and angels knew God was setting the stage for the greatest event in all human history. They didn't fully understand how God's plan of salvation would unfold. But they knew that whatever He did, it would be spectacular.

That's why the prophets and angels were eager to know more. They couldn't wait. They were thrilled by the promises of God's grace. They had seen the destruction and separation caused by sin. They longed to see the restoration and reunion that would come with salvation.

Of the many different promises that the prophets proclaimed, they knew that the promise of God's redeeming grace was supreme.

Looking back, we know how God's plan unfolded. The prophecies concerning His grace are no longer a mystery. Today, we have the benefit of reading the New Testament and seeing all that happened in Christ's life, death, and resurrection. Even though we have knowledge that the prophets didn't have, may we be just as eager as they were to take to heart the wonders and truths of the gospel story.

If the prophets and angels expressed such great enthusiasm and curiosity about how salvation would come about, we who have full revelation should marvel even more.

WHAT ANGELS LONG TO UNDERSTAND

…things into which angels long to look (1 Peter 1:12).

For God's angels, the prophecies of Christ's first coming provoked an amazement that will never cease. A key reason for this is they will never experience the wonders of salvation and forgiveness. Holy angels don't need these gifts, and fallen angels can't receive them. You'll recall that when Satan rebelled against God, many angels joined forces with him. These fallen angels are forever condemned, separated from their fellow holy angels with no hope of redemption. Their fate is permanent. This surely had a sobering impact on the angels who remained loyal to God. They saw firsthand the consequences of defying the Creator.

So when Adam and Eve sinned, severing all of humanity from God, the angels knew the seriousness of their offense. Yet God, in His infinite love and wisdom, had already planned a rescue operation. Through the cross, He would bridge the unbridgeable chasm between Himself and man. As God, He alone could make the impossible possible. So brilliant and so great and so miraculous is God's gift of salvation that the angels—who live in God's very presence and are eyewitnesses of what He can do—had an overwhelming passion to understand it.

The result of God expressing this grace toward mankind is that His "manifold wisdom" was "made known to the rulers and authorities in the heavenly places" (Ephesians 3:10). The angels marveled when God unveiled His plan, and they still do now. Their awe will continue into the future—in Revelation 4:11, we see them loudly proclaim, "Worthy is the Lamb who was slain, to receive power and wealth and wisdom and might and honor and glory and blessing!"

Luke 15:10 says, "There is joy before the angels of God over one sinner who repents." When you were saved, the angels rejoiced! From where they stand, they realize the greatness of salvation. Their joy should spur us to likewise exalt God and thank Him for what He has done.

THE PRECISION OF BIBLE PROPHECY IN CHRIST'S BIRTH

Behold, the virgin shall conceive and bear a son (Isaiah 7:14).

Typically, when people attempt to predict the future they are sufficiently vague, with hopes of increasing the likelihood that their so-called prophecies will come to pass. They offer broad and speculative guesses that rarely venture more than a year or two out.

In contrast, the prophecies God recorded in the Bible are specific and precise. Many were made hundreds or thousands of years in advance. So exact are the details that, humanly speaking, God increases the chances He will be wrong. But because He is God and He is sovereign, that will never happen. He alone knows the future, and He alone can orchestrate history in advance.

The extent of God's prophetic precision is evident in what He declared about the birth of Jesus. In both the Hebrew text of Isaiah 7:14 and the Greek text of Matthew 1:23, "the virgin shall conceive" pointedly states Jesus would be born of a *true* virgin, and born *only* of a woman, and not a man. From the very first messianic prophecy in the Old Testament—which says Jesus would be born from the seed of a woman (Genesis 3:15)—God was clear on this.

More than 700 years before Christ's birth, God said Jesus would be born in "Bethlehem Ephrathah"—the birthplace of David (Micah 5:2). The addition of Ephrathah distinguishes this town from a Galilean town also called Bethlehem. And remember that Joseph and Mary weren't in Bethlehem Ephrathah near the time of birth—it took a Roman census to direct them there.

The reason God was so exact in the many prophecies about Christ's birth was so there would be no mistaking His identity: This truly was the long-awaited Messiah. And the precise fulfillments of these prophecies leave no doubt as to their origin: Only an all-seeing, all-knowing, all-sovereign God could have uttered them. Only God the Father could speak those prophecies so accurately, and only God the Son could fulfill those prophecies so perfectly.

A LOVE FOR THE DOCTRINES
OF CHRIST'S COMING

What is our hope...before our Lord Jesus at
his coming? (1 Thessalonians 2:19).

The two letters Paul wrote to the church in Thessalonica are likely the first New Testament books he penned. Paul had spent only three weeks founding and teaching this church before he had to depart. This means he was writing to a young church filled with new believers.

Paul clearly felt it was vital for these new Christians to know the doctrines about Jesus' second coming. In every single chapter of 1 and 2 Thessalonians, he talks about one or more of these themes: the rapture, the tribulation, apostasy and the antichrist, or Christ's return. It's never too early for us as Christians to understand the end times. That's because it's never too early to let Bible prophecy motivate us toward holy living, sharing the gospel while there is time, and cultivating an eternal perspective that fills us with hope as we endure today's hardships.

What did Paul teach? In 1 Thessalonians, that believers would be delivered from the wrath to come (1:10), that they would be a source of joy to Paul at Christ's coming (2:18-20), that they would be blameless and holy when Jesus comes (3:13), that they would be raptured and taken to heaven (4:13-18), and that the day of the Lord would come without warning and they were to live soberly (5:1-11). In 2 Thessalonians, he taught that judgment was coming (1:5-10), that they were to be alert about the day of the Lord, that the antichrist would not rise until after the rapture (2:1-12), and that they would be protected from the evil one (3:1-5).

Paul was excited about sharing these truths with young believers. He knew Bible prophecy would build them up, equip them for challenging times, and point to the glorious future God had planned for them. Paul had a great love for the doctrines of Christ's return, and he wanted to pass that love on to others. We ought to have that same love so that we, too, will "eagerly await the revelation of our Lord Jesus Christ" (1 Corinthians 1:7 NASB).

THE PERSONAL NATURE
OF THE RAPTURE

I will come again and will take you to myself, that
where I am you may be also (John 14:3).

The Lord himself will descend...[we] will be caught
up to meet the Lord in the air, and so we will always
be with the Lord (1 Thessalonians 4:16-17).

In the two rapture passages above, a powerful truth stands out: It is the Lord Himself who will take us up to be with Him so that we can live with Him forever.

When the rapture takes place, it is Jesus who will come down from heaven to meet us in the air. From that moment onward, we will always be together with Him. This reveals the highly personal nature of the rapture. This isn't a task that Christ plans to delegate to the angels or some other intermediaries. Our miraculous transport to heaven will not be a formal or mechanical process in which we will observe the Lord at a distance. No, the rapture will bring us into the loving and direct presence of Jesus Himself. This will be the most spectacular face-to-face encounter ever!

The personal nature of the rapture is a powerful confirmation of just how greatly Christ loves us. The entire purpose of His going to the cross was so that we could one day dwell with Him. Ephesians 5:25 says it was out of love that He gave Himself up for us. First John 3:16 says, "By this we know love, that he laid down his life for us." As believers, we have been made "a people for his own possession" (1 Peter 2:9). *His own possession!* Scripture is abundantly clear in proclaiming just how precious we are to Christ.

When at last we are ushered into our Lord's presence, it will happen instantaneously. And Christ will carry out the task Himself. The rapture will be immediate and personal—all because of how much Jesus cherishes us. The Lord would have it no other way.

FACE TO FACE FOR THE FIRST TIME

I will...take you to myself (John 14:3).

Our pilgrimage here on earth is filled with longings. We are eager for the day when our bodies will be unshackled from the debilitating effects of sin. We look forward to shedding the perishable and taking on the imperishable. And we cannot wait for the time when our communion with the Lord is done not from an impassable distance but face to face.

Have you ever wondered about how marvelous that first moment in Christ's presence will be? Imagine, at long last, standing before the one who faced the brutal agonies of the crucifixion for you. Who, even when you were His enemy, was willing to die on your behalf and extend forgiveness to you. Who gladly set aside His glory, humbled Himself, and came to earth so that you could experience glory with Him in heaven.

Imagine coming face to face with the one who has guided your every step from the moment you became a believer. How little do we know of all that He does on our behalf! From our perspective, there are times when we are unsure of His designs and purposes for us. But every one of our days was written in His book before we were born—an affirmation of just how closely He pays attention to us each moment of every day.

At the rapture, when we first come face to face with Jesus in the air, the emotions that well up from within will be more overwhelming than anything we've ever experienced. We'll be so excited it will be as if we were walking on clouds. There will be no words adequate to describe the euphoria we feel. The love and gratitude in our hearts will crescendo as never before.

The more we ponder how incredible that first encounter with Jesus will be, the more we will grow in our anticipation of His return!

WHY THE RAPTURE IS OUR BLESSED HOPE

Our blessed hope...(Titus 2:13).

Have you ever thought about the many ways that the rapture is "our blessed hope"?

In context, here is what Paul wrote in Titus 2:11-13: "The grace of God has appeared, bringing salvation for all people, training us...to live self-controlled, upright, and godly lives in the present age, waiting for our blessed hope." God's grace compels us to live rightly as we await the rapture—a *blessed* event! Here, "blessed" speaks of a genuine happiness. And "hope" refers not to a mere wish, but to an absolute certainty.

Here are the reasons the rapture is our blessed hope:

- It promises our being taken up to our heavenly home prepared by Jesus Himself.
- It promises our reunion with beloved brothers and sisters in Christ who died before us.
- It promises that we will not face the wrath God pours out during the tribulation.
- It promises our transformation from mortality to immortality.
- It promises our living together with Christ—forever.

Every one of these promises is a blessing. It is for these reasons—and more—that the rapture is a powerful source of hope for us. This guaranteed event includes guaranteed benefits. That is why Paul wrote that we are to "encourage one another" with words about the rapture (1 Thessalonians 4:18). As we remind each other about the rapture, our hearts will be lifted up and we'll be reminded to live with an eternal perspective. The strength we need for the here and now can be drawn from the assurances of what lies ahead for us in the future.

Every thought about the rapture should thrill us. We have much to look forward to. While the blessings we anticipate tomorrow can easily be eclipsed by today's fears, we should live with a resolve to instead let our future blessings diminish our present anxieties.

GOD'S SOVEREIGNTY AND FULFILLED PROPHECIES

[He] works all things according to his will (Ephesians 1:11).

When it comes to understanding the extent of God's sovereignty, one question that inevitably arises is this: Does God actually control *all* things?

A key reason people ask this is because so much of what happens in the world doesn't make sense. We're unable to reconcile how the existence of evil and its many expressions fit with the premise that God is in control. So we place limitations on God, saying that He permits certain things, or that He is generally sovereign but not always, or that He works in response to or within circumstances rather than over them.

Scripture leaves no room for doubt about the totality of God's governance. He "works all things according to his will" (Ephesians 1:11). "Many are the plans in the mind of a man, but it is the purpose of the LORD that will stand" (Proverbs 19:21). "Who has spoken and it came to pass, unless the Lord has commanded it?" (Lamentations 3:37). Even when it comes to permitting things, Satan had to get permission from God before attacking Job (Job 1:6-12). The adversary had to go through Christ first when he wanted to sift Peter like wheat (Luke 22:31).

God's total sovereignty is an absolute essential when it comes to Bible prophecy. In Isaiah 46:9-10, He says, "I am God, and there is none like me, declaring the end from the beginning and from ancient times things not yet done, saying, 'My counsel shall stand, and I will accomplish all my purpose.'" If God weren't entirely sovereign, He would not be able to prophesy the future with exacting precision, then ensure the fulfillment of those prophecies.

God is able to fulfill every one of His prophetic promises because He is in full control of all. His sovereignty and His ability to fulfill prophecies go hand in hand. God's perfect track record of fulfilled prophecies is a testimony to the infinite reach of His sovereignty and will.

THE FULLNESS OF CHRIST IS OURS

From his fullness we have all received, grace upon grace (John 1:16).

In all that Christ has done for us, He has not done anything halfway. He has given fully of Himself. And when we realize what this fullness represents, we cannot help but be overwhelmed.

A great starting point for understanding all that we have in Christ is Colossians 2:9: "In him the whole fullness of deity dwells bodily." In Jesus is the fullness of God. Through Jesus, we have the fullness of God available to us. From a spiritual and eternal standpoint, we lack nothing!

What does the fullness available in Christ grant to us? "The blood of Jesus...cleanses us from *all* sin" (1 John 1:7). Because of this, we have *no* condemnation (Romans 8:1). We have received the *fullness* of His grace (John 1:16). We will be "united with him in a resurrection *like his*" (Romans 6:5). We have been "blessed...with *every* spiritual blessing in the heavenly places" (Ephesians 1:3-4). The "God of *all* comfort...comforts us in *all* our affliction" (2 Corinthians 1:3-4). "God will supply *every* need of yours according to his riches in glory" (Philippians 4:19). Second Corinthians 9:8-10 proclaims, "God is able to bless you abundantly, so that in *all* things at *all* times, having *all* that you need, you will abound in *every* good work" (NIV).

The fullness that is ours in Christ is all-encompassing. It is a fullness that is ours at all times in all things. It is a fullness that abounds and is beyond measure. It is in this context that the promises like "My grace is sufficient for you" awaken us to how much we have in Christ (2 Corinthians 12:9). We will never have too little; we will always have more than enough.

The longer we experience our Lord's fullness, the more we will realize it is inexhaustible. "His mercies never come to an end; they are new every morning" (Lamentations 3:22-23). That is why His provisions for us will always be fresh and bountiful. And it is why we will always have more to discover about Christ—and the thrill of abiding in Him will never cease.

WHY BIBLE PROPHECY
SHOULD BE PRECIOUS TO US

I have spoken, and I will bring it to pass (Isaiah 46:11).

For a variety of reasons, there are some Christians who shy away from Bible prophecy. But consider this: One of the most significant ways we show our love for God is by loving His Word. That means embracing all His Word, including the prophetic parts. All of Scripture should be precious to us, including Bible prophecy. That's because...

- every prophecy in the Bible comes from God Himself (2 Peter 1:21).

- prophecy informs us about who God is and how He works (Isaiah 46:8-11).

- as part of God's Word, prophecy equips us and makes us complete (2 Timothy 3:16-17).

- prophecy helps us to know more about Christ (every prophecy about Him!).

- prophecy creates within us a deeper love and gratitude for Christ (2 Corinthians 9:15).

- every prophecy is a promise God will fulfill (1 Kings 8:56; 2 Corinthians 1:20).

- God's prophets and angels were eager to understand Bible prophecy (1 Peter 1:10-12).

- prophecy brings blessing to us (Titus 2:13; Revelation 1:3).

- prophecy reminds us to encourage one another (Hebrews 10:24-25).

- prophecy increases our compassion for the lost (2 Peter 3:9).

- prophecy shines hope into a hopeless world (Isaiah 9:6-7).

- prophecy encourages us to have an eternal perspective (Colossians 3:2).

When Christ was born, most of Israel had no idea a miracle had occurred. Very few recognized that God had just sent the long-awaited Messiah. Those who understood the significance of Jesus' birth knew prophecy was being fulfilled. This tells us prophecy was dear to them. The same is true for us today. It's when Bible prophecy is precious to us that we will live with informed awareness and hope, making us ready for our Lord's return.

PART 2:

UNDERSTANDING THE BIG PICTURE OF BIBLE PROPHECY FROM GENESIS TO REVELATION

THE FIRST PROMISE OF A SAVIOR

*I will put enmity between you and the woman, and between
your offspring and her offspring; he shall bruise your
head, and you shall bruise his heel (Genesis 3:15).*

When Adam and Eve sinned in the Garden of Eden, their separation from God was immediate. A sinister darkness they had never known swept over and filled them. Instantly, they knew something was wrong. Plagued with guilt, they attempted to hide from God.

In that very dark moment, God proclaimed a promise that offered a lifeline of hope. As the first man and woman despaired over their separation from God, the Lord gave a prophecy that revealed a plan was already in place to make it possible for them to be brought back to Him.

In Genesis 3:15, God reassured Adam and Eve by telling them that someday, a Savior would come who would crush the enemy under His heel. As they sorrowed over the consequences of their disobedience, God gave a prophecy of future deliverance.

This first promise of a Savior wasn't a spur-of-the-moment idea. God wasn't caught by surprise. This wasn't a salvage operation. No, He had already planned for this in eternity past. Ephesians 1:4-5 proclaims, "He chose us in him *before the foundation of the world*, that we should be holy and blameless before him. In love he predestined us for adoption to himself as sons through Jesus Christ, according to the purpose of his will." God made plans for us to become His children—through Jesus Christ—before He created the world.

God's first promise of a Savior provided a glimmer of hope that grew brighter with time as He revealed more details about this future Rescuer. Never were we left without hope. Through every prophecy of a coming Savior, God declared, "Here is My plan to make restoration possible. This is how much I love you."

SEEING THE CROSS IN
THE GARDEN OF EDEN

He shall bruise your head, and you shall bruise his heel (Genesis 3:15).

Immediately after sin entered the garden, God gave the first prophecy of a Savior. In this promise, He revealed the outcome of what would be an ages-long battle between Christ and Satan—an outcome that was never in doubt.

God prophesied that Satan would bruise Christ's heel. All through the Old Testament, we read of the enemy's many attempts to bring an end to the people of Israel. Satan knew that if he could destroy the lineage that led to Jesus' birth, the Savior would never be born. But Satan was unsuccessful. When God became flesh, even Herod's order to kill all the baby boys in Bethlehem failed to achieve Satan's aim. Even the greatest of temptations in the wilderness failed to lure Christ into sin. Even the cross and death could not keep Jesus in the grave. All the attacks inflicted by Satan could do no more than bruise Christ's heel—blows that were not fatal.

God also prophesied that Christ would bruise Satan's head. Through Jesus' death and resurrection, the Lord delivered a fatal blow to the adversary. The devil's power was defeated not temporarily, but permanently. Death no longer had its sting and was swallowed up in victory.

At the cross, Jesus "disarmed the rulers and authorities and put them to open shame, by triumphing over them" (Colossians 2:15). He died to "destroy the one who has the power of death, that is, the devil" (Hebrews 2:14). And Satan's destiny is that he will be "thrown into the lake of fire and sulfur...tormented day and night forever and ever" (Revelation 20:10).

All through the Bible, the holy war between Christ and Satan is waged. But in the very first prophecy about the enmity that would exist between the two, God revealed who would have victory. And the God who assured that outcome is the same God who is at work in our lives today, assuring our ultimate victory too.

GOD SHOWS GRACE
EVEN DURING JUDGMENT

*The LORD said, "I will blot out man..." But
Noah found favor (Genesis 6:7-8).*

I n Noah's day, as people multiplied on the earth, they became more wicked, and the world was filled with violence. So grieved was God that He said, "My Spirit shall not abide in man forever, for he is flesh: his days shall be 120 years...I will blot out man" (Genesis 6:3, 7). Yet Noah "found favor in the eyes of the LORD"—he was "a righteous man" (verses 8-9). God said, "I have determined to make an end of all flesh" (verse 13), and He instructed Noah to build an ark.

The account of the flood makes for a grim read. The world was evil and deserving of judgment. Unfortunately, many who read this account see only God's judgment and overlook His grace. They view God as an angry ogre who smites the world nearly out of existence, and miss that God gave people another 100 years to repent before He sent the flood. They miss that Noah was "a preacher of righteousness" (2 Peter 2:5 NASB). For more than a century, as Noah built the ark, God used him to warn evildoers of coming judgment.

Though God extended an offer of grace, it was rejected by all except Noah and his family. Sinful mankind decided its own fate and spurned God, just as Adam and Eve had. Sin has consequences, and this made judgment necessary. Even so, God's grace shone brightly in those dark days by saving a family and some animals on the ark, and by giving earth a fresh start. It's because of that grace that we are here today.

The pattern we see all through the Bible is this: God uses prophecy to warn of future judgment. He allows time for repentance, though that time isn't unlimited. And before, during, and after He pours out judgment, He expresses grace. Should we ever doubt this, we need only to look to Christ, the Savior—the greatest expression of God's grace. God went to great lengths to make our salvation possible. He "is patient... not wishing that any should perish" (2 Peter 3:9).

THE PROMISE OF A GREAT NATION

The LORD said to Abram, "Go from your country...to the land that I will show you. And I will make you a great nation" (Genesis 12:1-2).

After Adam and Eve made the devastating decision that plunged all of humanity into sin and severed their relationship with their Creator, God wasted no time letting the couple know that someday, a Redeemer would come who would save them and defeat Satan.

In Genesis 12:1-3, we see the next big step forward in God's plan to rescue mankind. Abram was to become the beginning of a lineage through which the promised Savior would come. This lineage would run through a great nation that God Himself would build.

God's call to Abram is remarkable. He takes the initiative and reaches out to Abram. At the time, Abram is 75 and his wife, Sarai, is 65. Childless, they are getting older. They're asked to move 700-plus miles and are given no details about how this "great nation" would happen.

In hindsight, we now know that Israel truly did become great under the reigns of David and Solomon. More amazing is that even though Israel was wiped out in AD 70 and a remnant of Jews scattered to other lands, it became a nation again in 1948 and is now among the most powerful and influential in the world. And Israel's most glorious days are still ahead, when Jesus will sit on His throne and rule the earth from Jerusalem during the millennial kingdom.

God told Abram, "*I will* make you a great nation." Never in his wildest dreams could Abram have imagined the grand scale on which God would fulfill His promise. When God says, "I will," He means it. The pages of Scripture are filled with "I will" promises that are still in effect for Israel and that are given to those who follow Christ. To Israel, "not one word has failed of all his good promise" (1 Kings 8:56). To believers, "all the promises of God find their Yes in him" (2 Corinthians 1:20). Every single one of God's "I will" promises will come true.

THE PROMISE OF A GREAT NAME

I will make of you a great nation, and I will bless you and make
your name great, so that you will be a blessing (Genesis 12:2).

After God promises to make Abram a great nation, He gives more "I will" promises. He goes on to say He will make Abram's name great and explains why: so that Abram would be a blessing.

From Abram's perspective, the odds seemed heavily against him. He was to move to a land where he and his wife would start over from scratch. They had no children. How could he become great in a land where he was a nobody and when he had no offspring? If Abram had listed the reasons to decline God's call, he could have written several. The one and only reason he could possibly give for obeying God was because God had said, "I will do this."

The slender thread that Abram clung to as he stepped out on this venture was that of trust. All he had was God's word. Abram wasn't given a point-by-point plan backed by guarantees. Hebrews 11:8-9 says, "By faith Abraham obeyed when he was called to go out…not knowing where he was going. By faith he went to live…in a foreign land." How many of us would be willing to take such big steps that involved great risk, not knowing where we are going?

God was true to His word in many ways. He gave Abram a great legacy through material wealth (Genesis 24:35). He was with Abram in all he did (Genesis 21:22). Abram's stature grew so great that he was called "a prince of God" (Genesis 23:6). And across the centuries to today, Abram has been revered by Jews and Christians as a great man.

God's purpose for making Abram great was so Abram would be a blessing. God used Abram as a vessel to touch others. He desires to do the same through His people today. Among believers, we're to "stir up one another to love and good works" (Hebrews 10:24). Among unbelievers, we're to shine light (Matthew 5:16). God blesses us so that we may bless others.

THE PROMISE OF BLESSINGS OR CURSES

I will bless those who bless you, and him who
dishonors you I will curse (Genesis 12:3).

As God continues to proclaim His "I will" promises to Abram, He gives a prophecy that sets a remarkable standard that will continue all through the ages: "I will bless those who bless you, and I will curse those who curse you."

Beginning with the very first Bible passage in which God reveals His plans to establish the nation of Israel through Abram, He declares this truth: To do good to Israel is to invite God's blessing, and to go against Israel is to provoke His wrath. Every person and every nation will rise or fall based on how they treat Israel.

We have seen this evidenced powerfully all through history. Though the Assyrians and Babylonians took the Jewish people captive, in the end, God judged and destroyed them, as He did other ancient enemies. The supposedly invincible Roman Empire that destroyed Jerusalem and the temple in AD 70 eventually crumbled. Across the centuries, in the wake of hostilities against the Jews, the persecutors have declined or diminished. Germany's Third Reich, which was supposed to last 1,000 years, was swiftly eradicated. Israel has prevailed against all the Arab nations that have warred against it in modern times. The US, which has been an ally since Israel's rebirth in 1948, prospered for decades, but now that relationship is on rocky ground.

Most amazing of all is God's preservation and restoration of Israel after 2,000 years of exile. The nation, culture, and language have been revived. God's mighty hand is still on His people. "He who keeps Israel will neither slumber nor sleep" (Psalm 121:4). Later, during the millennial kingdom, God will exalt Israel, making it the center and source of blessing for all: "Nations will come to your light, and kings to the brightness of your rising" (Isaiah 60:3 NASB).

THE PROMISE OF BLESSINGS
TO ALL THE EARTH

In you all the families of the earth shall be blessed (Genesis 12:3).

The prophetic promises God made to Abram in Genesis 12:1-3 were meant for all time and are felt by us even now. God told Abram, "I will make your name great." This individual promise came true in Abram's time, and he is still widely revered today. God said that from Abram would come "a great nation." This was a national promise about Israel, which knew greatness in ancient times, was reborn in 1948, and is thriving today. And there is the global promise that through the bloodline of Abram and Israel "all the families of the earth shall be blessed." Through them, the world was given the Bible, a Savior, and the gospel, which continues to spread across the earth. Jesus has had a more transformational impact on history and people than any other person, and the Bible is, by far and away, the most published book on earth.

The dominant theme of God's prophetic promises is blessing. God said He would bless Abram so that Abram would be a blessing—to his descendants, to the nation of Israel, and to the world. The blessing God gave to Abram went on to bless *all* the people of earth through the birth, death, and resurrection of a Savior who could bring the lost back to God.

God's monumental blessings to one man have long since multiplied into many more blessings poured out through the ages to countless multitudes. Every person who receives Christ as Savior and Lord is another recipient and spreader of these blessings, which will continue to be felt and expand into the future, all through the coming millennial kingdom and eternity.

Galatians 3:8-9 says the gospel was preached "beforehand to Abraham, saying, 'In you shall all the nations be blessed.' So then, those who are of faith are blessed along with Abraham, the man of faith." Every believer—including you!—has been richly and eternally blessed by the blessings God first spoke to Abram in Genesis 12:1-3.

GOD'S "I WILL" PROMISES

Go…to the land that I will show you. I will make…you a great nation…I will bless you and make your name great…bless those who bless you, and him who dishonors you I will curse, and in you all the families of the earth shall be blessed (Genesis 12:1-3).

I n total, God gave eight promises to Abram in Genesis 12:1-3:

1. I will show you the land (that God would give to Abram).

2. I will make you a great nation.

3. I will bless you.

4. I will make your name great.

5. I will make you a blessing.

6. I will bless those who bless you.

7. I will curse those who curse you.

8. I will bless all the people of earth through you.

These promises were given to an individual, a nation, and the world, and their fulfillments will reach all the way into eternity. That makes Genesis 12:1-3 a remarkable treasure trove of prophetic promises, all clustered in the space of three verses.

God gave many other "I will" promises throughout the Bible. Two especially precious ones given to all believers are "I will never leave you nor forsake you" (Hebrews 13:5) and "I will come again and will take you to myself, that where I am you may be also" (John 14:3).

Because God always fulfills His promises, at heart, every single one is an "I will" promise. Every vow that God makes, He keeps. Oftentimes we won't know *how* or *when* God will carry out His promises, but we can know with certainty that He will *do* what He promised.

WHAT THE WORDS "I WILL" REVEAL ABOUT GOD

I will…(Genesis 12:3; John 14:3).

There is a lot of meaning packed into those two simple words "I will." When spoken by God, they ring with absolute certainty, and through them, we learn a lot about Him.

"I will" tells us God is faithful. God keeps His word. Hebrews 10:23 says, "He who promised is faithful." This faithfulness is new every morning (Lamentations 3:23), another way of saying it never ceases. Even when we are faithless, He remains faithful (2 Timothy 2:13). A promise given by God is a promise that will be fulfilled.

"I will" tells us God is trustworthy. We can count on God. His perfect character backs every word He says. Because He is unchanging, He will never change His mind about His promises. Because He is truthful, He will never lie to us. And because He is all-powerful, He is able to make His promises come to pass. When it comes to God's promises, we have no reason to waver in fear, doubt, or anxiety. Isaiah 26:4 tells us we can "trust in the LORD forever, for the LORD GOD is an everlasting rock."

"I will" tells us God is sovereign. For God to be able to fulfill His promises, He must possess the ability to orchestrate all things so they arrive at His predetermined outcome. This He can do, for Daniel 4:35 says that God "does *all* according to his will." If God were to make a promise and not be able to keep it, that would serve as evidence He isn't sovereign after all.

"I will" tells us God is loving. The very fact God is resolutely committed to keeping His promises to us shows the magnitude of His love for us. And when we consider how many promises God has given to us, the extent of His affection for us becomes clearer. So great is this love that He Himself has ensured we will be with Him for all eternity: "I will come back and take you to be with me that you also may be where I am" (John 14:3 NIV).

THE STRATEGY BEHIND
GOD'S PROMISE OF LAND

The LORD appeared to Abram and said, "To your offspring I will give this land" (Genesis 12:7).

After God promised that He would make Abram a great nation through which the Savior would be born and bless the peoples of the earth, He appeared to Abram again to unveil the next aspect of His master plan. He said, "To your offspring I will give this land."

In the simple words "I will give," God made it clear this was an unconditional promise. The land was a gift. No conditions were placed on Abram or his descendants. As we will soon see, God repeated and followed up on this promise many times—in some cases, making it clear this was an everlasting arrangement. This land would belong to Israel, period. God's promise itself serves as a title deed to the land. God, who owns all, was giving Israel the ownership.

At first, God's promise might not seem all that special. Why *this* land, of all places?

God was looking ahead to when His people would populate the land and He would task them with the responsibility of making Him known to others. He also wanted His Son to be born here and to minister here. This was the most strategic and central location in the ancient world for the Savior to be born. It formed a land bridge that served as the intersection between Europe, Asia, and Africa. All the world's traffic had to journey through Israel to go from one continent to another. This meant every traveler would potentially hear about the wonderful God of Israel. And when the church was born, the gospel would easily spread outward from here.

The land that would become Israel is where God chose to make Himself known to people everywhere. This was the ideal place for a spiritual lighthouse that would be able to shine its light outward to the surrounding nations in the ancient world. God's gift of this land to Abram's offspring was strategic, intentional, and motivated by His love for the lost.

A PERMANENT PROMISE
TO ABRAM'S OFFSPRING

To your offspring I will give this land (Genesis 12:7).

In Genesis 12:7, God promised a specific land to be given to a specific people—Abram's descendants. This promise was repeated many times all through the Old Testament—and it's fascinating to note the details God added to this promise as time went on. For example, in Genesis 13:15, God said, "All the land that you see I will give to you and to your offspring *forever*." In Genesis 17:8, He called this land "an *everlasting* possession."

God's promise was then given to the next generation. To Isaac, He said, "To you and to your offspring I will give all these lands" (Genesis 26:3). Jacob came next: "The land on which you lie I will give to you and to your offspring" (28:13). Later, Moses was promised the land that God "swore...to Abraham, to Isaac, and to Jacob" (Deuteronomy 6:10). See the continuity?

Hundreds of years later, even with Israel facing judgment and exile, God had the prophet Jeremiah tell the people He had given this land "to your fathers *forever*" (Jeremiah 7:7).

There are two reasons it's vital for God's promise of the land to continue today and into the future: First, many end-times prophecies would not be able to be fulfilled unless a nation of Israel was in place. Israel was destroyed and the people scattered in the Roman conquest of AD 70. But miracle of miracles, Israel was reborn in 1948. And now, there is a literal nation of Israel that can serve as a stage on which the end times play out. Only God could have done that!

Second, Christ will rule from Jerusalem in the future millennial kingdom. In Isaiah 60:3, God tells Israel that during those days, the nations will "come to your light." In that same millennial context, verse 21 adds that Israel will "possess the land forever."

When God says a promise is forever, He means it. Truly, "the gifts and the calling of God are irrevocable" (Romans 11:29).

THE ENDURING NATURE
OF THE LAND PROMISES

He guaranteed it with an oath (Hebrews 6:18).

Today, there are some who say that because the Jewish people rejected their Messiah, God's promise was made void and the land is no longer theirs. Therefore, He sent them out of the land. Some even believe that the promises God made to Israel now belong to the church.

But that is not supported by Scripture. As scholar Thomas Ice notes, "Every Old Testament prophet, except Jonah, speaks of a permanent return to the Land of Israel by the Jews. Nowhere in the New Testament are these Old Testament promises ever changed or negated."[4] When the Old Testament prophets condemned the Israelites for disobeying God, they followed with promises of Israel's future restoration—Amos 9:14-15 is a great example.

In the book of Hebrews, we find this: "When God made a promise to Abraham, since he had no one greater by whom to swear, he swore by himself...when God desired to show more convincingly to the heirs of the promise the unchangeable character of his purpose, he guaranteed it with an oath" (6:13, 17-18).

This bears repeating: God swore by *Himself*—the highest authority in all the universe. Why? To show *more convincingly* the *unchangeable* character of His purpose. He *guaranteed* His words with an oath. His word can always be trusted, but He did this to show He meant it.

God did this for the benefit of "the *heirs* of the promise." Who are Abraham's heirs? Genesis repeatedly described them as his "seed" or "offspring"—always in a literal sense, speaking of Abraham's physical descendants, the nation of Israel, and not the church.

If God's land promises were not everlasting and no longer applied to Israel, it would mean hundreds of His prophecies were wrong. But God's plans and purposes have always endured and will continue onward. He never changes, and His prophecies will always stand.

ADVERSITY CANNOT
STOP GOD'S PLANS

Your offspring will be sojourners in a land that is not theirs...
And they will be afflicted for four hundred years (Genesis 15:13).

On the evening that God walked between the animal halves and sealed His promise with Abram, He revealed a new prophecy informing Abram of what would happen to his descendants. They would go to Egypt, be enslaved there for 400 years, then return home with great possessions (Genesis 15:13-16). In the space of four verses, God gave a brief outline of a history that would extend from the last part of Genesis to Joshua—roughly 160-plus chapters of the Bible.

Long before any of this happened, God had already planned out every detail—working even with all the adversity that would occur along the way! It was through the hatred of Joseph's brothers that Joseph ended up in Egypt. It was because of a woman's fury that Joseph ended up in prison, where he interpreted a dream and went on to become second in power only to Pharaoh. It was through a famine that Abram's descendants were driven to move to Egypt. It was because of the Hebrews' slavery that they cried out to God for deliverance. When they were being chased by the powerful Egyptian army, God did a miracle at the Red Sea. When they wandered for 40 years in a vast desert, God provided manna, quail, and water. When it came time to conquer powerful enemies in the Promised Land, God gave them victory.

One of the patterns we see all through the Bible is how frequently adversity arises as God's prophetic plans are put into motion. But no matter how much the forces of evil and the hands of evildoers fight against God's rule, God overrules them. Joseph famously told his brothers, "You meant evil against me, but God meant it for good" (Genesis 50:20). As prophecies unfold and are fulfilled in the face of even the worst opposition, the infinitude of God's sovereignty is put on glorious display. God has and always will prevail.

GOD SEALS HIS PROMISE TO ABRAM

On that day the LORD made a covenant with Abram, saying,
"To your offspring I give this land, from the river of Egypt
to the great river, the river Euphrates" (Genesis 15:18).

In Genesis 15, God repeats to Abram His Genesis 12 promises of greatness, many descendants, and a specific land. This time, however, He not only states the promises, but seals them.

God told Abram to cut some animals in half (except for two birds) and lay them out so there was a path between them (Genesis 15:9-10). The custom in ancient times was that when two parties made a covenant with each other, both would walk between the cut halves, which pictured what would happen to them if they broke their end of the deal. But when it came time for God and Abram to carry out this act, it was God alone who "passed between these pieces" (verse 17) as Abram slept. This means God took upon Himself the entire responsibility of carrying out the promises, making them unconditional. Abram was not bound in any way.

As Hebrews 6:13 says, God "swore by himself." There is nothing Israel could have done to cancel God's promises. God did this because He knew His fallen people were destined to fail. This is also true about God's gift of salvation to us. Christ did it all; we contribute nothing.

God's action of walking between the animal parts sealed for all time His vows to Abram. From Genesis 12 to the last chapter of Revelation, God's promises form continuous threads moving toward their ultimate fulfillment. We know there is more to come because God said Israel's boundaries would go "from the river of Egypt to the great river...Euphrates." That hasn't happened yet; that will occur during Christ's reign in the millennial kingdom.

Through Israel, we see that God's prophecies are still in motion today. This makes us eyewitnesses of His ongoing work and assures us that all God's future promises *will* be fulfilled!

TRUSTING GOD TO DO
WHAT HE PROMISED

Sarai, Abram's wife, had borne him no children (Genesis 16:1).

A bram was puzzled. More than 10 years had gone by since God had prophesied to him, "Look toward heaven, and number the stars, if you are able to number them…So shall your offspring be" (Genesis 15:5). Yet Abram and Sarai still had no children. And they were older than ever.

Out of desperation, Sarai devised a plan, and Abram went along with it. She offered her handmaid, Hagar, to Abram in the hopes of producing an heir. Surely this would help move God's promise along! Their intentions may have been good, but their actions backfired—badly.

Hagar became pregnant…and Sarai became jealous. Even though Sarai came up with the idea, she went into blame mode and, in anger, told Abram, "May the wrong done to me be on you!" (Genesis 16:5). From Hagar came Ishmael, and the damage caused by Abram and Sarai's foolish decision still has ramifications today. Ishmael went on to father the Arab peoples, who have been in conflict with the Jewish people for the past 4,000 years.

What lesson can we learn from all this?

When God makes a promise, He will keep and fulfill it—in His way, in His timing. Anytime we assume an unfulfilled prophecy should come to pass in a certain way or time, we end up second-guessing God and we may find ourselves attempting to make His plan happen apart from His provision.

There's great danger in imposing our expectations upon God's prophetic promises. This is one reason for some of the incorrect views of Bible prophecy today—views that cause a lot of confusion among believers. A key part of "rightly handling the word of truth" (2 Timothy 2:15) is to take God's promises exactly as they are, trust His ways and His timing, and watch Him carry out their glorious fulfillments.

WATCHING FOR GOD'S GRACE IN PROPHECY

I am God Almighty (Genesis 17:1).

Even after Abram and Sarai made a big mess by attempting to fulfill God's promise of an heir, God's mercy and grace abounded to them. Though they had failed to trust Him and the results led to serious consequences, in love and compassion, God reaffirmed His commitment that He would follow through on His promises to them.

From our perspective, what Abram and Sarai had done would seem like a setback that would have required God to overhaul His plans. But because God is all-knowing, their actions did not take Him by surprise. And because He is all-sovereign, even their attempt to take the situation into their own hands did not remove it from His hands.

After Ishmael's birth, another 13 years went by. God visited Abram again when he was 99, and Sarai 90. Upon greeting Abram, the Lord said, "I am God Almighty" (Genesis 17:1). This is the first time this title appears in Scripture, and it refers to God's unlimited power. It's as if He was telling Abram, "Nothing can derail My plans." And in light of Abram and Sarai's age—which now made childbearing impossible—God was saying, "Nothing is too hard for Me."

Within the year, Isaac was born—the first of many millions of descendants. The long wait was over. Looking ahead, Abraham still had no idea of the magnitude of what God would do. Looking back, we cannot help but marvel at the countless blessings this world has experienced because God has carried out and continues to fulfill His promises to Abraham.

Beginning with the first promise of a Savior in Genesis 3:15, we see a consistent pattern: When God announces or fulfills His prophecies, we see expressions of His grace. This teaches us to be on the lookout for ways He evidences His grace as His prophetic plans unfold. Whenever we celebrate God's amazing prophecies, we'll find reason to celebrate His amazing grace.

GOD'S FAITHFULNESS CONTINUES

I will be with you and will bless you...and I will establish the
oath that I swore to Abraham your father (Genesis 26:3).

After Abraham died, God appeared to Isaac and prophesied,

> I will be with you and will bless you, for to you and to your
> offspring I will give all these lands, and I will establish the
> oath that I swore to Abraham your father. I will multiply
> your offspring as the stars of heaven and will give to your
> offspring all these lands. And in your offspring all the nations
> of the earth shall be blessed (Genesis 26:3-4).

Here, God reaffirmed all three promises He made to Abraham:
(1) numerous descendants, (2) permanent possession of the land, and
(3) a universal blessing of all the earth through his descendants, from
whom would come the Savior.

As God passed these promises on to Isaac, He made these three
points clear:

- All the promises I gave to Abraham, I am giving to you.

- Just as I have been faithful in the past, I will be faithful in
  the present and the future.

- I have taken upon Myself the responsibility for fulfilling
  these promises.

Here's what we should notice: Isaac had times when he failed God,
just as Abraham did. Yet God promised blessing to Isaac—not because
of anything Isaac had done, but because He is faithful.

The same is true for every believer: God saves and blesses us not on
account of anything we have done, but what Christ has done. He saved
us "not according to our works, but according to His own purpose
and grace which was granted us in Christ Jesus" (2 Timothy 1:9 NASB).
Because God keeps His promises, and because we are saved in Christ's
power and not our own, we have the assurance that even our unfaithfulness will not cause God's faithfulness to cease.

THE REASON GOD REPEATS HIS PROMISES

The land on which you lie I will give to you and to your offspring. Your offspring shall be like the dust of the earth…and in you and your offspring shall all the families of the earth be blessed (Genesis 28:13-14).

The prophecies and promises that God spoke to Abraham were handed down to Isaac, then to Jacob. Once again, the Lord guaranteed many descendants, ownership of the land, and blessings to all the earth through the family line that would one day culminate in the Messiah's birth.

With each successive generation and the passage of time, a lot changed. But God's promises did not. As we review what God said to Abraham, Isaac, Jacob, and others after them, His words may sound like a broken record. But by repeating His promises, God firmly establishes these important truths:

1. When He makes a promise, He keeps it. *He is faithful.*

2. The failures of God's people would not cancel God's promise of a future Savior that would bless the earth. *He is loving and merciful.*

3. The land would belong to Abraham's descendants, period. *He is sovereign.*

When it comes to God's promises to be faithful, there is a reason He is repetitious: We are forgetful, and our failures often cause us to doubt that God still loves and cares for us.

Remember that Abraham and Sarah waited 25 years for a child. Isaac and Rebekah waited 19 years. Jacob had to flee the land for 21 years, but God promised he would return. For many people, difficult circumstances like these are what causes them to question God.

The trials we face in life can easily give birth to doubt, and God's reminders of His faithfulness serve as a lifeline of hope. In times of uncertainty, the prescription is to remember and cling to God's promises. As we do so, our unsettled hearts will be filled with peace.

FAITHFUL EVEN WHEN WE FAIL

I am with you and will keep you wherever you go...I will not leave you until I have done what I have promised you (Genesis 28:15).

The words above were spoken by God to Jacob, the next generation after Isaac. God declared His commitment to remain faithful to Jacob and never leave him, regardless of what might happen. And a lot did happen. Jacob, whose name means "deceiver," lived up to his billing.

In those days, when a father died, the firstborn son was given twice the inheritance of the other sons and became the family authority. Jacob's brother, Esau, was the firstborn, meaning he possessed this birthright.

When Isaac became ill and thought he was dying, he asked to see Esau so he could give the birthright and blessing. But Isaac's wife Rebekah wanted the birthright for Jacob. Through a combination of lies and deceit, Rebekah and Jacob plotted to fool Isaac—who had poor vision—into thinking that Jacob was Esau. Through this wicked scheme, Jacob got the birthright and blessing. When Esau found out what happened, he vowed to kill his brother.

Jacob suffered greatly for his deception. His brother's fury forced him to move some 500 miles away from home and family for the next 21 years. During this exile, though God promised to stay with Jacob, He did not bail Jacob out of the consequences of his wrong actions. Though God was faithful, Jacob had lessons to learn.

We can always count on God's faithfulness, which overrides our failures but not necessarily their effects. His faithfulness does not promise relief from our troubles. Rather, God assures us that He will stay with us through them. While it's often hard to see God's faithfulness as we struggle with the consequences of our sins, we have His promise that He will never abandon us.

FORESHADOWS OF JESUS

Joseph's brothers came and bowed themselves before him (Genesis 42:6).
At the name of Jesus every knee should bow (Philippians 2:10).

The theme of the entire Bible is Jesus. The Old Testament points toward Him, the Gospels depict His years of ministry on earth, and the rest of the New Testament proclaims the wonders of all that He has done and will do for us.

In addition to the many direct Old Testament prophecies that speak about Jesus, there are what are known as *types*—illustrative or symbolic portrayals of God's plan of salvation. A remarkable example of this are the many parallels between Joseph and Jesus, which makes Joseph a foreshadow of Christ. Here are just a few examples:

- Joseph's brothers rejected him; the people of Jesus' day rejected Him.
- Joseph was sold for silver; Jesus was sold for silver.
- Joseph was jailed with two accused criminals; Jesus was crucified between two criminals.
- Joseph was falsely accused; Jesus was accused by false witnesses.
- Joseph's brothers did not recognize him; Jesus' own did not recognize Him.
- Joseph's brothers eventually bowed before him; someday, the world will bow to Jesus.
- God used Joseph's suffering to save many; God used Jesus' suffering to save many.

In these ways and more, Joseph foreshadowed Jesus, although no one realized this until after Jesus' ministry took place. A type remains unknown until *after* the parallels have occurred. For this reason, we shouldn't attempt to find supposed types that have no parallels yet and force prophetic significance upon them. It is only in hindsight that we can marvel over the many ways God was revealing certain elements of His plan of salvation. While types are not prophecies, they are prophetic in character, and many of them affirm just how full the Bible is of Jesus.

THE FUTURE SAVIOR AND KING

The scepter shall not depart from Judah…until tribute comes to him;
and to him shall be the obedience of the peoples (Genesis 49:10).

B efore Jacob died, he called his 12 sons to his bedside. To all 12 he prophesied "what shall happen to you in the days to come" (Genesis 49:1). The prophecy he gave to his son Judah stands out from all the others because in it, God unveils new details about the coming Savior.

Jacob began by referring to the tribe of Judah as a lion (verse 9)—and Revelation 5:5 calls Jesus "the Lion of the tribe of Judah." Jacob then said, "The scepter shall not depart from Judah, nor the ruler's staff from between his feet, until tribute comes to him; and to him shall be the obedience of the peoples." This scepter is a sign of kingly authority, and it would stay within the tribe of Judah until the coming of the one who holds all authority. This prophecy points to the future rule of King David, who came from the tribe of Judah. And it foreshadows Christ—a descendent of David—sitting on David's throne in a kingdom with no end (Luke 1:32-33).

God revealed that from the line of Judah would come kings for the nation, as well as the ultimate king, the Messiah, who will rule over all people in a future and prosperous kingdom.

This prophecy brings the book of Genesis to a glorious crescendo—it threads a direct line from Judah to King David to the final ruler, the King of kings and Lord of lords. This is the first glimpse God gives of the fact that the promised Savior would also be King.

As the Old Testament unfolded, God revealed more details about His grand plans for mankind. Most amazing of all is that along the way, He chose to work through flawed vessels. He still does that today. We fail God and don't always understand His will or His ways, but He has privileged us with active roles in what He is doing. And despite our shortcomings, He has granted for us to someday rule alongside our Savior and King in His kingdom.

TRUSTING GOD ABOUT THE FUTURE

You meant evil against me, but God meant it for good, to bring it
about that many people should be kept alive (Genesis 50:20).

God promised Abraham a land for his descendants—a land in which they would become a great nation and prosper. In His perfect wisdom, He determined that first, His chosen people should grow in numbers while in Egypt before they moved to the Promised Land.

After Abraham, Isaac, and Jacob came Joseph—the latest heir of this promise. And the path that God ordained for getting His people safely into Egypt called for Joseph to be sold into slavery, wrongly accused, and put into prison. Though Joseph suffered greatly, he never questioned God. He was unwavering in his commitment to live rightly, with integrity, even when there was a high price for doing so.

What explains Joseph's willingness to submit to whatever happened to him? He trusted that God's hand was upon him at all times, even when he couldn't see it. It was this trust that sustained him. His mature understanding of God's sovereignty had taught him this: God can work through *all* our present circumstances—good and bad—to accomplish His future purposes.

In life's dark hours, we cannot see ahead to what will happen. Only God knows the outcome. This requires trust on our part; He asks that we rest in the truth that no matter what our present circumstances, He can use them toward our future good—whether on earth or in eternity.

That's why Joseph was able to tell his brothers, "Do not be distressed or angry with yourselves because you sold me here…it was not you who sent me here, but God" (Genesis 45:5-8). Joseph then said, "You meant evil against me, but God meant it for good" (50:20).

When we trust God's sovereignty, we are better able to submit to adversity. From this trust comes a settled confidence that we are firmly in God's hands, the safest place we can be.

HOW PROPHECY REVEALS
GOD'S CHARACTER

I have come down to deliver them out of the
hand of the Egyptians (Exodus 3:8).

The people of Israel had been in Egypt for 400 years. They had grown from a family of about 70 to an estimated two million. Pharaohs had arisen who had forgotten about Joseph. They didn't know Joseph had saved Egypt during a famine. Fearing the fast-growing numbers of Abraham's descendants, Egypt's rulers turned them into slaves.

The cruelty of the slave taskmasters drove the children of Israel to beg God for deliverance. Using a burning bush to get Moses' attention, God revealed to Moses that it was time for His people to leave Egypt and go to "a land flowing with milk and honey" (Exodus 3:8). God then told Moses, "Come, I will send you to Pharaoh that you may bring my people, the children of Israel, out of Egypt" (verse 10).

In the words of this monumental prophecy, God revealed these truths about Himself:

- "I am the God of your father, the God of Abraham, the God of Isaac, the God of Jacob" (verse 6). God had not forgotten the promises originally given to Abraham long ago. He still identified Himself as the God of the very people He had made promises to. In this way, He confirmed He would still keep those promises.

- "I have heard their cry...I know their sufferings" (verse 7). God is compassionate. He hears the cries of those who hurt.

- "I will be with you" (verse 12). God is faithful. Moses responded in fear, saying, "Who am I to do this?" But God said, "Trust Me; I will go with you."

When God reveals His plans for the future, He also reveals His character. A study of Bible prophecy is a study of God Himself. Through prophecy, we learn the ways God intervenes in circumstances to make Himself known and to do His will.

LEANING UPON GOD'S ADEQUACY

I will be with you, and this shall be the sign for you, that I
have sent you: when you have brought the people out of Egypt,
you shall serve God on this mountain (Exodus 3:12).

Moses didn't like what he was hearing. God wanted him to go to Pharaoh and ask that the Israelites be permitted to leave Egypt. This was no small request. Pharaoh was powerful, had a massive army, and wasn't about to release the huge numbers of slave laborers who were vital to Egypt's interests. Moses was also a marked man—he had killed an Egyptian 40 years earlier.

Moses tried to back out, but God was firm. He promised, "I will be with you, and this shall be the sign for you, that I have sent you: when you have brought the people out of Egypt, you shall serve God on this mountain." God was willing to prove His trustworthiness to Moses by bringing the Israelites out of Egypt and back to this specific mountain for worship (a prophecy that was fulfilled in Exodus 17:6).

Moses gave further objections, insisting he was inadequate. His resistance contrasts sharply with the willingness displayed earlier by Joseph. Why the different responses?

When we're confronted by challenges beyond our capabilities, we have two choices: be emboldened by focusing on God's adequacy, or be paralyzed by focusing on our inadequacy. Looking Godward fills us with courage because we're reminded God is sovereign over all outcomes. To do this is to rely on His sufficiency, which is more than enough—as opposed to our own sufficiency, which is never enough.

We should have the heart of the apostle Paul, who wrote, "Our sufficiency is from God" (2 Corinthians 3:5). In our own power, we can accomplish nothing. Only in God's power can we be useful and effective. That is where we should pour all our trust.

FORESHADOWS OF JESUS
THE SACRIFICIAL LAMB

Every man shall take a lamb... Your lamb shall
be without blemish (Exodus 12:3, 5).

When Pharaoh refused to let the people of Israel leave Egypt, God sent a series of ten plagues. In the final plague, God sent an angel of death to slay the firstborn of every Egyptian family. Beforehand, God commanded the Israelites to sacrifice a lamb and brush its blood on the doorframe of their homes before nightfall. This would tell the avenging angel to "pass over" the house, protecting the Hebrew firstborns.

Much of what happened that first Passover foreshadows our Lord's death on the cross:

- A lamb was to be sacrificed; Jesus was the Lamb of God sacrificed on our behalf.

- The lamb had to be without blemish; Jesus was without sin.

- The sacrifice was to be killed on Passover; Jesus was crucified on Passover.

- The Israelites were saved by the blood on their doorposts; we are saved by the sacrificial blood of Christ.

The prophetic accuracy of these parallels and others is amazing. The lesson God wanted to teach Israel was this: Deliverance from judgment requires the death of an innocent substitute.

Some 1,400 years later, when John the Baptist saw Jesus, he declared, "Behold, the Lamb of God, who takes away the sin of the world!" (John 1:29). He made sure to let Israel know its long-awaited sacrificial substitute had arrived.

In a plague that brought judgment and death, God powerfully declared His love for Israel and mankind. Through many more Old Testament prophecies and foreshadows to come, He repeated that message of love and His desire to save people. It's a message God never tires of proclaiming—and it's why He has given so many prophecies about our future with Christ!

PROPHECY AS A
SOURCE OF CONFIDENCE

Fear not, stand firm, and see the salvation of the Lord (Exodus 14:13).

When God first approached Moses about leading the people of Israel out of Egypt, Moses made it clear he didn't want the job. He was resistant and unwilling.

But after the ten plagues occurred and God's people were freed, Moses was a different man. He had seen God at work. Repeatedly, God had given prophecies of plagues to come, and every single time, God fulfilled those prophecies. Moses had learned that whatever God speaks, it will happen. Moses could not help but be awed…and convinced.

The magnitude of the plagues would have increased Moses' confidence as well. So overwhelming were they that there was only one possible explanation: God was behind all this. No mere mortal could have brought about such miracles.

It didn't take long for Moses' newfound courage to manifest itself. After the Israelites left Egypt, Pharaoh sent his army after them. Ahead was the Red Sea, which blocked the people's path. Behind was Pharaoh's army. The Israelites panicked and cried out to Moses, "What have you done to us in bringing us out of Egypt?" (Exodus 14:11).

Moses answered, "Fear not, stand firm, and see the salvation of the Lord, which he will work for you today" (verse 13). Even *before* Moses was given instructions about parting the Red Sea, he was already convinced God would come to the rescue.

A key part of Moses' transformation was fulfilled prophecies that only God could have brought about. One of God's key purposes in proclaiming and fulfilling prophecies is to prove that He really is God. So grand and perfect are the fulfillments that the only possible answer is that He is behind them. Anytime we face the unknown and need help, God's track record of fulfilled Bible prophecies serves as evidence that He knows all and is able to do what is needed.

PROPHECY LESSONS
FROM THE TEN PLAGUES

By this you shall know that I am the Lord *(Exodus 7:17).*

Not only did God prophesy each of the ten plagues in advance, but there are wonderful prophecy-related insights we can glean from the account of the plagues in Exodus 7–12:

The plagues fulfilled God's prophecy that He will curse those who curse Israel. The Egyptians were brutal in their treatment of the Hebrew slaves. The plagues were payback. As early as Exodus, we see God judge Israel's enemies, as promised in Genesis 12:3.

The plague judgments have some similarities to the tribulation judgments. There are some striking parallels between Exodus 7–12 and Revelation 6–19: water turning to blood, boils on skin, hailstorms, and darkness. Also, God could have sent one swift judgment on Egypt, but He didn't. He gave people multiple chances to repent—as He will do during the tribulation. In addition, God fulfilled all the prophecies about the plagues literally. With that as a pattern, we should expect the tribulation judgments to be literal and not allegorical, as some people say.

The plague judgments support the argument for a pretribulation rapture. When God judged the Egyptians, He spared the Israelites (see Exodus 8:22; 9:4, 26; 10:23; 11:7). Earlier, when God judged the world through the flood, He preserved Noah's family (Genesis 7:23). Similarly, during the end times, because believers are not the object of God's wrath, it makes sense that He would remove them before the tribulation by taking them up in the rapture (see John 14:3; 1 Thessalonians 1:10; 5:9; Revelation 3:10).

The fulfilled prophecies about the plagues confirmed God's sovereignty over people, nature, and nations. God had the power to carry out His punishments on the Egyptians. He specified exactly what would happen and made all of it come to pass. As He pinpointed the recipients of His wrath, He exhibited complete control over people, nature, and nations.

A PERSONAL GUIDE FOR THE JOURNEY

Behold, I send an angel before you to guard you on the way and
to bring you to the place that I have prepared (Exodus 23:20).

In Exodus 23:20-21, God gave a deeply touching prophecy about the personal nature of His presence with the people of Israel as they traveled to the Promised Land. He said He would "send an angel" who would "guard" them. The Hebrew term for "angel" here is *malak*, which means "messenger." A closer look reveals this is no ordinary angel. Some important clues before and within this passage help identify this angel.

At the start of Israel's journey, we're told, "The LORD went before them by day in a pillar of cloud…and by night in a pillar of fire" (Exodus 13:21). Exodus 14:19 then adds this new detail: "the *angel of God*… was going before…and went behind them." Returning to Exodus 23, verse 21 says this angel had the power to "not pardon your transgression." In all of Scripture, only God has the authority to forgive—never angels. Then God said of this angel, "My name is in him." God's name is never said to be "in" an angel, indicating this must be God Himself.

Together, these clues point to the angel in Exodus 23:20 being what's known as a Theophany, or a pre-incarnate appearance of Christ. This was the Angel of the Lord, the second person of the Trinity, Jesus Christ, who would personally accompany His people in the wilderness and bring them to the Promised Land. God's care for Israel was not merely symbolic. It was real, intimate, and personal. Christ Himself would take them under His wings!

This same watchfulness is promised to every believer. As children of Christ, we are promised Jesus' devoted care for every step of life's journey. In the vow "I am with you always" (Matthew 28:20), the phrase "I am" is vigorous and literally translates to "I Myself am." Christ's presence is near and unceasing. There is no greater Shepherd we could ask for.

GOD'S UNCONDITIONAL PROMISES ARE FOREVER

When they are in the land of their enemies, I
will not spurn them (Leviticus 26:44).

In Genesis 15:17-18, God walked alone between the animal parts while Abraham slept. He was making it clear that His promises to Abraham in Genesis 12:1-3 were unconditional. They were guaranteed regardless of what Abraham did. The same is true about the gift of salvation: Christ did all the work on the cross. There is nothing we can contribute to our redemption.

It's true there are Bible passages in which God said He would bless the Israelites when they obeyed Him and discipline them when they disobeyed. But it's important to recognize that when God punished His people for doing wrong, that did *not* negate the promises He made to Abraham in Genesis 12:1-3. God Himself made this clear in Leviticus 26. After He listed the severe consequences of disobedience in verses 14-39, including expulsion from the land, He said, "When they are in the land of their enemies, *I will not spurn them*" (verse 44). Then God added, "I will for their sake *remember the covenant* with their forefathers" (verse 45).

God's prophetic "I will" statements here are powerful. He was saying, "Even when I punish My people, I will not abandon them. I will remember My covenant." This dovetails with God's vows He would restore and regather His people (Amos 9:14; Zephaniah 3:20).

God's promises in Genesis 12:1-3 still stand. If the Jewish people's sins could have broken God's unconditional promises to Abraham, then our sins today would be able to break God's unconditional gift of salvation to us. Yet if we could not earn God's gift in the first place, then how can we possibly unearn it?

God's unconditional promises stay unconditional. That makes them prophetic certainties. He will never break those promises—they are forever secure.

THE DANGER OF IGNORING "LITTLE" SINS

If you do not drive out the inhabitants of the land...
they shall trouble you...And I will do to you as I
thought to do to them (Numbers 33:55-56).

As the Israelites prepared to enter the Promised Land, God told Moses they were to "drive out all the inhabitants of the land from before you and destroy all their figured stones and destroy all their metal images and demolish all their high places" (Numbers 33:51-52).

God's instructions were clear: The wicked and godless Canaanites were to be removed, along with every element of their idol worship. God warned that if Israel didn't do this, "those of them whom you let remain shall be as barbs in your eyes and thorns in your sides" (verse 55). While barbs and thorns are minor irritants, if not removed, they can cause major infections.

Tragically, Israel didn't keep God's command. Pockets of Canaanites and their idolatrous influences remained and were not dealt with. Over time, the small irritants spread and infected the Hebrews to the point they abandoned God, and "everyone did what was right in his own eyes" (Judges 21:25). As forewarned in Numbers 33:55-56, God later did to His own people what He had commanded be done to the Canaanites: He drove Israel out of the land.

This powerfully illustrates the danger of permitting even a small sin to fester in our lives. When sin isn't dealt with, it grows. Ignored, it spreads its cancerous influence and makes us callous to God's desire for us to be holy and set apart for Him.

The Lord used strong language in Numbers 33:55-56 about the need for the Israelites to purge the land. In Colossians 3:5, God used strong language about the need for us to purge sin from our lives: "Put to death therefore what is earthly in you: sexual immorality, impurity, passion, evil desire, and covetousness." "Put to death" means eliminate it all. With love and good reason, God urges us to not take sin lightly because its consequences are so devastating.

SEEING THE END TIMES
FROM DEUTERONOMY

When you are in tribulation, and all these things come upon you in the latter days, you will return to the LORD your God (Deuteronomy 4:30).

As far back as Deuteronomy 4, God delivered a prophecy about Israel during the end times. He said that "in the latter days," the people of Israel would return to Him after having rejected Him. The phrases "in tribulation" and "the latter days" point to the end times. God wasn't describing Israel's return to the land after the Babylonian captivity, hundreds of years before Christ's birth. Rather, He was speaking of a return that is still in the future.

This prophecy in Deuteronomy 4 describes a widespread repentance that will occur in a time of great distress. This same event is prophesied in Zechariah 12:10, when God will "pour out on the house of David and the inhabitants of Jerusalem a spirit of grace and pleas for mercy, so that, when they look…on him whom they have pierced, they shall mourn." The context of Zechariah 12 is the tribulation, when "all the nations of the earth will gather against" Jerusalem (verse 3). This corresponds with Revelation 19:19, where we read that "the kings of the earth with their armies [will be] gathered to make war" against Christ at His second coming.

The Israelites had barely left Egypt when God gave this prophecy. Little did they know that over the next many centuries, they would abandon God repeatedly. But the Lord reveals in Deuteronomy 4 that ultimately, His people would return to Him.

Why is this so important? God wants us to know that even after Israel repeatedly rejects Him all through history to the end times, He will keep His covenant promises to Abraham and never abandon His people. He wants us to know He is forever trustworthy, faithful, loving, and merciful. He also wants us to know He is sovereign. No amount of interference from a wayward and sinful humanity will prevent God from carrying out His promises and plans.

JESUS, THE GREATEST PROPHET

The LORD your God will raise up for you a prophet like me from among you...it is to him you shall listen (Deuteronomy 18:15).

Moses told the people of Israel that someday, God would "raise up for you a prophet like me." Who was this prophet? Moses' use of the singular "a prophet" is a clue that he was referring to the ultimate prophet. Later, in Acts 3, when Peter spoke to a large audience about "the Christ appointed for you," he quoted Moses' words, saying, "The Lord God will raise up for you a prophet like me" (verses 20, 22). Peter reveals that Jesus was the prophet Moses spoke of.

Moses said this prophet would be "like me." The similarities between Moses and Jesus include evading death as a baby (Exodus 2:1-10; Matthew 2:13-23), being an intercessor between God and His people (Exodus 20:19; Hebrews 7:25), having the compassion of a shepherd (Numbers 27:17; Matthew 9:36), mediating a covenant with the people (Deuteronomy 1:29; Hebrews 8:6-7), and being a deliverer and leader. Also, Moses was the only prophet who, like Jesus, spoke with God face to face (Deuteronomy 34:10).

What made Jesus the ultimate prophet? The duty of Old Testament prophets was to be mouthpieces for God—they spoke for Him. Jesus, however, was God Himself speaking. Because of His divine nature, He alone was the perfect prophet. Every word Jesus spoke was true, and His deity and perfection enabled Him to speak with an authority like no other. Jesus was also the only prophet who *knew* the future rather than having it told to Him.

Because Jesus was all that a prophet could possibly be, He was the ultimate and perfect prophet. As part of the Godhead, Jesus is the source of all prophecy, a prophet Himself, and the one who fulfills all prophecy. He perfectly revealed God to mankind, and He will perfectly bring to pass all that He said He would do.

YOU WILL LISTEN TO HIM

The LORD your God will raise up for you a prophet like me from among you...it is to him you shall listen (Deuteronomy 18:15).

When Moses spoke about a future "prophet like me," he was pointing to Jesus. Peter confirms this connection in Acts 3:22-23; Moses had said of Jesus, "It is to him you shall listen."

But Jesus was not welcomed by the people of Israel. John 1:11 tells us, "He came to his own, and his own people did not receive him." Not only did they reject the greatest prophet Himself, but the prophets who had preceded Him over the course of many centuries. Shortly before His crucifixion, our Lord cried out, "Jerusalem, Jerusalem, who kills the prophets and stones those who are sent to her! How often I wanted to gather your children together, the way a hen gathers her chicks under her wings, and you were unwilling" (Matthew 23:37 NASB).

That unwillingness persisted even beyond the resurrection. So when Peter had the opportunity to tell a crowd about Jesus, he said, "What God foretold by the mouth of all the prophets, that his Christ would suffer, he thus fulfilled" (Acts 3:18). Peter was saying that the very prophets whom the Israelites had killed had been accurate in their prophecies about Jesus. This was a powerful indictment—the prophets had been right, and the people had been wrong.

Peter then repeated Moses' prophecy in Deuteronomy 18:15: 'The Lord God will raise up for you a prophet like me from your brothers. *You shall listen to him*" (Acts 3:22). Peter pointed to Moses because the Jews revered him as a prophet. And Moses himself had said to listen to this Jesus!

Peter was saying, "If you believed in Moses, you should also believe in Jesus." He quoted a prophecy from a trusted prophet—Moses—as evidence that Jesus was the Messiah. Peter used prophecy to confirm Jesus' identity. We can do the same today, urging people to listen to Him.

EVIDENCE OF GOD'S FAITHFULNESS

*Arise, go over this Jordan, you and all this people, into the land
that I am giving to them…you shall cause this people to inherit the
land that I swore to their fathers to give them (Joshua 1:2, 6).*

The Israelites now stood on the eastern bank of the Jordan River,
looking into the land God had promised to Abraham 400-plus
years earlier. This promise, which was unconditional and everlasting,
had been repeated to Isaac, Jacob, and Moses. God said Israel would
own this land forever. Sure enough, Scripture reveals Israel will be in
the land during Christ's millennial kingdom. Christ will rule from Jerusalem, and at last, Israel will possess all the borders God described in
Genesis 15:18: "from the river of Egypt to…the river Euphrates." We
see the fulfillment of this in Ezekiel 47:15-20, which describes Israel in
the millennial kingdom.

In Joshua 1:6, God said He would give this land as an *inheritance*—
and during the millennial kingdom, it will again be described as an
inheritance (Ezekiel 47:13-14). While Israel's *ownership* of the land is
permanent, the people's *presence* in the land required obedience to God.
Disobedience would see the people temporarily removed.

As the Israelites looked across the Jordan River at the land of promise, they were also looking at God's faithfulness. Despite all the times
they had questioned God and disobeyed Him during their wilderness
journeys, God had kept His promise. In front of them, God's faithfulness was on full display. This was God's gift to them—not deserved, but
lovingly granted.

As you look around you, what evidences do you see of God's faithfulness to you? How has God made His love known to you, tangibly
and intangibly? Be intentional about treasuring these evidences in your
mind and heart so that they will inspire and encourage you in your wilderness moments. They will remind you that you can always count on
God's faithfulness.

THE WISDOM OF
EXAMINING OUR HEARTS

I said, "I will never break my covenant with you…" But you
have not obeyed…So now I say, I will not drive them out
before you, but they shall become thorns in your sides, and
their gods shall be a snare to you (Judges 2:1-3).

It didn't take long for the Israelites to respond to God's faithfulness with unfaithfulness. His allegiance to them would never be broken, but their allegiance to Him was broken again and again.

In Judges 2, God prophesies that because the Israelites had not driven all the wicked Canaanites out of the land, they would become a snare, pulling God's people away from Him. Upon hearing this prophecy, the people "lifted up their voices and wept" (Judges 2:4). But their sorrow didn't last long. Within a few verses, we read that "the people of Israel did what was evil in the sight of the LORD…They went after other gods" (verses 11-12). This happened repeatedly all through the book of Judges: The people would indulge in evil and idolatry, be oppressed by their enemies, cry out to God for help, and be rescued…only to stray again. Though God delivered His people several times, sadly, by the end of Judges, we read that "everyone did what was right in their own eyes" (21:25).

How often do we find ourselves doing what is right in our own eyes? We let seemingly harmless sins take root within us and grow. In time, we find ourselves living in defeat and feeling distant from God.

Our all-too-human tendency to let sins—no matter how small—wedge their way between us and God proves the wisdom of ongoing self-examination. Like the psalmist, we should plea, "Search me, O God, and know my heart! Try me and know my thoughts! And see if there be any grievous way in me, and lead me in the way everlasting!" (Psalm 139:23-24).

THE MESSIANIC LINE CONTINUES

Ruth...bore a son...They named him Obed. He was the
father of Jesse, the father of David (Ruth 4:13, 17).

There are no prophecies in the book of Ruth, but within it is much of messianic significance.

In search of sustenance, widows Naomi and her daughter-in-law, Ruth, travel from Moab to Bethlehem. Naomi is an Israelite returning home, and Ruth chooses to leave her Moabite family to follow Naomi. Upon arriving in Bethlehem, Naomi informs Ruth of the Israelite custom of providing food for the poor by leaving remnants of grain after the harvest is done. Ruth ends up working in a field that belongs to Boaz, who is related to Naomi.

Deuteronomy 25:5-10 stipulated that a deceased man's relative was to marry his widow so they could raise a son in the deceased man's name. The person who did this was called a kinsman-redeemer. Boaz was willing to be a kinsman-redeemer for Ruth. They married, and gave birth to a son, Obed—the grandfather of the future King David.

As a kinsman-redeemer, Boaz was willing and able to pay the price of redeeming Ruth. This foreshadows Christ, the ultimate kinsman-redeemer, who was willing and able to pay the price for our redemption. Boaz and Ruth's union also continued the messianic line that wove a path through the tribe of Judah to King David, whose future descendant would be Jesus:

- From Adam and Eve came the woman's seed (Genesis 3:15)
- From Abraham came the seed that would bless the earth (Genesis 22:18)
- From Jacob this lineage would continue (Genesis 25:23; Numbers 24:17-19)
- From Judah came the scepter—the right to rule (Genesis 49:10)
- From Obed came Jesse, David...and later, Jesus (Ruth 4:22)

In Ruth, the family line that would bring about the Messiah becomes clearer than ever.

GOD'S GOODNESS IN DIFFICULT CIRCUMSTANCES

For this child I prayed, and the LORD has granted me
my petition that I made to him (1 Samuel 1:27).

Hannah was brokenhearted because she had long been childless. She pleaded for God to give her a son, promising that she would "give him to the LORD all the days of his life" (1 Samuel 1:11). After she lifted up this prayer during one of her visits to the house of the Lord in Shiloh, she became pregnant, and later gave birth to Samuel.

This brought such great joy to Hannah that she lifted up a song of praise and thanksgiving to God for His goodness. Overflowing with gratitude, she declared God as her Savior, and acknowledged Him as holy, mighty, all-knowing, sovereign, caring, and just (1 Samuel 2:1-10).

True to her word, as soon as Samuel was weaned, Hannah took him to the house of the Lord for a lifetime of service. God then blessed Hannah with five more children.

Hannah is an example of exceptional loyalty to God while enduring great distress. She remained faithful in prayer and devotion even when her prayers had long gone unanswered. As it so happened, God desired to raise up a faithful priest, and He chose Hannah to bear this child.

In times of persistent grief or pain, we often become discouraged and tempted to give up on God. But it's in those very times that we need to stay fervent in prayer. God will always prove Himself faithful to us, but not necessarily in the ways we hope for or request. He will uphold us, but He will also do His will. When we place our full trust in God, we will find ourselves able to rejoice no matter what outcome He chooses because it's His will that we desire, and not ours.

When we stay connected in prayer and make ourselves available to God, He is able to use us to accomplish His good purposes. When we're dedicated to being a vessel God can use, we will experience a deep and satisfying joy regardless of what happens with our circumstances.

FAITHFULNESS BRINGS INFLUENCE

I will raise up for myself a faithful priest, who shall do according
to what is in my heart and in my mind (1 Samuel 2:35).

Israel had been in a long downward spiral. Not only were the people spiritually and morally corrupt, but so were the priests at the Lord's house in Shiloh. Idolatry was rampant, and the sins of the high priest's two sons were "very great in the sight of the LORD" (1 Samuel 2:17).

God rebuked the high priest for failing to discipline his sons and warned that judgment would come upon them. God then prophesied that they would be replaced by "a faithful priest"—Samuel. Adding more details to this prophecy, God said this priest would have "a sure house" and "go in and out before my anointed forever" (verse 35). Evidently Samuel was the initial fulfillment of this prophecy, and "a sure house" and "my anointed forever" point to Jesus as the final fulfillment, for He would be a priest forever (Psalm 110:4; Hebrews 5:6).

As Daniel 2:21 says, God "removes kings and sets up kings." Here, He removed corrupt priests and raised up a faithful one. Samuel exhorted the Israelites to return to the Lord with all their heart, and said, "I will pray to the LORD for you" (1 Samuel 7:5). In this way, Samuel showed his devotion to both God and the people. The people loved Samuel for this—so much so that when he died, "all Israel…mourned for him" (1 Samuel 25:1).

Here is what's amazing: Hannah had very little time to train up her little boy before turning him over to the Lord's service. So dedicated was her love and instruction that she set Samuel on the right path for life. This, in turn, had a powerful influence on an entire nation.

We may think our faithfulness and influence are small, but in God's hands, their effects can be great. When we content ourselves with focusing solely on His immediate calling for us and doing it well, God will take care of the rest.

A KEY TRANSITION IN PROPHETIC HISTORY

Your kingdom shall not continue. The LORD has sought out a man after his own heart…to be prince over his people (1 Samuel 13:14).

I srael's first king had been a disappointment. He had refused to do what the Lord commanded. Through Samuel the priest, God told King Saul, "The LORD has torn the kingdom of Israel from you this day and has given it to a neighbor of yours, who is better than you" (1 Samuel 15:28). Just as God had earlier removed corrupt priests and raised up a faithful one, God was about to remove a rebellious king and replace him with a man after His own heart: David.

This brings us to one of the greatest transitions in God's prophetic timetable. From the Garden of Eden until now, God had gradually revealed details about the coming Messiah, the salvation He would bring, and His everlasting kingdom. But as Samuel and David usher in the age of the kings and the prophets, there is an explosion of prophetic revelation. From here onward, a surge of new prophecies are given about Christ's first and second comings.

What's more, both Samuel and David were major foreshadows or types who pointed to Christ. Samuel is the only person in the Old Testament who filled the roles of priest, prophet, and ruler (he was Israel's final judge, before the coronation of Israel's first king). Likewise, Scripture revealed that the Lord Jesus Christ would be a priest (Jeremiah 31:31-34; Hebrews 2:17), prophet (Deuteronomy 18:15; Matthew 21:11), and king (Genesis 49:10; Matthew 22:42-45).

King David prefigured the King of kings and Lord of lords. God told David, "I will raise up your offspring after you…and I will establish his kingdom. He shall build a house for my name, and I will establish the throne of his kingdom forever" (2 Samuel 7:12-13).

Satan continued to do all he could to corrupt and destroy Israel. But God's promises of a Messiah multiplied all the more, with every single one a declaration that God would prevail.

GOD LOOKS AT THE HEART

I have provided for myself a king (1 Samuel 16:1).

King Saul had failed miserably, and God had a replacement waiting in the wings. God told Samuel, "Go, I will send you to Jesse the Bethlehemite, for I have provided for myself a king among his sons" (1 Samuel 16:1).

Samuel took with him a horn of oil, which he would use to anoint Israel's next king. Upon arriving at Jesse's house, he asked for the sons to be brought to him. Seven came forward. As soon as Samuel saw Eliab, he thought, "Surely the LORD's anointed is before him" (verse 6). But God said, "Do not look on his appearance or on the height of his stature, because I have rejected him. For the LORD sees not as a man sees; man looks on the outward appearance, but the LORD looks on the heart" (verse 7).

One by one, the remaining sons were rejected. Puzzled, Samuel asked, "Are all your sons here?" As it turned out, the youngest was in the fields watching sheep. Samuel sent for him, and David was called before the priest. God said, "Arise, anoint him, for this is he" (verse 12).

Little would anyone have anticipated that Israel's next—and greatest—king would be the youngest of eight sons, a teen who did the dirty, difficult, and lowly job of a shepherd. Even the wise and faithful Samuel had guessed wrongly and was rebuked by God for his assumption about Eliab. David surely had the shortest resume of Jesse's eight sons, but he had the one qualification God sought for the nation's highest leader: He was a man after God's own heart.

When our heart is entirely set apart for God, we become a vessel through which He can work. As we fully yield ourselves to Him, we become pliable to whatever His will calls for. A wholehearted obedience to God occurs only when we possess a wholehearted love for Him and the things He desires. That's what it looks like to be a person after God's own heart.

WAITING ON GOD'S TIMING

The Lord will strike him (1 Samuel 26:10).

Nearly 15 years went by between the time David was anointed king and he actually became king. Then another several years passed before David was king over all of Israel.

At the time David was anointed, God had already rejected Saul. This would seem to indicate David could rightfully ascend to the throne anytime he wanted.

But David knew otherwise. Just as he had been divinely anointed by God, he knew Saul had been divinely anointed. He recognized that just as the raising up of kings is in God's hands, so is the taking down of kings.

Before long, Saul became jealous of David and repeatedly attempted to kill him. Saul and his army chased after David, forcing David and his warrior friends to flee into the wilderness. On two occasions, David had the opportunity to kill Saul, and was even urged to do so. But he refused. The first time, David rebuked his fighting men, saying, "The Lord forbid that I should…put out my hand against him, seeing he is the Lord's anointed" (1 Samuel 24:6). The second time, David declared, "As the Lord lives, the Lord will strike him, or his day will come to die, or he will go down into battle and perish" (1 Samuel 26:10). No matter how Saul died, it would not happen at David's hand.

David waited a long time to become king, but was committed to God's timing, which is always right. God had appointed Saul, and David would let God remove him. David knew that to go against Saul would have been to go against God.

There are times when we will look at a situation and wonder why God hasn't acted sooner. Yet His timing and reasons are always perfect. It's as we wait upon God that our character, trust, and patience are built—and we stay in sync with His will and His ways.

GOD'S FOREVER PROMISE TO DAVID

Your throne shall be established forever (2 Samuel 7:16).

As far back as Genesis 49:10, God had promised Israel a king whose dynasty would last forever. This king would come from the line of Judah. This means Saul could not have fulfilled this prophecy because he was from the tribe of Benjamin. David, however, was from Judah.

David's conquest of Israel's enemies ushered in an era of peace to the land. This freed him to deal with another concern: How could the ark of God dwell in a mere tent while he lived in a palace? David was eager to build a house for the Lord, but God told the king he wasn't the one to make this happen. However, God promised David, "Your house and your kingdom shall be made sure forever before me. Your throne shall be established forever" (2 Samuel 7:16).

David wanted to build for God a house built with human hands; God said He would build for David a house built with divine hands. A house built with human hands would be destructible and temporary, but a house built by God's own hands would be indestructible and eternal.

Repeatedly in 2 Samuel 7, God said David's kingdom would last forever. Jesus came from the lineage of David, and clearly, it is Jesus' future kingdom that is in view here.

Genesis 12:3 was a prophetic high point in human history because God chose for Himself a *nation* through which the Messiah would come. Second Samuel 7:16 marks a new prophetic high point because God chose a *king* on whose throne the Messiah would rule forever.

After the people of Israel spent 2,000 years in exile, God orchestrated the rebirth of Israel in 1948. He is now setting the stage for the King's return. Just as surely as God fulfilled all the prophecies about Israel's regathering, He will fulfill all the prophecies of a forever kingdom. In these last days, we stand on the verge of the rapture, tribulation, and second coming. All of prophetic history is reaching a crescendo—and we have the privilege of watching it unfold!

THANKFUL FOR THE PAST, PRESENT, AND FUTURE

Who am I, O Lord GOD, and what is my house, that
you have brought me thus far? (2 Samuel 7:18).

King David was overwhelmed. God had said, "I will make for you a great name...And your house and your kingdom shall be made sure forever before me" (2 Samuel 7:9, 16). So astounding were God's promises that David prayed, "Who am I, O Lord GOD, and what is my house, that you have brought me thus far?" In these words, David revealed that he felt unworthy of the honors God was granting to him.

In David's prayer, we see patterns emerge that are instructive for our own prayers:

First, David thanked God for blessing him in the *present* (verses 18-21). He gave God full credit, saying, "You have brought about all this greatness."

Second, David praised God for His faithfulness to Israel in the *past* (verses 22-24). He said, "You established for yourself your people Israel to be your people forever."

Third, David exalted God for His promises about the *future* (verses 25-29). He told God, "Your name will be magnified forever...you are God, and your words are true."

In awe, David recognized that God's goodness was unceasing—it encompassed the past, present, and future. And in the prayer, David referred to himself as "your servant" ten times. He had a proper perspective of God's sovereign authority over his life and knew He could trust whatever God chose to bring his way. Finally, David concluded the prayer by saying, "You, O Lord GOD, have spoken" (verse 29). He knew God's every promise was settled and secure.

When we remember to thank God for His past, present, and future work, we are more likely to recognize the ongoing nature of His goodness. And when we pray with the attitude that we are God's servants, we are more likely to receive His goodness with trust and humility.

CHRIST'S ULTIMATE TRIUMPH

I will make the nations your heritage, and the ends
of the earth your possession (Psalm 2:8).

Psalm 2 describes the ongoing battle of the ages: The kings of the world plot in vain against God and shake their fists at Him. But "he who sits in the heavens laughs" (verse 4). Then with fury, God declares, "I have set my King on Zion, my holy hill" (verse 6). Who is this king? God reveals more in the next verse: "You are my Son; today I have begotten you. Ask of me, and I will make the nations your heritage, and the ends of the earth your possession." From these clues we know this King is God's "begotten" Son, Jesus, who will rule the world from Zion.

The prophecy continues, "You shall break them with a rod of iron and dash them in pieces like a potter's vessel" (verse 9). This matches the description of Jesus at His second coming: "From his mouth comes a sharp sword with which to strike down the nations, and he will rule them with a rod of iron" (Revelation 19:15). God then urges the rebellious to "be wise" before judgment comes and promises blessing if they "take refuge in him" (Psalm 2:10-12).

All of Psalm 2 is a prophecy about Christ's future reign on earth and the ultimate destruction of those who oppose Him. Worldly authorities have long deceived themselves into thinking they will prevail against God, but God warns that their defeat is sure. When Christ returns, He will triumph and rule as the supreme authority over all.

Because the wicked flourish, it may seem as if God is not sovereign. But with loving patience, God calls the rebellious to submit to His authority before He crushes theirs. God's power to determine the fate of those who defy Him affirms He truly is sovereign after all. And the absolute certainty of Christ's future victory and rule gives us this confident hope: There is coming a day when evil will never again exist on earth, and righteousness will reign forever.

A PROPHECY ABOUT
CHRIST'S RESURRECTION

You will not abandon my soul to Sheol; You will not allow
Your Holy One to undergo decay (Psalm 16:10 NASB).

Psalm 16:10 was penned by King David 1,000 years before Christ arose from the grave. In this short but powerful passage, David expressed complete confidence that when he died, he would immediately go into God's presence. And the Spirit inspired David to prophesy that "Your Holy One"—the Messiah—would rise from the dead. In this messianic psalm, we have a prophecy of the resurrection.

David knew that when he died, his body would go to the grave, but not his soul. Rather, he would immediately be ushered into heaven. Every believer has this wonderful assurance. In Philippians 1:23, Paul wrote that "to depart" is to "be with Christ." Second Corinthians 5:8 says that to "be away from the body" is to be "at home with the Lord."

Next, David wrote, "You will not allow Your Holy One to undergo decay." This clearly does not refer to David, for his body went to the grave and decomposed. And in Scripture, the phrase "Your Holy One" clearly points to the Lord Jesus Christ. He is called the Holy One in Mark 1:24 and Acts 3:14. Also, in Acts 2:25-28, Peter quoted David's prophecy in Psalm 16:10 and said Jesus' resurrection fulfilled it. Paul said the same in Acts 13:34-35.

Psalm 16:10 weaves together these two great truths: For believers, life does not stop with death—our souls will go directly into God's presence. For Christ, it was impossible for death to keep its grip on Him—and His resurrection guarantees our resurrection.

Because of Christ's resurrection, death is no longer a reason for fear. Rather, death can be faced with peace and confidence. Our souls will go to heaven immediately. Our bodies will later be raised in glory. Death will not pause nor cease the relationship we enjoy with God.

WHEN THE FATHER FORSAKES THE SON

My God, my God, why have you forsaken me? (Psalm 22:1).

Psalm 22 is made special by the rare glimpse it provides into the special nature of the relationship between the Father and the Son. The psalm opens with a heartbreaking cry that Jesus would utter from the cross: "My God, my God, why have you forsaken me?" A thousand years before the crucifixion, the deep agony Messiah would experience at the cross is made known. These prophetic words in Psalm 22:1 were fulfilled in Matthew 27:46.

Then in Psalm 22:2, the Savior laments, "I cry...but you do not answer." Here, we witness the anguish Jesus would suffer when He was separated from the Father at the cross. As Jesus took our sins upon Himself, God, who is holy and cannot look upon sin, had to turn away. For the first and only time, the precious and eternal fellowship between Father and Son was disrupted as Jesus "loved us and gave himself up for us, a fragrant offering and sacrifice for God" (Ephesians 5:2). As the psalm continues, the words are thick with pain and despair.

But when we reach Psalm 22:21, "You do not answer" changes to "You have rescued me." Jesus had taken upon Himself God's wrath, which was now satisfied. The Father was no longer silent toward His Son. The penalty was paid, and victory was won. And the rest of Psalm 22 is an exuberant song filled with celebration and praise.

Jesus' willingness to endure wrath on the cross had a profound effect on the intimate relationship between the Father and Himself. Never had He experienced silence from heaven, nor fury from His Father. Stunningly, the very cross intended to close the gap between God and man created a gap between Father and Son. Yet that moment of separation made possible an eternity of deliverance. For that, we can be exceedingly grateful and rejoice.

GOD'S DEVOTION TO REDEEMING US

In the midst of the congregation I will praise you (Psalm 22:22).

In Psalm 22, God revealed more prophetic details about Jesus' crucifixion and resurrection than in any other chapter of the Old Testament.[5] Written 1,000 years before Jesus came to earth, every prophetic aspect of this psalm was fulfilled with stunning accuracy.

Many centuries in advance, God provided this descriptive portrait of how the high point in all human history would play out. What's even more amazing is that Scripture tells us that every part of how God's redemptive plan would unfold was predetermined even before creation. In Ephesians 1:4-5, we read that "before the foundation of the world... [God] predestined us for adoption to himself as sons through Jesus Christ." In Acts 2:23, when Peter spoke to a large crowd about the crucifixion that had taken place weeks earlier, he said that Jesus was "delivered up according to the definite plan and foreknowledge of God."

Not only were Jesus' crucifixion and resurrection the high point of redemptive history, they were the turning point. Beforehand, we were in bondage to sin and the enemy, with no access to God. Afterward, the power of sin and the enemy were broken, and access to God became possible.

So vivid is Psalm 22 in its description of what Christ would do on our behalf that we cannot help but be filled with deep reverence. As the redemptive drama unfolds in this passage, we are not only reading about it, but experiencing it.

Everything God did from creation onward was designed to set the stage for Christ's crucifixion and resurrection. All of history was orchestrated in a way that the cross stands at the very center. The many messianic prophecies in the Old Testament are meant to draw our eyes to this focal point. That's how devoted God was to making it possible for us to return to Him.

FORESHADOWS OF CALVARY

It shall be told of the Lord...that he has done it (Psalm 22:30-31).

Even though Psalm 22 was penned several centuries before Calvary, it reads like an eyewitness account written at the foot of the cross. Take a careful look for yourself in your Bible, and the parallels between David's words and what took place at the crucifixion are striking:

- The words in verse 1— "My God, my God, why have you forsaken me?"—are the very words Jesus cried out from the cross (Matthew 27:46).

- Verses 6-7 detail the mockery and hatred the crowd would hurl toward Jesus (Matthew 27:39-42).

- Verse 8 prophetically proclaims the taunt, "He trusts in the Lord; let him deliver him; let him rescue him, for he delights in him!" (Matthew 27:43).

- Verses 12-13 compare the people at the crucifixion with bloodthirsty beasts (Matthew 27:27-50).

- Verses 14-17 describe the physical torment Jesus would suffer at the cross (Matthew 27:27-50; John 19:28).

- Verse 16 prophesies the piercing of Jesus' hands and feet (John 19:18; 20:25).

- Even the casting of lots for Jesus' clothes is accounted for (Psalm 22:18; Matthew 27:35).

The many messianic foreshadows in Psalm 22 are extraordinary. They go beyond merely reporting what would happen. We are even given insight, from within Christ Himself, to the thoughts that would fill His mind and the pain that would rage through His body.

The mind-boggling accuracy of the many Old Testament prophecies about Christ's crucifixion and resurrection tell us we have a Bible that can be trusted, a Messiah whose claims to be Savior and Lord are true, and a God who is sovereign and reigns over all.

THE MESSIAH IN THE PSALMS

The LORD of hosts, he is the king of glory! (Psalm 24:10).

The book of Psalms is most famously known for being a collection of Hebrew poetry that includes prayers, pleas, praises, and worship. There are also a good number of prophecies in the Psalms, many having to do with the first and second advents of Christ, as well as Jesus' 1,000-year kingdom on earth. Those that reveal specific prophetic truths about Christ are often called messianic psalms.

Jesus Himself told His disciples, "Everything written about me in the Law of Moses and the Prophets and the Psalms must be fulfilled" (Luke 24:44). He was saying that there were prophecies within the Psalms that pointed specifically to Him and either had been fulfilled or awaited fulfillment. There are some who say these passages are merely allegorical. But all the psalms about the first coming of Christ were fulfilled in ways that make it clear they were literal prophecies with literal fulfillments. This applies to all the second-coming psalms as well.

One special trait about some of the prophetic psalms is that they don't merely provide information, but they include heart-moving descriptions of actual events, causing us to grieve or rejoice as we read them. Great examples of this are the portrayals of the crucifixion in Psalm 22 and the millennial kingdom in Psalms 96–99.

The prophetic psalms are an ever-flowing wellspring of hope. They promise a Savior who delivers and a Messiah who will rule the world in righteousness. They also give glimpses of Israel's glorious future. As we take these psalms to heart, we are comforted and encouraged. In the psalms about Christ's suffering, we are reminded of His love and grace. And in the psalms about Christ's kingship, we are reminded of His sovereignty and majesty. Every psalm that points to our Lord fills our hearts with adoration for the one who alone is worthy of all praise.

GOD'S PROVIDENCE
OVER JESUS' WOUNDS

He keeps all his bones; not one of them is broken (Psalm 34:20).

This prophecy in Psalm 34:20 not only looks forward to what would happen at the cross, but also looks back at a foreshadow that appeared in the book of Exodus.

In preparation for the final plague upon Egypt, God told the Israelites to select a Passover lamb that would be sacrificed so its blood could be brushed on their doorposts. This blood would inform God's angel of death to "pass over" their homes, delivering the people within from death. God also gave strict instructions to not break any of the lamb's bones (Exodus 12:46).

The Passover lamb prefigured Jesus, whom John the Baptist called "the Lamb of God" (John 1:29). Three years later, Jesus was nailed to the cross as the sacrificial Lamb who would deliver us from death. Because the Mosaic law forbade executed people from being left out overnight on the Sabbath, the Jews asked Pilate to have his soldiers break the legs of Jesus and the two thieves so their deaths would be hastened. This would make it impossible for them to use their legs to push themselves upward and breathe. Instead, they would quickly suffocate and die.

After the soldiers broke the legs of the thieves, they noticed Jesus was already dead. This made it unnecessary to break His legs. John 19:36 tells us that "these things took place that the Scripture might be fulfilled: 'Not one of his bones will be broken.'" Instead, to ensure Jesus was dead, the soldiers thrust a spear into His side. That Christ would be pierced in this way was prophesied in Isaiah 53:5. None of this was accidental; all of it was by God's design.

At the cross, God providentially guided everything that happened to Jesus to ensure Scripture would be fulfilled—down to the exact wounds He received. These scars will remain with our Savior even in heaven (Revelation 5:6). They will serve as eternal reminders of God's sovereignty over the actions of men, and of the great price Jesus paid to bring us home.

THE PRICE OF DOING GOD'S WILL

In sacrifice and offering you have not delighted...
Burnt offering and sin offering you have not required. Behold,
I have come; in the scroll of the book it is written of me:
I delight to do your will, O my God (Psalm 40:6-8).

Psalm 40:6-8 is a messianic prophecy that anticipates Christ's perfect sacrifice on the cross. His sacrifice was permanent and superior to the animal sacrifices required by Mosaic law, which were temporary and ineffectual. It was Jesus' delight to go to the cross because that was the Father's will for Him.

Hebrews 10:5-7 confirms for us that Psalm 40:6-8 was fulfilled by Christ. The focal point of Hebrews 10 is that animal sacrifices could never cleanse God's people from their sins. Their purpose had always been to point toward the future sacrifice that would once for all please God and be able to remove sin. Hebrews 10:5 tells us, "When Christ came into the world, he said, 'Sacrifices and offerings you have not desired, but a body have you prepared for me.'" When Jesus was ready to take on human flesh and be born on earth, He acknowledged to the Father that the "body...prepared for me" was meant to become a sacrifice.

The cross was Jesus' mission. He came to earth to do the Father's will—to obey the Father. He was born to die on our behalf. Shortly before He was nailed to the cross, He told the Father, "Not my will, but yours, be done" (Luke 22:42). And "he humbled himself by becoming obedient to the point of death, even death on a cross" (Philippians 2:8).

For Jesus, doing the Father's will and going to the cross came at a very high price. But for us, the outcome meant the difference between heaven and hell. This is a powerful affirmation that no matter how greatly it costs us to do the Father's will, the outcome will always be worth it.

ARE YOU READY TO MEET THE KING?

Your throne, O God, is forever and ever...
at your right hand stands the queen (Psalm 45:6, 9).

I n its entirety, Psalm 45 looks ahead to the day when Jesus will come to reign as King over the earth. And according to Hebrews 1:8, it is David's descendant, Jesus Christ, who will fulfill Psalm 45:6: "Of the Son he says, 'Your throne, O God, is forever and ever.'"

The first half of Psalm 45 focuses on the King. Then verse 9 introduces us to the King's bride: "At your right hand stands the queen." Can you guess who this is? It's us! In the New Testament, the relationship between Christ and the church is likened to that between a bridegroom and bride (Ephesians 5:25-27; Revelation 21:9). And as one Bible commentator puts it, the emphasis of the next several verses—Psalm 45:10-15—is "Here comes the bride!"[6]

While this psalm appears to describe one of David's weddings, it serves as a foreshadow of the wedding in Revelation 19:6-10: "Let us rejoice... for the marriage of the Lamb has come, and his Bride has made herself ready" (verse 6). So Psalm 45 portrays the church—Christ's bride—as coming into the King's presence on His wedding day.

In Psalm 45:10-15, we get a clear sense of how greatly the bride prepared herself for the King. Similarly, in Revelation 19:6, we read that "his Bride has made herself ready."

As the bride, how ready are we to meet our King? Ephesians 5:26-27 describes how Christ desires to cleanse us "by the washing of water with the word, so that he might present the church to himself in splendor, without spot or wrinkle...that she might be holy and without blemish." It's as we let God's Word purge us of sin and impurity that we become a holy and blameless bride, ready for our Lord.

This spells out Christ's foremost desire for us. Is it your foremost desire as well?

HATED WITHOUT A CAUSE

More in number than the hairs of my head are those
who hate me without cause (Psalm 69:4).

The theme of Psalm 69 is unjust suffering. It begins, "Save me, O God! For the waters have come up to my neck…and the flood sweeps over me. I am weary with my crying out, my throat is parched. My eyes grow dim with waiting for my God" (verses 1-3).

Though the psalm recounts the persecution David faced, it finds its ultimate fulfillment in Christ. The disciples quoted parts of Psalm 69 and applied them to Jesus,[7] for He is the supreme example of being unjustly rejected. Jesus applied Psalm 69:4 to Himself, saying, "The word that is written in their Law must be fulfilled: 'They hated me without a cause'" (John 15:25).

In David's response to the many injustices he faced, we find wisdom for ourselves: "As for me, *my prayer is to you*, O LORD. At an acceptable time, O God, in the abundance of your steadfast love answer me in your saving faithfulness. Deliver me" (verses 13-14). David placed his full trust in God, knowing that deliverance would come from Him alone at the right time.

Jesus did the same: "When he was reviled, he did not revile in return; when he suffered, he did not threaten, but continued *entrusting himself to him who judges justly*" (1 Peter 2:23).

What stirred all this opposition? In Psalm 69:9, David said, "Zeal for your house has consumed me." Remember Jesus' zeal for His Father's house and His cleansing of the temple? When we do what is godly and right, we will face animosity.

When we are hated without a cause, the answer isn't vengeance. Rather, it is to entrust ourselves completely to God. As we are treated unjustly by a hostile world, it's encouraging to know that it's our devotion to God that stirs negative reactions. It is far better for us to suffer for pleasing God, than to evade persecution by lacking any zeal for Him and for what is right.

A GREATER KING AND
A GREATER KINGDOM

May the king's name endure forever (Psalm 72:17 NLT).

P salm 72 is known as a coronation psalm. While it is attributed to King Solomon, it may have been written for him as an intercessory prayer from the people of Israel, asking for God's blessings and favor upon a newly enthroned king.

As we read through the psalm, we become aware of clear references not just to Solomon and his kingdom, but also to a greater king and a greater kingdom. For example, in verses 5-7, we read, "May they fear you as long as the sun shines, as long as the moon remains in the sky. Yes, forever!" (verse 5). Solomon was a mortal man, and these words clearly point to an immortal ruler—the Lord Jesus Christ, a future descendant of David.

Verse 8 speaks of a kingdom that extends "to the ends of the earth." Solomon's kingdom was regional. Not until Christ becomes king will there be a kingdom that encompasses the entire world, beginning with His millennial reign and extending into the eternal state.

The rest of Psalm 72 continues in these two veins—Solomon's reign, and Christ's. And it concludes with this exuberant doxology: "Praise the LORD God, the God of Israel, who alone does such wonderful things. Praise his glorious name forever! Let the whole earth be filled with his glory" (verses 18-19).

A greater king and a greater kingdom are coming. Jesus is rightly called the King of kings and Lord of lords because He will reign supreme over all people and all places for all time. Nothing can even remotely compare to the wonders that await us. This will be an amazing new experience for us because the whole earth will be *filled* with God's glory. We will be blessed as we experience the fullness of every single one of God's perfect attributes. The more we dwell on what is to come, the more we cannot help but want to shout, "Amen! Come, Lord Jesus!"

GOD'S STEADFAST LOVE

I will not remove from him my steadfast love or be false to my faithfulness. I will not violate my covenant (Psalm 89:33-34).

One of the most important truths taught in the Bible about God and the people of Israel is this: Just because they disobey Him and He finds it necessary to discipline them doesn't mean He will abandon them.

Through the ages, Christians have assumed that because the people of Israel rejected their Messiah and were later cast out of their land for the next 2,000 years, God has likewise rejected them, removed His covenant promises from them, and given those promises to the church.

Yes, God warned that disobedience would mean removal from the land. But God has *not* revoked His covenant promises. Psalm 89, a messianic psalm, gives powerful confirmation of that. Speaking about His promises to David, God said, "I will not remove from him my steadfast love or be false to my faithfulness. I will not violate my covenant or alter the word that went forth from my lips. Once for all I have sworn by my holiness; I will not lie to David. His offspring shall endure forever, his throne as long as the sun before me" (verses 33-36).

Later in the psalm, we read the writer's response to God's judgments: "You have renounced the covenant with your servant...How long, O LORD? Will you hide yourself forever?" (verses 39, 46). Note the contrast: Though from a human perspective it *seemed* God's faithfulness had ended, God made it clear that He would *never* violate His covenant.

When God disciplines His own, His goal is restoration. When we let sin come between us and God, that sin and its consequences will distort how we perceive Him. We may interpret His discipline as abandonment, but it is lovingly meant to pressure us to leave our sin and return to Him. It's when we stop hiding behind our sin that we discover God has never hidden Himself.

WHEN IT SEEMS A PROPHECY WON'T BE FULFILLED

*I will not violate my covenant or alter the word that
went forth from my lips. Once for all I have sworn by my
holiness; I will not lie to David (Psalm 89:34-35).*

Numerous times, God promised that King David's house and kingdom would last forever. This raises a big question: Ever since the Jewish people were taken captive to Babylon (605–586 BC), there has not been a king over Israel. And after the Roman destruction of Jerusalem in AD 70, the people were scattered over the earth, not to become a nation again until nearly 2,000 years later. Does this mean God changed His mind? Did He revoke His promise to David?

When it comes to Bible prophecy, it's important to realize there can be interruptions, pauses, or gaps in the prophetic timetable. God's promise to David of a forever kingdom didn't mean there would be an uninterrupted succession of kings on David's throne all through the ages. Rather, God was saying that one of David's descendants—Jesus—would eventually sit on his throne, in Jerusalem, and rule from it forever.

Daniel 7:13-14 provides clarity for us. Here, we are told that at the second coming, when the Son of man comes on the clouds of heaven, He will be presented with "glory and a kingdom...an everlasting dominion." Zechariah 14:4, 9 tells us Christ will descend and set His feet on the Mount of Olives before he becomes "king over all the earth." Not until our Lord returns to earth will He sit on David's throne and rule for all of eternity.

There are other prophecies in the Bible that have gaps in them. The temporary interruption of a promise should not be interpreted as a permanent cancellation of that promise. As Psalm 89:34-35 says, God's covenant to David was unconditional. The King *will* come. His rule *will* be established when He returns. And we *will* dwell in His glorious kingdom forever.

THE ULTIMATE SAVIOR
AND SOVEREIGN

*The LORD says to my Lord: Sit at my right hand, until I
make your enemies your footstool (Psalm 110:1).*

Psalm 110 takes us on a giant prophetic leap all the way to Christ's ascension to heaven after His resurrection—and then another leap to His future millennial kingdom. King David opens this psalm with words spoken by God the Father to God the Son: "Sit at my right hand, until I make your enemies your footstool."

Because of Jesus' triumph at the cross, when He ascended to heaven, the Father invited His Son to sit at His right hand—a position of highest authority and honor. Christ will remain there until His return to earth, when He will conquer all His enemies. Ancient kings often spoke of making their defeated foes a footstool, representing their total power over them. When Christ comes back and sets up His kingdom, He will become the final king for all time.

In Psalm 110:4, the Father told the Son, "You are a priest forever." Because Christ's sacrifice on the cross is good for all time, He is the final priest. For Christ to be the final king and final priest means He will have no successors. His kingship and priesthood are forever.

After Jesus asked the Pharisees, "Who do you think I am?" (see Matthew 22:42), He identified Himself by quoting Psalm 110:1. For Jesus to say that He fulfilled Psalm 110 was to say, "I am your Messiah, King, and Lord." This was a declaration of His deity and supreme authority. They knew Psalm 110 was about the Messiah but didn't recognize Him.

Jesus alone is able to claim the titles Messiah, King, and Lord—and He alone is able to combine and fulfill those roles perfectly. So supreme is He that there will be no successors. His future reign is certain, as is the forever defeat of His enemies. In Him, we have the ultimate Savior and the ultimate Sovereign.

WHAT MEN REJECTED, GOD ACCEPTED

The stone that the builders rejected has become
the cornerstone (Psalm 118:22).

I n Psalm 118:22-23 is a major Old Testament prophecy about Jesus: He would be rejected by the very people who should have recognized who He was.

After the crucifixion and resurrection, Peter pointed this out to the Jewish ruling elite. Peter and John had been arrested by these leaders for healing a beggar and proclaiming the gospel. The rulers asked, "By what power or by what name did you do this?" (Acts 4:7).

Peter responded, "By the name of Jesus Christ...whom you crucified...This Jesus is the stone that was rejected by you, the builders" (verses 10-11). What a sharp rebuke! The very ones responsible as "builders" of Israel and the Jewish people had spurned their Messiah!

Peter then said this same Jesus "has become the cornerstone." A cornerstone is the chief foundation stone upon which all the rest of a building is established. God made Christ the cornerstone of the church He continues to build today (Ephesians 2:20).

The very stone that the leaders had rejected, God accepted. The psalmist then wrote, "This is the LORD's doing; it is marvelous in our eyes" (Psalm 118:23). Even the extreme evil of putting Christ to death could not alter God's plans. His sovereignty overruled man's actions.

The crucifixion and resurrection are the supreme example of God's ability to override man's evil with His good. The cross that appeared to bring a disastrous end to Christ's mission was used by God to accomplish that mission. If God could prevail over the outcome of the crucifixion, we can trust Him to ultimately prevail over anything that people do with an evil intent. "The light shines in the darkness, and the darkness has not overcome it" (John 1:5). All the powers of darkness were defeated by the person and work of Christ at the cross.

FREQUENT REMINDERS
OF GOD'S PROMISES

The LORD has chosen Zion; he has desired it for his dwelling place: "This is my resting place forever; here I will dwell" (Psalm 132:13-14).

D avid wanted to build a temple, a house for the Lord. But God told His beloved servant, "I've chosen your son, Solomon, to build the temple." David was disappointed by this news, but what God said next compensated for that many times over: "Your house and your kingdom shall be made sure forever before me. Your throne shall be established forever" (2 Samuel 7:16). Though David was forbidden to build a temporary structure for God, the Lord promised that He would dwell in Jerusalem forever and rule the earth from David's throne.

God repeated this promise to David and the people of Israel several times—including here in Psalm 132:13-14, saying, "I have chosen Zion—Jerusalem—as my forever dwelling place." This raises a natural question: Why all the repetition?

When we see a promise repeated in Scripture, it's all too easy for us to quickly skim the words and move on. But when God repeats a truth, He always has reasons for doing so. Through repetition, God affirms the truthfulness and certainty of a promise and directs our attention to it.

A key reason God repeats His promises is because He knows that life's negative circumstances cause us to take our eyes off Him. When that happens, we're prone to become disillusioned and forget His assurances to us. Repeated promises are meant to renew our hope in life's dark moments. Through them, God says, "Though your circumstances change, My promises have not." God's desire is to replace our discouragement with hope.

In Psalm 132, God wanted to remind His people that no matter how dark their future looked, their Messiah absolutely *would* come to establish His kingdom and rule forever from Jerusalem. There *is* coming a day when "all Israel will be saved" (Romans 11:26).

PROPHECY ENCOURAGES HOLINESS

Where there is no prophetic vision the people cast off restraint,
but blessed is he who keeps the law (Proverbs 29:18).

In the book of Proverbs are hundreds of practical principles for wise living. Though there are no prophecies in this book, Proverbs 29:18 does tell us what happens to those who have "no prophetic vision." The Hebrew term used here is *chazon*, which literally translates to "prophetic vision" and can refer to divine communication, revelation, vision, or prophecy.

The principle here is that a lack of God's Word leads to a lack of restraint. When people aren't guided by God's instructions, they will indulge in sin and selfishness. But when they delight in keeping the Scriptures, they will be blessed.

Because much of God's Word is prophetic in nature, Bible prophecy can have a role in motivating people toward right living. Frequently in the Old Testament, God's prophets warned the Israelites—and others—of the future consequences they would experience if they kept rebelling against God. These prophecies were given to urge people to turn back to God.

When people lack any expectation of future judgment, they will live as if they'll never be called to account before God. This can apply to believers as well. Those who aren't reminded to live with the expectation Christ could return at any time may find themselves lacking spiritual fervor. Because they don't have eternity on their minds, they aren't motivated toward holiness.

Our spiritual well-being hinges on our exposure to God's Word. The more we feed on Scripture, including Bible prophecy, the more we are spurred to holy living. The more mindful we are of the future that awaits us, the more that influences how we live today. As 1 John 3:3 says, everyone who lives in anticipation of our Lord's appearance "purifies himself as he is pure." Living in expectation of Christ's return motivates us toward Christlikeness.

GOD'S PLANS WILL ENDURE

I will give you a wise and discerning mind (1 Kings 3:12).

I will surely tear the kingdom from you (1 Kings 11:11).

When God asked Solomon, in a dream, to choose whatever he desired, Solomon said, "Give your servant therefore an understanding mind to govern your people" (1 Kings 3:9). God was so pleased with Solomon's humble request that He prophesied, "I will not only make you the wisest of men, but also the richest of kings" (see verses 12-13).

Solomon rose quickly in power and fame. He built a temple for the Lord, and he enriched Israel through trade with foreign nations. But in time, these alliances led Solomon to marry foreign wives. This may have been politically advantageous, but it was spiritually destructive. "When Solomon was old his wives turned away his heart after other gods, and his heart was not wholly true to the LORD his God" (1 Kings 11:4). In anger, God declared: "I will surely tear the kingdom from you" (verse 11). After Solomon's death, the nation split into two kingdoms.

Solomon's reign began with prophecies of wisdom and riches but came to a sad end with a prophecy of destruction. As the wisest man in the world, he should have known better. What had gone wrong between the prophecies of blessings and a curse?

Solomon went from wanting to please God to wanting to please people. The concessions he made led to compromise, and to a collapse with repercussions that lasted for centuries.

God "removes kings and sets up kings" (Daniel 2:20-21). Even the most brilliant and powerful man in the world could do nothing to salvage his kingdom. Thankfully, in mercy, God said, "I will afflict the offspring of David...*but not forever*" (1 Kings 11:39).

Even when people fail, God's purposes will endure. His plans will march onward. The detours may be many, but nothing will keep God's everlasting promises from being fulfilled.

GOD'S GREAT PATIENCE

The Lord *warned Israel and Judah by every prophet…saying, "Turn from your evil ways and keep my commandments" (2 Kings 17:13).*

As the people of Israel spiraled downward into sin and the nation split into two, God sent prophets to warn the kings and the people of coming judgment. Both the northern and southern kingdoms had a long succession of kings who, with rare exceptions, followed other gods and filled the land with evil. It got to the point where the people were offering child sacrifices.

In response to the ever-worsening rebellion, God sent prophets who pleaded with the people to depart from their sins and idolatry, and to return to Him. The Lord showed great patience and provided an abundance of warnings over the next 200 years for the northern kingdom, Israel, and more than 300 years for the southern kingdom, Judah.

God would have been justified in bringing immediate judgment, but He didn't. In an outpouring of grace and mercy, from the ninth to the seventh centuries BC, He sent the prophets Obadiah, Joel, Amos, Hosea, Jonah, Micah, Isaiah, Nahum, Zephaniah, Habakkuk, and Jeremiah. Through these messengers, God sent many calls for His wayward people to change their minds and hearts. "The Lord was gracious to them and had compassion on them and turned to them because of his covenant with Abraham, Isaac, and Jacob" (2 Kings 13:23 NASB).

The common stereotype of God in the Old Testament is that He was vengeful, swift to anger, and itching to pour out wrath. But the pages of Scripture show God to be exceedingly patient, exceedingly gracious, and exceedingly merciful. After He warned, He wept and waited.

How wonderful is God's eagerness to show mercy and forgive! "He does not treat us as our sins deserve" (Psalm 103:10 NIV). When we repent and He forgives, He remembers our sins no more.[8] As God overwhelms us with His grace, may we overwhelm Him with our gratitude.

CALLED TO SHARE GOD'S GRACE

I know that you are a gracious and merciful God (Jonah 4:2 NKJV).

Jonah is famously known as the reluctant prophet. Called by God to go preach to the people of Nineveh in Assyria, he refused. The Israelites despised the Assyrians morally and politically, thinking themselves superior because God had chosen to bless them through Abraham.

Sadly, Jonah—who himself was a prophet!—missed the entire point of his calling. From the beginning, God chose the Israelites to be a light and a witness to the surrounding nations. He didn't show favor to them because they were better than anyone else, but because He desired to reach other peoples through them. Before they had entered the Promised Land, God said, "Do not say in your heart…'It is because of my righteousness that the LORD has brought me in to possess this land.'" Rather, "it is because of the wickedness of these nations that the LORD is driving them out" (Deuteronomy 9:4).

After a failed escape, Jonah reluctantly went to Nineveh—and the largest, most wicked city in the ancient world repented and turned to God. Still clinging to his mindset of superiority, Jonah admitted the reason he had fled: "I knew that you are a gracious God and merciful, slow to anger and abounding in steadfast love, and relenting from disaster" (Jonah 4:2).

Jonah knew God was a God of grace, but he didn't want it to be so.

Though the Jews were God's chosen people, God's desire all along was to invite Gentiles to salvation too. Some of the Egyptians left Egypt with the Israelites. God had shown mercy to Jethro, Rahab, Ruth, and other Gentiles not named in Scripture—and now, to Nineveh.

How big is our vision of God's grace? In the times we self-righteously assume someone is unworthy of or beyond His grace, we need to think again. God is the judge, not us. Our calling is to shine His grace. As we celebrate God's grace to us, let's eagerly show it to others.

GOD'S ENDURING LOVE

*If the LORD of hosts had not left us a few survivors, we should
have been like Sodom, and become like Gomorrah (Isaiah 1:9).*

G od's coming judgment upon Judah and Jerusalem would be so devastating that it could be compared to the destruction that came upon Sodom and Gomorrah. But because of God's grace for the Jewish people, as Isaiah 1:9 says, there would be a remnant of survivors.

This remnant would ensure the survival of the Jews, which was necessary for the bloodline of Jesus to continue. As we look through Old Testament history, we see that God has always had a remnant who preserved the ongoing existence of Israel. This is God's faithfulness on display! Later in Isaiah, God said about His people, "I will not contend forever, nor will I always be angry" (57:16). This confirms God will never entirely cast off the Jews.

At Christ's second coming, there will be a remnant of Jews who eagerly receive Him as their Messiah. On that day, there will be "pleas for mercy...when they look...on him whom they have pierced, they shall mourn" (Zechariah 12:10). It is this event that Paul referred to when he said, "In this way all Israel will be saved" (Romans 11:26).

No matter how great Israel's rebellion, God's grace has always permitted a remnant that made sure His promises to Abraham would be fulfilled. In the Old Testament, anytime we see the word *remnant* in relation to the Jewish people, it represents God's enduring love for them.

We who have come to faith in Christ as our Savior and Lord are the recipients of God's enduring love. We see it in Romans 8:38-39, which says nothing can separate us from His love. We see it in John 10:28-29, which says nothing can snatch us out of His hand. When we sin, we may suffer consequences, but we will never suffer the loss of our salvation. There is nothing we can do to make God love us more, and there is nothing we can do to make Him love us less.

TRUE SPIRITUALITY
STARTS WITH THE HEART

Bring no more vain offerings; incense is an abomination to me...even
though you make many prayers, I will not listen to you (Isaiah 1:13, 15).

The people in the southern kingdom of Judah were guilty. Their spiritual corruption offended God. Through the prophet Isaiah, God listed the many crimes that demanded His judgment.

The crime God condemned first might surprise us: spiritual hypocrisy. Even as the people indulged in the most abhorrent evils, they still made a show of external rituals that gave the appearance they worshipped God. They went to the temple, offered sacrifices, and lifted up prayers. But God said they were trampling the temple courts and going through the motions. They performed all the ceremonies as prescribed, but their hearts were void. Their hypocrisy angered God so much that He said, "My soul hates [it]" (Isaiah 1:14). It wasn't right actions that God wanted, but a right heart.

Scripture says that spiritual hypocrisy will worsen as this world draws nearer to Christ's return. "In the last days...people will be lovers of self... having the *appearance* of godliness" (2 Timothy 3:1-2, 5). They will look godly, even infiltrating the church. But at heart, they will be "lovers of pleasure rather than lovers of God" (verse 4).

While the above kinds of spiritual hypocrisy result from unbelief, true believers need to exercise caution as well. In the sincere and earnest desire to "do what is right" in the Christian life, we can easily pay too much attention to our actions and not enough to our hearts. Any deed that we carry out *for* God is meaningless and ineffective when it doesn't originate from a heart that is right *with* God. True spirituality has everything to do with the state of our heart, and not our actions. Only when our heart is right will our actions have meaning and be effective.

PROPHECY A LIFELINE OF HOPE

Come, let us walk in the light of the LORD (Isaiah 2:5).

Through much of the book of Isaiah, God condemned the people of Judah for their sinfulness. Because of their disobedience, God warned of judgment and expulsion from the land. The spiritual darkness was great, and God's proclamations were grim.

Remarkably, even during this bleak time, God gave promises that shone bright with hope. It is within Isaiah that we find some of the most powerful prophecies about the coming Messiah. Against the blackest of backdrops, these prophecies shine like brilliant stars. Though the near future was dismal, the distant future wasn't. Not wanting to leave His people in despair, God spoke of eventual restoration and a promised king and kingdom.

It is in this context that Isaiah gave these beloved prophecies: "Behold, the virgin shall conceive and bear a son, and shall call his name Immanuel" (7:14). And, "To us a child is born, to us a son is given; and the government shall be upon his shoulder, and his name shall be called Wonderful Counselor, Mighty God, Everlasting Father, Prince of Peace. Of the increase of his government and of peace there will be no end, on the throne of David and over his kingdom" (9:6-7).

In these prophecies and others, Jesus is clearly in view. He will be the heir to David's throne and rule over an everlasting kingdom. These are wonderful examples of how the Old Testament prophets spoke not only of doom, but of great blessings to come.

As today's world approaches its darkest hours, we're able to see more readily than ever how Bible prophecy can serve as a lifeline of hope. As we struggle with the challenges of being surrounded by evil, God's promises about the future are meant to sustain us. As we dwell on them, any discouragement present in our hearts will be ousted by encouragement.

THE REASONS GOD BRINGS JUDGMENT

They have rejected the law of the LORD of hosts (Isaiah 5:24).

As we read Isaiah chapter 5, we see today's culture unfold before us. The world Isaiah lived in is the world we live in now. The sins that led to God's judgment upon Judah are overwhelmingly present in our society, making it ripe for God's judgment as well:

- Uncontrolled greed (verses 8-10)—an obsession with gain
- Selfish pleasure (verses 11-12)—an addiction to drink and entertainment
- Flagrant evil (verses 18-19)—an eagerness to indulge in sin
- Twisted immorality (verse 20)—a blindness that calls good evil, and evil good
- Arrogant pride (verse 21)—a conceit that exalts self and despises others
- Corrupt leaders (verses 22-23)—a perversion of power and justice

For these reasons, God warned Judah of judgment (verse 25). Even so, God still offered forgiveness if the people would turn back to Him.

Isaiah had a similar compassion. When God sought a messenger who would represent Him to the people, unlike Jonah the reluctant prophet, Isaiah said, "Here I am! Send me!" (Isaiah 6:8). Then for the next 60 years, he shone God's light into a dark culture.

So depraved is today's culture that by every biblical measure, we can expect that judgment is near. But until it comes, we're to exhibit the patience shown by God. Rather than conclude that all is hopeless, like Isaiah, we should willingly say to the Lord, "Here I am! Send me!" Philippians 2:15 calls us to live as "children of God without blemish in the midst of a crooked and twisted generation, among whom you shine as lights in the world." No matter how grim the darkness, as long as there is still time, that's God's cue to keep our light shining.

GOD WITH US: OUR GREATEST NEED

Behold, the virgin shall conceive and bear a son, and
shall call his name Immanuel (Isaiah 7:14).

When Isaiah gave this prophecy, Israel and Judah were in great peril. The forecast was judgment, destruction, and captivity. At a time when it seemed as if the Jewish people's survival was seriously in doubt, Isaiah proclaimed the best news God's people could possibly hear—as well as people everywhere and through all time. Not only was the forecast grim for Israel and Judah, it was terminal for all of mankind and the entire universe. Ever since man's fall into sin, all of creation had been hopelessly severed from God and destined for eternity apart from Him.

Only Immanuel could change all that. Only He could reverse the effects of the curse and return everything to its original pristine glory. Only He could change the human heart with its default setting toward sin and make it a new heart that hungers and thirsts for God. What Israel, Judah, and all of mankind needed most was not a physical deliverance that would end up being temporary, but a spiritual salvation that would be eternal.

If any prophecy could get people's attention, it would be Isaiah 7:14. A virgin give birth? Impossible—only a divine miracle could do this. This would have to be a very special child.

God with us? Sadly, that's not what the people wanted. They loved their sin more than they loved Him and pushed Him away. Even so, He expressed His longing to draw near to them. God with us would make relationship possible again.

God with us. In times of crisis or despair, there is no better helper. When we need protection or provision, there is no better shepherd. When we're lonely or afraid, there is no better companion. When we need wisdom and guidance, we have no better counselor.

Whatever the need, God with us is always the best answer.

LAMB AND LION IN ONE PROPHECY

To us a child is born, to us a son is given; and the
government shall be upon his shoulder (Isaiah 9:6).

In the space of just a few words, the prophet Isaiah pointed to Christ's first coming as Savior and His second coming as King. The Jewish people clearly recognized Isaiah 9:6 as a promise of their Messiah. What they didn't realize was that many centuries would separate "a child is born" and "the government shall be upon his shoulder." The people wanted a geopolitical king—a Lion—who would free them from oppressive human governments and set up His kingdom immediately. But their greater need was for a spiritual Savior—a Lamb—who would free them from the bondage of sin and make possible their restoration to God.

"To us a child is born, to us a son is given" has already happened. The Father, by His marvelous design, sent the Son to die on the cross and rise again so that we would no longer be held captive by sin and the grave. Through the Lamb, we have been given spiritual victory and brought back to God. We have been taken from death to life.

"The government shall be upon his shoulder" is yet to come. But just as the baby Jesus arrived in the fullness of time (Galatians 4:4), so will King Jesus return in God's perfect timing. Every human ruler and empire in history has failed and is destined to. Only Christ's rule and kingdom will endure, and they will do so forever. Only He will successfully bring about the perfect justice and peace that so many people through the ages have longed for.

As both Lamb and Lion, Jesus offers everything we need. In meekness, He made our spiritual restoration possible, opening the way to a personal relationship with God. In power, He will return physically, setting up a glorious kingdom for us to dwell in. When at last He rules over our hearts as well as all the nations, we will experience life as God meant it to be.

WONDERFUL COUNSELOR

His name shall be called Wonderful Counselor (Isaiah 9:6).

As Isaiah 9:6-7 unfolds, wonderful new details are revealed about the coming Messiah. Here, we see His majestic attributes described: He is the Wonderful Counselor, Mighty God, Everlasting Father, and Prince of Peace. We'll unpack these amazing titles over the next few days, starting with Wonderful Counselor.

Daily, we are faced with decisions to make and issues to resolve. Some are simple and can be settled quickly. Others we struggle with for weeks or even months.

Especially difficult are concerns of a deeply personal nature. We may feel as though seeking counsel is futile because no one will understand. Or maybe the hurt we're feeling is too painful to share. And with the passage of time, these burdens accumulate, and they weigh us down because we don't know where to turn for help.

Wonderful Counselor is one of Jesus' titles. There is no greater counselor. He is always ready to listen. His perfect wisdom understands our needs better than we do. He is able to sympathize with our troubles and temptations because He faced them while in human flesh. His love seeks our best, and His constant presence assures we are never alone.

In the name Wonderful Counselor, the Hebrew word translated "Wonderful" means "extraordinary." It's a term Scripture uses frequently to describe God's extraordinary acts. To use this same word in connection with Jesus is a clear declaration of His deity.

In Jesus, we have an extraordinary counselor. Because He is God, there is no higher wisdom, no higher love, no higher compassion we can appeal to when we need help. He walks with us through life's hurts and circumstances, providing the strength to endure and a peace that calms our hearts. We can always count on Him to stay near and remain faithful.

MIGHTY GOD

His name shall be called...Mighty God (Isaiah 9:6).

When it comes to describing Christ's attributes, we can rightly say that because He is perfect, every expression of His attributes is perfect.

As Mighty God, Christ possesses perfect might. Not only does His power infinitely exceed human power, but because it is perfect, it doesn't make any sense for us to attempt to live life in our own strength.

This has amazing implications for us. When we find ourselves in an impossible situation, Christ alone can make rescue possible. When we're defenseless, there is no better shelter we can go to for protection. When we have a need, He is infinitely able to supply it.

How great is Christ's power?

- He is "able to do far more abundantly than all that we ask or think" (Ephesians 3:20).
- "He who is in you is greater than he who is in the world" (1 John 4:4).
- "All authority in heaven and on earth has been given to me" (Matthew 28:18).
- "His divine power has granted to us all things that pertain to life and godliness" (2 Peter 1:3).
- "He is before all things, and in him all things hold together" (Colossians 1:17).

It is with very good reason, then, that in 1 Corinthians 2:5, Paul urges that we not let our faith "rest in the wisdom of men but in the power of God."

Because Christ possesses perfect might, we have no need to rely on our own. We can rest in total dependence upon Him because He is all-sufficient. In Him, we find all our answers. No matter how great the obstacles we face, He is mightier.

This is the power that resides in every person who believes!

EVERLASTING FATHER

His name shall be called...Everlasting Father (Isaiah 9:6).

How is it that a prophecy about the *Son* of God would say that one of His names is "Everlasting *Father*"? In saying this, Isaiah was not mixing up the persons of the Trinity. Rather, he was speaking of Jesus as being like a compassionate father to His own. After Jesus died and rose again, He invited us to become His children and to experience His fatherly love.

In ancient times, kings were sometimes called "father" because of their role as overseer and caretaker of their subjects. As Jesus reigns from His kingly throne during the millennial kingdom, He will do for us what a father does for His children: He will lead us, watch over us, and provide for our needs.

The term "Everlasting Father" can be translated "the father of eternity," and refers to Jesus as the author of eternity. Because He is the cause, possessor, and sustainer of eternity, He truly does reign supreme over everything. As with the names Wonderful Counselor and Mighty God, the name Everlasting Father is another proclamation of His deity.

Because Jesus is the Everlasting Father, the fatherly care that He lavishes on us will continue forever. As believers, we are already experiencing His parental love right now. And this love will extend for endless ages, without interruption.

In the name Everlasting Father, we are made aware of this powerful truth: The father of all eternity is the one who extends to us the fatherly love we know as believers. The one who is so mighty as to have created eternity is the one who will attentively care for even the least of our needs forever. It is humbling to think that as exalted and transcendent as our Lord is, He willingly lowered Himself to the point of death on the cross so that we could become His children. Only the greatest of fatherly hearts would do that.

PRINCE OF PEACE

His name shall be called...Prince of Peace (Isaiah 9:6).

As the Prince of Peace, Jesus is not only the greatest bearer of peace ever, but the only source of peace. Apart from Him, peace cannot be known. And the peace He offers is powerful—note the ways it changes everything for us:

Peace with God. With sin's entrance into the world, we became enemies of God. Sin's presence within us makes us, by nature, hostile toward God. Christ's sacrifice on the cross changed that. As Romans 5:1 says, we who have been "justified by faith...have peace with God through our Lord Jesus Christ." When we ask Jesus to cleanse us of our sin and its resulting enmity with God, we can enjoy peace with God.

Peace with Others. Sin has not only divided mankind from God, but people from one another. From the moment sin tore apart Adam and Eve, no relationship has been left unaffected. Turmoil and strife have been constants. Every human interaction has been damaged by conflicts ranging from arguments to wars. Sin makes peace impossible. Not until Christ reigns on His throne in the millennial kingdom will there be true and enduring peace in this world.

Peace Within Ourselves. Apart from Jesus, we cannot experience inner peace. When we surrender the throne of our hearts to the Prince of Peace, His peace will rule over us and shape our thoughts and actions.

As the Prince of Peace, Jesus is the source and giver of peace. It is appropriate that of the four titles ascribed to Him in Isaiah 9:6, Prince of Peace is last, for earth's final kingdom will be the first to know true peace. As He ascends His throne in Jerusalem, He will usher in a peace that brings a climactic end to the turmoil and chaos that has plagued our world since that dark day in Eden. With the government on His shoulders, peace will prevail forever and ever.

INCREASE WITH NO END

*Of the increase of his government and of peace
there will be no end (Isaiah 9:7).*

Our first day in Christ's millennial kingdom will be far more amazing than any previous day in our lives. And as exciting as it will be, Isaiah 9:7 tells us that "of the *increase* of his government and of peace there will be no end." As time goes on, our Lord's rule in power and majesty and peace will continue to ascend and expand.

This raises an interesting question: How can a kingdom that is already perfect become even better?

This tells us that from the millennial kingdom onward, we will never tire of the "same old same old." Some people speculate that life will become routine and boring, but it won't. It's hard to imagine, but the already-wonderful future that awaits us will grow even more wonderful as eternity goes on.

In Christ's millennial kingdom—and in the New Jerusalem after that—we will never exhaust all there is to know and experience about God and His universe. Think about the space telescopes and cameras that continue to peer deeper than ever into the cosmos, unveiling for us galaxies we never knew existed. Just as the vast reaches of an infinite universe will always leave us with more to learn, so will we never run out of wonders to discover about our infinite God.

Scripture tells us, "Oh, the depths of the riches and wisdom and knowledge of God! How unsearchable are his judgments and how inscrutable his ways!" (Romans 11:33). Even when we become eternal immortals, we will still be the created creatures of the all-transcendent Creator. The more we experience of God's many splendors, the more we will want to worship, praise, and exalt Him. In eternity, our lives with God will unceasingly grow fuller, richer, and deeper—without end.

A PEACE WITHOUT END

The wolf shall dwell with the lamb (Isaiah 11:6).

The curse of sin is all we have ever known. With sin came everything that is opposed to God's created order, including pain, destruction, enmity, and death. These weren't what God intended for us to experience. That is why, instinctively, we recognize the many things that are wrong with our world, and we long to correct them. This explains mankind's never-ending search for utopia. No matter how hard people try, the paradise they yearn for is unattainable because of sin's suffocating—and humanly irremovable—presence.

In the book of Isaiah, not only are there prophecies about the coming Messiah, but also about His coming kingdom on earth. Many first-time revelations are given that promise a glorious future—revelations meant to let God's people know that even though they would soon be punished and taken into exile, God's promises of future blessing would not be taken away.

Never has this world known real peace. That will change when the Prince of Peace sits on David's throne in Jerusalem. One of the more exciting prophecies about the millennial kingdom is this: "The wolf shall dwell with the lamb, and the leopard shall lie down with the young goat, and the calf and the lion and the fattened calf together; and a little child shall lead them" (Isaiah 11:6). That kind of peace is incredible to ponder, isn't it?

When Christ returns and the curse is lifted from all creation, the animal world will be transformed and restored to the peace it knew in the Garden of Eden. Not only will all animals get along, but we will get along with them. Because peace reigns over all creation, everything that is contrary to peace will vanish.

With Christ's return will come a peace that changes everything. So powerful is this peace that we truly will live in a new world. The best part? This peace will never end!

PREPARING FOR THE LORD'S ARRIVAL

A voice cries: "In the wilderness prepare the way of the Lord; make straight in the desert a highway for our God" (Isaiah 40:3).

Beginning in Isaiah 40 is a major shift that continues to the end of the book. Up to this point, Isaiah's prophecies have mostly emphasized judgment. Now comes a refreshing and continuous stream of prophecies about deliverance, restoration, and blessing.

Isaiah 40 opens with God's promise to make forgiveness available to His people even though they had sinned greatly against Him. Then comes a remarkable prophecy that points ahead to John the Baptist, the voice in the wilderness who will call people to "prepare the way of the Lord" (verse 3). All four Gospel writers later confirmed that Isaiah's prophecy spoke of Jesus' forerunner, John the Baptist (Matthew 3:3; Mark 1:3; Luke 3:4-6; John 1:23).

In the strongest possible terms, Isaiah was telling anyone who would listen, "God Himself is coming to you! Prepare the way for Him. He is bringing the forgiveness you so desperately need." In ancient times, before kings traveled, heralds were sent in advance and roads were repaired. For someone truly special, a new and smooth highway would be built.

Isaiah's prophecy about John the Baptist was meant to serve as a call—for the next 700 years—for God's people to be ready to welcome their King. Out of great love and mercy, God gave more than enough advance notice. All through the Old Testament, He gave many alerts that preceded the first coming of His Son. And for 2,000 years now, the Bible has made known many more alerts for the world to be ready for Christ's second coming.

God has spoken. When it comes to what the future holds, no one can plead ignorance. One of prophecy's grand purposes is to prepare believers and unbelievers for what is to come. Are we paying attention? Are we ready?

HOW A HIGH VIEW OF GOD HELPS US

Behold your God! (Isaiah 40:9).

When God's people were lured away from Him by the entice-
ments of this world, Isaiah knew what they needed to hear most:
"Behold your God!" (Isaiah 40:9). The people had taken their eyes off
Him, forgetting all that He had done for them and could do for them.
This calls our attention to an important truth: Our trust in God's greatness and His sufficiency can do much to help us resist the temptations
that try to pull us away from Him.

Had Abraham fully trusted God's ability to do the impossible, would
he have attempted to fulfill God's promise of offspring through a woman
other than Sarah? Had Moses recognized God's power was infinitely
greater than Pharaoh's, would he have turned down God's call to lead
the Israelites out of Egypt? Had Jonah looked beyond his pride to recognize the greatness of God's plan of salvation to include Gentiles, would
he have avoided going to Nineveh?

When we are plagued with doubt and uncertainty, the answer is to
look to God's sufficiency and greatness. When we struggle with our lot
in life and look for solutions apart from God, we need to turn our gaze
to Him alone. When our thoughts and feelings tempt us to seek satisfaction outside of what God offers, we need to remember that only He
can satisfy.

Scripture is filled with reminders of God's incomparable greatness
and sufficiency. In 2 Chronicles 14:11 is the cry, "O LORD, there is none
like you to help…Help us, O LORD our God, for we rely on you." Such
reminders call us to always depend on God.

A high view of God is what enables us to stay anchored when life's
temptations and trials threaten to send us adrift. It's as we are convinced
of His exceedingly great wisdom, power, and love for us that we will
want to stay close to Him and not wander.

The higher our view of God, the more we gladly trust Him and will
find rest in Him.

GOD'S INCOMPARABLE GREATNESS

To whom then will you compare me? (Isaiah 40:25).

With the dark clouds of judgment and exile hanging over them, God's people needed words of comfort and hope. That's what Isaiah delivers in chapters 40–66. He begins by saying that God's offer of forgiveness would always be available to those who seek it. And He repeats God's promise of a coming Messiah who would make that forgiveness possible.

The rest of Isaiah chapter 40 then soars to proclaim—to anyone who would hear—that absolutely no one and nothing compares to God. To the people who had forgotten His greatness, Isaiah shouts, "Behold your God!" (verse 9). He describes God's power over all nature, and how God's wisdom far exceeds ours. "Whom did he consult?" Isaiah asks rhetorically (verse 14). "All the nations are as nothing before him" (verse 17). God is far above all.

"To whom then will you compare me?," God asks (verse 25). No one can rival Him. Why, then, would anyone disregard Him? No one is greater or more powerful. "Have you not known? Have you not heard? The LORD is the everlasting God, the Creator of the ends of the earth" (verse 28). Again and again, Isaiah pleads to God's rebellious people, "How could you turn from and abandon God? No one and nothing can fulfill your needs as He can."

Because God is so incomparably great, He alone is worthy of all our devotion and trust and love. Nothing outside of God can satisfy. He is all-sufficient. Our every human need is met in Him alone. Because we are wholly inadequate, we need Him who is wholly adequate.

It is because God is so great that He is able to fulfill the promise in Isaiah 40:31 that is so dear to many: "They who wait for the LORD shall renew their strength; they shall mount up with wings like eagles; they shall run and not be weary; they shall walk and not faint."

For every longing in your heart, the answer is always the same: Behold your God!

BRINGING DELIGHT TO GOD

Behold, my servant...my chosen, in whom my soul delights (Isaiah 42:1).

Though God's people had failed to be a light to the nations around them, that would not thwart His plan to bring salvation to the world. After Isaiah's incredible tribute to God's greatness in chapter 40, we read about what this great—and wise!—God will do next: "Behold, my servant, whom I uphold, my chosen, in whom my soul delights. I have put my Spirit upon him; he will bring forth justice to the nations" (Isaiah 42:1).

God tells Israel and Judah, "What you couldn't accomplish, I will accomplish. I will send My servant to proclaim salvation not only to you, but the rest of the world." Here, God prophesies of the coming Messiah. Isaiah 42 then describes how this servant will carry out His mission: "He will not cry aloud or lift up his voice, or make it heard in the street" (verse 2). The Jews wanted a Messiah who would start a revolution and overthrow enemy powers. Instead, at His first coming, Jesus came meekly and quietly to offer peace with God through salvation.

Isaiah 42:3 then adds, "A bruised reed he will not break, and a faintly burning wick he will not quench." This prophecy speaks of the gentle nature of Jesus' ministry. He will reach out to the lowly and oppressed. He will bring comfort and encouragement to the weary and desolate.

As we look back on Jesus' ministry, we see in Him a model for what God had hoped the Jews would do, and what He desires the church to do today. As long as there is still time for people to turn to God, we are to proclaim the message of salvation and to do so with gentleness.

In Isaiah 42:1, God said of Jesus, "Behold, my servant...in whom my soul delights." Why did God delight in Jesus? Because He carried out the mission given to Him. Do you desire to delight God as well? That will happen as you carry out God's purpose for you: to be His loving messenger to others. As you fulfill God's design for you, you'll bring delight to Him.

APPOINTED FOR A PURPOSE

He shall fulfill all my purpose (Isaiah 44:28).

God's exactness with Bible prophecy is breathtaking. This is especially evident in Isaiah 44:28, a climactic prophecy given to God's people in Judah: "I am the Lord, who...says of Cyrus, 'He is my shepherd, and he shall fulfill all my purpose; saying of Jerusalem, "She shall be built," and of the temple, "Your foundation shall be laid"'" (verses 24, 28).

Nearly 200 years before it happened, God not only *predicted* that a future king of Persia would free the Jewish people to leave Babylon and return home, but He *named* the king—far in advance of his birth! Also, God promised restoration *before* the people of Judah had even been taken captive, and *before* Jerusalem and the temple were destroyed.

Two other levels of amazing happen here: In calling Cyrus the "shepherd" who would give the decree for the Jewish people to go back to their land in 538 BC, God prophetically prefigured Jesus as the Shepherd who would regather the Jews again in the distant future for His millennial kingdom (Micah 5:4). Also, God chose a pagan monarch to "fulfill all my purpose"!

God knows, reveals, and guarantees the future—not in some vague sense where He "fills in the blanks" as the fulfillment of a prophecy draws near, but to the point of even knowing the names of who will do what. That God would orchestrate His plans to this extent shows a highly personal side to Bible prophecy. Not only is God sovereign and providential, but he is detailed and deliberate. He knows who He will use, and when and where He will use them.

So intentional is God in carrying out His purposes that we were "created in Christ Jesus for good works, which God prepared beforehand" (Ephesians 2:10). All our days "were written, every one of them...when as yet there was none of them" (Psalm 139:16). This makes every one of us specially appointed. Our place in God's timeline is by His design. What an honor!

THE SUFFERING SERVANT

Behold, my servant (Isaiah 52:13).

For Isaiah to provide one of the grandest Old Testament previews of the Savior's time on earth is appropriate because *Isaiah* means "the Lord is salvation." So significant are Isaiah's words that Jesus and the New Testament writers quote or allude to him an estimated 65 times. And because there are so many passages in Isaiah that have to do with redemption, some call it the "fifth Gospel," for Matthew, Mark, Luke, and John are foreshadowed in Isaiah.

Of all the prophetically rich content in the book of Isaiah, chapter 53 stands out. The prophecies here about Christ's ministry, crucifixion, burial, and resurrection are so detailed and so accurate that it's as if Isaiah wrote the words as an eyewitness. But this chapter was written more than 700 years before Jesus' birth. It is here, within this chapter, that we read one of the most graphic and moving descriptions of the crucifixion in all the Old Testament.

In Isaiah 53 we are introduced to Jesus, the suffering servant. We know it's Jesus because of how perfectly these words describe what happened at the cross: The brutal nature of His wounds (52:14), the iniquities of all being laid on Him (53:6), His silence when He was accused and led as a lamb to the slaughter (verse 7), His innocence (verse 9), His being an offering for guilt and His resurrection (verse 10), and His justifying many and being an atonement to make us righteous (verse 11).

Isaiah 53 really begins at Isaiah 52:13, where God said, "Behold, my servant." Here, the Father solemnly points our attention to His Son. In this prophetic passage, we see the entirety of the gospel. The extent of Jesus' love for us and the cost of the sacrifice He made are put on full display. Jesus truly gave His all more than we'll ever understand. We will never be able to thank Him enough. That's why we will never tire of praising and worshipping Him for all eternity.

THE BRUTALITY OF THE CROSS

His appearance was so marred, beyond human semblance (Isaiah 52:14).

At the time Isaiah was written, there was no Roman Empire. Nor had crucifixion been invented yet. But once this means of execution was devised, it became popular because it was so savage and so shameful that it had a strong deterring effect on people.

The words Isaiah used to describe the torture Jesus experienced are painful to read. He was "stricken" and "afflicted" (Isaiah 53:4). Before going to the cross, He was severely beaten and flogged. Then Jesus was "pierced" and "crushed" (verse 5). His wounds were excruciating. To be nailed to a cross was a barbaric way to briefly stall inevitable death.

Not only was Jesus' physical anguish great, He was also "despised and rejected by men" (verse 3). The crowds mocked and jeered at Him. It's possible this prophecy has in view the fact He was abandoned even by His own disciples, except for John.

Especially agonizing for Jesus is that He was "smitten by God," and "upon him was...chastisement" (verses 4-5). He willingly took the full brunt of God's wrath—on Him was laid "the iniquity of us all" (verse 6). In doing this, He "brought us peace" (verse 5).

Words are not adequate to describe the enormity of the torment Jesus endured on the cross. We cannot imagine the horror of the cumulative effects He felt from the unbearable physical pain, the hatred of the crowd, the fury of God's wrath, and the weight of our sins upon Him. The punishment humanity inflicted upon Jesus was the worst injustice ever to take place in the universe. Yet through it, God brought about the justice that would make it possible for us to come back to Him. The pain of the cross was great, but Jesus' love for us was greater.

In a hymn written in 1707, Isaac Watts described the best possible response we could have to what Jesus did: "Love so amazing, so divine, demands my soul, my life, my all."[9]

THE GOSPEL AT THE CENTER OF ISAIAH 53

He was pierced for our transgressions; he was crushed for our
iniquities; upon him was the chastisement that brought us
peace, and with his wounds we are healed (Isaiah 53:5).

In Isaiah 52:13, God says, "Behold, my servant." Then from Isaiah 52:13 to 53:12 are 15 verses that form the entirety of Isaiah 53. The middle-most verse in this passage is Isaiah 53:5, which appears above. This verse is at the exact center of the passage—it is the heart of Isaiah 53, and it is the heart of the gospel. Here, Isaiah describes the core of the gospel message: Christ's substitutionary death on our behalf paid for our sins and made possible our forgiveness.

On the cross, Jesus took the punishment we deserved for our guilt. The sinless one became the substitute for sinners. Our sin was credited to Him so that His righteousness could be credited to us. As our substitute, Christ made possible a miraculous transformation:

- Before, we were enemies with God, but now we're friends.
- Before, we were condemned, but now we're forgiven.
- Before, we were destined for hell, but now we're destined for heaven.

Hebrew scholars say the terms translated "pierced" and "crushed" are the strongest words in Hebrew to describe a violent and excruciating death. "Chastisement" and "wounds" speak of punishment and physical affliction. Christ suffered God's intense wrath on our behalf so that we could know peace with God and spiritual healing.

At the cross, the great exchange took place. Jesus was our substitute. He took on our sin so we could be given His righteousness. This is why God "does not deal with us according to our sins" (Psalm 103:10). It is why we can draw near to God's throne of grace (Hebrews 4:16).

A NEW AND BETTER WORLD

Behold, I create new heavens and a new earth (Isaiah 65:17).

First and foremost, the book of Isaiah is about God's unfailing love for His people. Though they have wandered far from Him, He will not abandon them. Though they will be punished, God promises to preserve them. Someday, they will recognize the Messiah whom they pierced and claim Him as their Savior. This will happen at Christ's return. Afterward, He will usher this Jewish remnant into His glorious millennial kingdom.

Isaiah prophesied more about the millennial kingdom and eternity than any other Old Testament prophet. The themes of Isaiah chapters 40–66 are restoration and deliverance. It all comes to a climactic peak in Isaiah 66:22, where God says, "As the new heavens and the new earth that I make shall remain before me...so shall your offspring and your new name remain."

Just as the new heavens and new earth will endure, so will Israel. The nation will be restored, the Messiah will rule on His throne at Jerusalem, and the Gentile nations surrounding Israel will come to Jerusalem to worship the Lord (Isaiah 66:23). Yes, the promise God made way back in Genesis 17:7 is true: God's covenant with Israel is everlasting!

The book of Isaiah ends on the same triumphant note as the book of Revelation: It looks ahead to the new heavens and new earth. Both Isaiah and the apostle John remind us that the world we live in is temporary. It's not our real home. Someday, the remnant of Israel and the Gentiles who have salvation in Christ will dwell in a new and glorious place.

All of God's people are destined for a glorious future. A world is coming that is far better than the one we're in today. We may think we will miss some of what we enjoy now, but we won't. Life will be so incredible in God's presence and His kingdom that we will never look back. Our heavenly gains will be so great that our earthly losses will become as nothing.

FAITHFUL TO THE TASK

I appointed you a prophet to the nations (Jeremiah 1:5).

Jeremiah witnessed Judah's darkest days. Three times, he watched as the Babylonian army invaded the land and took his fellow Jews into captivity. The third time, the enemy soldiers ransacked and destroyed Jerusalem and the temple.

Nicknamed "the weeping prophet," Jeremiah's heart weighed heavily for God's people. He grieved over their refusal to return to God. So great was the opposition against him that he struggled with wanting to quit (20:9), and he cursed the day he was born (verses 14-18).

Up front, God told Jeremiah that his efforts would be fruitless: "Do not pray for this people, or lift up a cry or prayer for them, and do not intercede with me, for I will not hear you" (7:16). Forty years of ministry would yield zero results. From our perspective, it would seem Jeremiah was a failure. But he wasn't. He did exactly what God had called him to do.

When it comes to doing the Lord's work, our role is to be faithful and serve. The results aren't our responsibility, but God's. As 1 Corinthians 3:7 says, "Neither he who plants nor he who waters is anything, but only God who gives the growth." Only God can bring faith to the spiritually dead. Salvation has always been a work of God's grace—in both the Old and New Testaments, and all through the church age.

Our usefulness to God is measured not by the size of our ministry or its results, but our faithfulness to the task He has given us. It's when we stay true to God's assignment that our service is most pleasing to Him.

When we place our full trust in God to bring forth the fruit, we will free ourselves from the temptations to take credit for the results and to do things in our own strength. Staying wholly dependent upon God ensures that His purposes are accomplished, and not our own.

GOD'S PERFECT JUSTICE

These nations shall serve the king of
Babylon seventy years (Jeremiah 25:11).

By the time we reach Jeremiah 25, the prophet had been warning the people of Judah for 23 years. If they turned back to God, then they could stay in the land. But if not, God said He would bring "Nebuchadnezzar the king of Babylon, my servant...against this land and its inhabitants" (verse 9). For God to call Nebuchadnezzar "my servant" was not a compliment, but a confirmation of His ability to work through even ungodly leaders to achieve His purposes.

God then revealed the punishment: The Jews would remain captive in Babylon for "seventy years" (verse 11). Why 70? Because for 490 years, the people had not given the land its Sabbatical-year rest. Every seven years, they were to abstain from raising crops so the soil could be replenished. Over the course of 490 years, 70 of these rests had been ignored. If the people wouldn't allow the soil to rest, then God would make it happen by removing the people.

Then, in the very next verse, Jeremiah gave this stunning prophecy: At the end of the 70 years, God would bring swift judgment against the Babylonians (verse 12). Though God used Babylon to chastise Judah, He would not let the wicked Babylonian Empire off the hook.

The back-to-back prophecies about Israel's 70-year exile and Babylon's subsequent judgment reveals that God always executes justice rightly and perfectly. The punishment He imposed on His people was measured according to their wrongdoing. And though the wicked may prosper temporarily (as did the Babylonians), judgment *will* come.

God's standard of justice is perfect in all its expressions. He does not play favorites, and He does not overlook evil. With righteous love He chastises His own, and with righteous indignation He punishes evildoers. We can rejoice in the truth that no injustice ever escapes His attention, and rest in the promise that He will always deal with us, His children, righteously.

GOD'S PROMISES ARE SECURE

The days are coming...when I will fulfill the promise I made to
the house of Israel and the house of Judah (Jeremiah 33:14).

God has reasons for repeating His promises. He doesn't want us to forget them, and He wants to make it clear He will never break them. One of the most powerful and deeply moving examples of this in the Old Testament occurs in Jeremiah 33—not once, but twice!

Centuries earlier, God promised to Abraham land that would belong to Israel forever. Later, He promised to David a descendant who would sit on his throne eternally. Both promises were unconditional. Their fulfillments rested fully on God's character and not people's actions.

If God were to break just one of His promises, it would mean He couldn't be trusted to keep any of them. On a whim, He could change His mind and betray us. Or it would mean He is less than God and less than perfect, leaving no reason for us to believe or follow Him.

How committed is God to keeping His promises to Israel and Judah? "I would no more reject my people than I would change my laws that govern night and day, earth and sky" (Jeremiah 33:25 NLT). God made the same declaration in verses 20-21. Twice, He said His promises to Abraham, Isaac, Jacob, and David were as fixed as the laws of nature, which were established at creation.

Just as the laws of nature will never collapse, God's promises will never fail. Just as night reliably becomes day, God reliably follows through on what He says He will do. The greatest promise in Scripture—of a Messiah who would come through Israel, bless the world, and reign forever—is backed by the very power that upholds the cosmos. That is how secure God's promises are. When God wanted to guarantee the permanence of His promises to Israel, there was no greater example of certainty He could point to than the fixed laws of the universe He created.

THE MIRACULOUS REBIRTH OF ISRAEL

The cities shall be inhabited and the waste places rebuilt (Ezekiel 36:10).

The Israel we see today is the Israel described 2,600 years ago in a prophecy given by Ezekiel. We are eyewitnesses to the fulfillment of one of God's greatest prophetic promises in the Bible: the regathering of the Jewish people from all over the earth to the land God had given them.

The story of Israel's miraculous rebirth has God written all over it. Never in the history of the world has a people been so thoroughly uprooted and yet preserved for nearly 2,000 years, eventually to become a nation again. Humanly speaking, the impossible happened. That's because with God, nothing is impossible.

Not only did God promise to bring His people back to their ancestral homeland, but He also said He would make them prosperous. Through Ezekiel, God declared, "You, O mountains of Israel, shall shoot forth your branches and yield your fruit to my people Israel, for they will soon come home. For behold, I am for you, and I will turn to you, and you shall be tilled and sown. And I will multiply people on you, the whole house of Israel, all of it. The cities shall be inhabited and the waste places rebuilt" (Ezekiel 36:8-10). What was once barren desert and useless swampland is now covered with prolific farmland and gleaming cities.

Now that the physical restoration of the *land* has taken place, next comes the spiritual restoration of the *people*—the spiritual awakening that will occur at Christ's return, as prophesied in Ezekiel 37:1-14 and Zechariah 12:10.

We live in exciting days. The rebirth of Israel is a clear sign that God's prophetic plans are moving forward. The nation of Israel must literally be in place for the end times to occur. And during the millennial kingdom, Christ will rule from His holy city: "At that time Jerusalem shall be called the throne of the LORD, and all the nations shall gather to it" (Jeremiah 3:17).

THE FUTURE SPIRITUAL RESTORATION OF ISRAEL

They shall be my people, and I will be their God (Ezekiel 37:23).

The "valley of dry bones" prophecy in Ezekiel 37 is one of the more unusual passages in the Old Testament. In a vision, the prophet Ezekiel stood before a valley. The bones littered on the ground are identified as "the whole house of Israel," who say, "Our bones are dried up, and our hope is lost." This represents the destitute state of Israel after God scattered the Jewish people for what would end up being nearly 2,000 years.

In the vision, Ezekiel was told a day was coming when the bones would rise to life. They would come together and grow tendons and flesh. But at first, there would be "no breath in them" (verse 8). Then later, "breath came into them" (verse 10) "that they may live" (verse 9). As if rising from the dead, the nation of Israel would come back to life again.

Today, the Jewish people have been physically restored to their homeland. But the spiritual restoration won't occur until Christ returns. At that time, the Jews will have a miraculous awakening that leads to repentance. They will acknowledge Christ as their Messiah. God says, "I will pour out on the house of David and the inhabitants of Jerusalem a spirit of grace and pleas for mercy, so that, when they look on me, on him whom they have pierced, they shall mourn for him, as one mourns for an only child" (Zechariah 12:10).

Paul mentions this awakening in Romans 11:26-27: "In this way *all Israel will be saved*, as it is written, the Deliverer will come from Zion, and…I [will] take away their sins."

Here's the best part: God says that when Israel's spiritual renewal occurs, the Jews "shall know that I am the LORD" (Ezekiel 37:14). For the Jews to have been scattered worldwide for 2,000 years, be regathered, then come to spiritual life will be such an astounding miracle that the obvious explanation will be "God did this." He will get all the credit… and all the glory.

GOD IS PROPHETICALLY ACTIVE TODAY

I will show my greatness…and make myself known (Ezekiel 38:23).

In Ezekiel 38 is a prophecy that is being fulfilled right now before our very eyes. The prophet spoke of a massive military attack that will come against Israel in the last days (verses 8, 16). These warring forces will "go against the land…whose people were gathered from many peoples upon the mountains of Israel" (verse 8). This attack will be against a nation of *regathered* people—which describes Israel today. The enemy forces will be so massive that they "will be like a cloud covering the land" (verse 9).

Amazingly, the nations that take part in this war are identified for us. Ezekiel 38:2-6 lists the ancient place names whose modern-day equivalents include Russia, Iran, Turkey, Sudan, Libya, Tunisia, and Algeria.[10] For centuries, this prophecy didn't make sense because these nations had no real ties with each other. But that is changing rapidly. Several of them are now building highly dangerous alliances—especially Russia, Iran, and Turkey.

The invaders will descend swiftly upon Israel, and just as swiftly, God will destroy them (verses 19-22). Intent on annihilating Israel, instead, the enemies will be wiped out. God says, "I will show my greatness and my holiness and *make myself known* in the eyes of many nations. *Then they will know* that I am the LORD" (Ezekiel 38:23). God's intervention will be the only possible explanation for Israel's survival of such an overwhelming attack.

God is prophetically active right now. He is doing a lot of stage-setting for the end times. Israel is a nation again, and the countries that will attack Israel in the last days are building military alliances. God is coordinating countless other details as only He can. In Isaiah 46:11, He said, "I have spoken, and I will bring it to pass." His plans are unfolding exactly as He ordained. He is at work, and we have front-row seats to all the action.

THE PRICE OF TAKING A STAND

Daniel resolved that he would not defile himself (Daniel 1:8).

It's hard to be a Christian in today's world. We experience constant pressures to compromise our faith. In a society hostile toward God, we can likewise expect to face rejection. In our desire to avoid opposition, the temptation is great for us to blend in with everyone else.

The prophet Daniel knew what it was like to face pressure to conform to an ungodly culture. In 605 BC, the first group of Jews were deported to Babylon. The young teenager Daniel and a few of his friends were taken captive along with other select nobles. King Nebuchadnezzar wanted to train and integrate them into Babylonian society.

Because Daniel was willing to stand by his convictions no matter the cost, he serves as a great example for how we can resist compromise. We may get frustrated over the decline of morality in our day, but it's exactly what we should expect, and it's an opportunity for us to shine brightly and point people Godward. Blending in with the world may appear to be the safer option, but we'll be miserable because we're living contrary to God's calling. And if that blending in means accommodating sin, we'll be even more miserable from a guilty conscience.

One of the most important lessons we can learn from Daniel and his friends is that taking a stand will cost us. That's how Daniel ended up in the lions' den, and his friends ended up in a fiery furnace. God spared all of them, but it doesn't always happen that way. In Hebrews 11:36-37, we read that some of God's great servants "suffered mocking and flogging, and even chains and imprisonment. They were stoned, they were sawn in two, they were killed with the sword."

Jesus warned that we will face tribulation (John 16:33). Rather than try to avoid it, we're called to persevere. Let's gladly be willing to pay the price, for "our present sufferings are not worth comparing with the glory that will be revealed in us" (Romans 8:18).

EXPRESSING OUR CONVICTIONS WITH GRACE

Let us be given vegetables to eat and water to drink (Daniel 1:12).

The story of what happened to Daniel when he first arrived in Babylon is well known. Select Jewish youths who had been taken captive were to eat the king's food and drink the king's wine as part of their immersion into Babylonian society.

But Daniel and his friends Hananiah, Mishael, and Azariah did not want to defile themselves with this menu. Daniel asked one of the king's chief servants to instead give them a diet of vegetables and water. Most likely, the king's food violated Jewish dietary laws, or it had earlier been offered to pagan gods, which would have made it impure to eat.

There are two valuable lessons we can learn from how Daniel handled this situation. First, for Daniel and his friends to be concerned about the king's food may seem trivial. Why not just go along? Why not be accommodating over the little things, and save the strong stands for bigger issues? Daniel recognized the importance of honoring God's standards at all times. He also knew that a minor compromise would pave the way to major ones. By not giving in to a smaller matter, his resolve would remain intact, and others would know where he stood.

Also, we read that "God gave Daniel favor and compassion in the sight of the chief [servant]" (verse 9). Clearly, the king's servant liked Daniel—probably because Daniel was kind and gracious to him. When Daniel was asked to go against his convictions, he could have been combative and defiant, but he wasn't. As he declined the food, he befriended the servant.

When we stand for our convictions, we need to do so clearly and consistently. Otherwise, we will confuse others and hurt our testimony. And as we exhibit our convictions, we should do so by displaying godly attitudes that are more likely to win the ears of our enemies. Even when we're opposed for our faith, we want to keep our faith attractive so that people are drawn to it.

GOD, THE SUPREME SOVEREIGN

He removes kings and sets up kings (Daniel 2:21).

King Nebuchadnezzar was deeply troubled. A recurring dream was bothering him. He recognized that it was significant and wanted to know its meaning. None of his occultists or wise men could interpret it, so he threatened to kill them. Upon hearing this news, Daniel asked the king to "appoint him a time, that he might show the interpretation to the king" (Daniel 2:16).

Daniel then went home to his friends Hananiah, Mishael, and Azariah. He asked them to pray for mercy, that God would reveal the meaning of the dream to Daniel—for they were among the wise men endangered by the king's death edict. That night, their prayers were answered, and God revealed Nebuchadnezzar's dream to Daniel in a vision.

As it turned out, the dream—which featured a statue made of gold, silver, bronze, iron, and clay—revealed a sweeping panorama of the rest of human history, all the way to Christ's return. It offered fascinating prophecies about the future, all of which have been accurately fulfilled to date. But what often gets overlooked is Daniel's prayer and praise to God before he went to the king. As he acknowledged God's wisdom and might, he made this powerful statement: God "changes times and seasons; he removes kings and sets up kings" (verse 21).

In every Bible prophecy about history, two truths are made clear: God knows the future, and He determines it. He is the supreme sovereign over all sovereigns. Not even earth's mightiest powers can circumvent His will. The destiny of every ruler and nation is in His hands.

Daniel is our example for how to live under worldly governments. Rather than be distressed by the wrongs and abuses of human powers, we can rest in the knowledge that God is in control. Every human empire will collapse, and Christ's future kingdom will prevail. As we await its arrival, we should pray, trust God, thank Him for His sovereignty, and live honorably.

THE ONE TRUE GOD

There is a God in heaven who reveals mysteries (Daniel 2:28).

King Nebuchadnezzar had asked for the impossible. He demanded that his magicians and wise men tell him what he had dreamed, and to interpret the dream. But they couldn't. They pleaded, "Tell your servants the dream, and we will show the interpretation" (Daniel 2:4). They figured that once they knew the details, they could make up a seemingly plausible explanation.

But the king saw through their trickery. If they truly had the powers that they claimed to possess, they should be able to do what he asked. The king did not budge: Tell me the dream or be put to death. In fear, they said, "The thing that the king asks is difficult, and no one can show it to the king except the gods, whose dwelling is not with flesh" (verse 11). In other words, the Babylonian gods were distant and impersonal. This, said the wise men, left them helpless.

When Daniel prepared to explain the dream, he set the stage by saying no man could have done what the king asked. Then he said, "There is a God in heaven who reveals mysteries, and he has made known to King Nebuchadnezzar what will be in the latter days" (verse 28).

"There is a God in heaven" made it clear this God was above all gods. And "he has made known to King Nebuchadnezzar" showed this God was accessible and had a personal message for the king. Daniel drew a stark contrast between the living God of the universe and the false gods of Babylon. The God of heaven wanted the attention of earth's most powerful king.

Daniel then told the king, "God revealed the mystery to me not because I possess greater wisdom than others, but because He wants to speak to you" (see verse 30). Daniel gave God all the credit and glory. Nebuchadnezzar was eager to know about the dream; Daniel was eager for the king to meet the one behind the dream. The role of anyone who speaks for God is to point to God and not self, so that God may be heard clearly and draw people to Himself.

GOD IS SOVEREIGN
OVER BIG AND SMALL

You, O king…the God of heaven has given the kingdom, the
power, and the might, and the glory (Daniel 2:37).

D aniel had Nebuchadnezzar's full attention. So perfectly had he revealed the details of the dream that the king was spellbound. Then as Daniel transitioned to explain the interpretation, he made this important declaration: "You, O king…the God of heaven has given the kingdom, the power, and the might, and the glory" (Daniel 2:37).

At the time, Nebuchadnezzar was the most powerful monarch on earth. Everyone in his empire answered to him, and no other kingdoms could compare. It's clear the king thought highly of himself, for later, while walking on the roof of his palace, he boasted, "Is not this great Babylon, which I have built by my mighty power…?" (Daniel 4:30).

In one of the most sweeping prophecies in all the Bible—one that covered world history from the Babylonian Empire to Christ's return—God revealed the extent of His sovereignty. Through the ages, every human kingdom portrayed by the statue in Daniel 2 has risen and fallen, as ordained by God. Every one of them owed their power to the God of heaven. We now await the final kingdom—antichrist's future empire, which will be destroyed by Christ Himself.

The one truth proclaimed by every prophecy in the Bible is this: God is absolutely sovereign. He has supreme power and unlimited authority over everything. He planned all things, spoke all things into existence, governs all things, has determined the outcome of all things, and has ruled and will rule over all things from eternity past into eternity future.

So great and wonderful is God's sovereignty that the same God who upholds the universe and directs history also upholds us and directs our path. He is not so busy orchestrating the big picture that He overlooks us. It is because God is totally sovereign that He can love us so totally!

HUMAN LEGACIES WON'T LAST

The toes of the feet were partly iron and partly clay (Daniel 2:42).

I n a dream, God revealed to Nebuchadnezzar a statue with a head of gold, chest and arms of silver, midsection and thighs of bronze, legs of iron, and feet and toes of iron and clay. Each section of the statue represented a major world kingdom. Daniel equated the head of gold to the Babylonian Empire. And history has since revealed the other kingdoms to be Medo-Persia, Greece, and Rome—all of which have long since collapsed and vanished.

This brings us to the final part of the statue: the feet and ten toes of iron and clay. The presence of the iron tells us that remnants of the Roman Empire are present, but it's broken into parts mingled with clay. The ten toes represent a confederacy of ten powers that cover the same geographical area as the ancient Roman Empire. Never in history has this existed, which tells us the feet and toes are still future. They point to a *second* phase of the Roman Empire. And in today's European Union, we see efforts being made to cobble together lands that have long been splintered. Slowly but surely, earth's final kingdom is taking shape right now.

There is a lot of speculation about the identity of the ten toes. With the help of the ten horns mentioned in Daniel 7:24, we know that the toes represent ten powers. At this time in prophetic history, it's too early to figure out who or what the ten toes are.

But we do know this: Iron and clay don't mix. Not even earth's most powerful ruler—the antichrist—will be able to hold earth's final kingdom together. It, too, will collapse.

The temporary nature of earth's kingdoms brings Psalm 127:1 to mind: "Unless the Lord builds the house, those who build it labor in vain." Every work done apart from God will fail. Only the labors we do in accord with God's purposes will endure. As we make choices about what we'll build here on earth, may our focus be on Christ's legacy and not our own.

A REMARKABLE CONFESSION

Truly, your God is God of gods and Lord of kings (Daniel 2:47).

As Daniel interpreted the meaning of King Nebuchadnezzar's dream, two details surely stood out to the king: First, Babylon would someday be replaced by another kingdom (Daniel 2:39). This news had to be distressing. Second, a stone cut "by no human hand" would destroy the statue and bring an end to all human kingdoms (verse 45). Then, "the God of heaven will set up a kingdom that shall never be destroyed" (verse 44).

Daniel's repeated use of the phrase "the God of heaven" was intentional. The same God who revealed the mystery behind the dream (verse 18), and the same God who had given the king his kingdom and power (verse 37) would one day destroy all human empires and set up His own forever kingdom.

Nebuchadnezzar couldn't miss the point. This God was supreme. He had seen it for himself. God had enabled Daniel to describe the dream and interpret it. Nebuchadnezzar's gods were no match. In response, the king "fell upon his face and paid homage…and said to Daniel, 'Truly, your God is God of gods and Lord of kings'" (verses 46-47).

Daniel could have taken the credit for explaining and interpreting the dream. He could have pridefully sought the king's favor. Instead, he said that no man could have done this—including himself. This drove Nebuchadnezzar to give the praise where it belonged—to God.

Matthew 5:16 says, "Let your light shine before others, so that they may see your good works and give glory to your Father who is in heaven." When we seek the credit and glory for ourselves, a watching world's eyes are brought low and deprived of the opportunity to realize that God is at work. But when we make it clear that God gets the credit, the world's eyes are raised to where they should be—and God gets the rightful recognition and glory.

DANIEL'S CONNECTION TO JESUS' BIRTH

The king gave Daniel high honors...and made him ruler over the whole province of Babylon and chief prefect over all the wise men (Daniel 2:48).

Nebuchadnezzar was thrilled. Daniel had interpreted his dream. So grateful was the king that he lavished Daniel with honors and made him "chief prefect over all the wise men of Babylon."

God placed Daniel in this position of influence for a reason. If you've ever wondered how it was that the magi—the wise men from the East—knew about the birth of Jesus, it's because of Daniel. As chief over all the wise men, we can be certain Daniel taught them about the God of Israel, the Scriptures, and God's plans for Israel's future—including His promises about the future Messiah. Because the wise men were expected to be experts in all subject matters, they would have listened willingly as Daniel informed them about the one true God.

When the Jewish exile in Babylon ended, many of the Jews opted to stay instead of returning to Jerusalem. Their continued presence assured an ongoing awareness of Hebrew beliefs in that part of the East long after Daniel's death.

More than 500 years later, this happened: "After Jesus was born in Bethlehem...behold, wise men from the east came to Jerusalem, saying, 'Where is he who has been born king of the Jews? For we saw his star when it rose and have come to worship him'" (Matthew 2:1-2). How the magi knew the star pointed to Jesus' birth, we don't know. But they said they had come to worship Daniel's Messiah, the king of the Jews.

We never know how God might use our influence on the people around us—even those who have no interest at all in the one true God. But when we are faithful to make Him and His truth known, God says His word will not return empty. Rather, it will "accomplish that which I purpose" (Isaiah 55:11).

CHOOSING CONVICTION
RATHER THAN COMPROMISE

*If you do not worship, you shall immediately be
cast into a burning fiery furnace (Daniel 3:15).*

King Nebuchadnezzar had not learned his lesson. In Daniel 2, he dreamed of a statue and demanded that his wise men interpret the dream's meaning. None could do so. When Daniel explained the dream, its message was clear: In the future, a succession of kingdoms would rise, then fall—including Nebuchadnezzar's. In response, the king told Daniel, "Truly, your God is God of gods and Lord of kings, and a revealer of mysteries" (Daniel 2:47).

Then Daniel 3 opens with another statue—90 feet tall—built by Nebuchadnezzar as a tribute to himself and his greatness. He orders all the important people in his empire to gather and worship the statue or be cast into a fiery furnace. It's as if he thought this statue could overrule the prophecies connected to the statue in Daniel 2. He didn't want his kingdom to end.

When the order is given for all to bow down, everyone does...except for Daniel's three friends Shadrach, Meshach, and Abednego. Given a second chance to bow, they refuse. The angry king has them thrown into a fiery furnace—and unexpectedly, God spares them.

Once again, the King of heaven prevails, and the king of Babylon is humbled. Daniel's friends are delivered, and God is glorified. But in the midst of all this, a disturbing question arises: Only three brave Israelites stood. What were all the other Israelites at the scene doing?

All through the Bible, we see example after example of how compromise is chosen over conviction. What can we do to protect ourselves from this temptation? It all comes down to fearing God more than people. As Proverbs 29:25 says, "The fear of man lays a snare." When we're confronted with a choice, we need to apply the Galatians 1:10 test: "Am I now seeking the approval of man, or of God?" When we fear God more than people, conviction will prevail.

THE CONNECTION
BETWEEN LOVE AND COURAGE

He was faithful, and no error or fault was found in him (Daniel 6:4).

Daniel feared God more than he feared man. And in Daniel 6, we see his faithfulness to God severely tested. The officials who served King Darius resented Daniel and plotted to get him sentenced to death. Approaching the king, they said, "We propose that anyone who prays to a god other than you be cast into a lions' den" (see Daniel 6:7). The king foolishly agreed, not realizing this was a scheme to trap Daniel.

When Daniel heard the news, he returned to his chamber and continued to pray to God three times a day, as always. From Daniel's courage, we learn these life lessons:

Prayer should be our first action when we face a crisis. When Daniel realized his life was in danger, his first response was to pray. He put his life in God's hands. He didn't know what would happen to him, but he knew who to approach for help.

Never be ashamed of your faith. Daniel had always prayed visibly. He could have changed his habit to hide his prayers, but he didn't. His desire to honor God exceeded his fear of what people might do to him. When we hide our faith, it's because we want to please people.

No matter what the consequence of following God, be willing to pay the price. Daniel knew that to pray to God meant certain death. This reveals just how greatly he loved God. He preferred death to compromise. God had been faithful to him; he wanted to be faithful in return. Looking back on this event, we know that God spared Daniel. But Daniel had no assurance that God would deliver him. He was willing to die, and trusted God with the outcome.

Daniel's fear of God was motivated by a deep love for Him. The more we love God, the greater our desire to please Him, and the more willing we will be to express our convictions. There is a definite connection between our love for God and the courage we exhibit as believers!

THE ANTICHRIST'S RISE...AND DEFEAT

He shall speak words against the Most High (Daniel 7:25).

The book of Daniel has more prophecies about the antichrist than any other book in the Old Testament.

Daniel 7:8 describes him as a "little horn." The term "horn" can be translated "king" or "power." The word "little" tells us he will rise from obscurity. Verse 24 adds more details, saying he will go on to rule over ten kings. After that, he will take complete control of the world. Verse 25 says, "He shall speak words against the Most High, and shall wear out the saints of the Most High." He will blaspheme God and persecute believers as well as the Jewish people.

The antichrist's power will be great, but it won't be his own; he will "make deceit prosper" and "destroy many" (Daniel 8:24-25). He will come from the people who destroy the temple (Rome did this in AD 70), meaning he will rise in Europe, or the revived Roman Empire. This "prince who is to come" will promise peace and establish a seven-year treaty with Israel, which he will break at the midpoint (9:26-27). He will "magnify himself above every god" (11:36).

A fearsome and evil master of deceit, the antichrist will do all that is contrary to Christ and righteousness. That's why, in 2 Thessalonians 2:8, he is described as "the lawless one."

Daniel also reports that God will limit the antichrist's global reign of terror to three-and-a-half years (7:25). His end has already been determined and is sure. Though he will do all he can to prevent Christ's return, he will fail—spectacularly.

Believers have no reason to fear the antichrist. He will not come to power until after the rapture,[11] after we're taken up to heaven. Though he will kill multitudes who become Christians during the tribulation, God will exact fierce judgment against him. At Christ's return, the antichrist will be captured and cast into the lake of fire—never to deceive or harm anyone again.

LETTING PROPHECY
COMPEL YOU TO PRAYER

In the first year of Darius...king over the realm of the Chaldeans...
I, Daniel, perceived in the books the number of years that...must pass
before the end of the desolations of Jerusalem, namely, seventy years. Then
I turned my face to the Lord God, seeking him by prayer (Daniel 9:1-3).

Daniel was a teenager when the Babylonian army conquered Jerusalem. He and many other Jews were taken as captives to Babylon. When King Nebuchadnezzar asked Daniel and his three teenage friends to conform to the Babylonian lifestyle, they chose commitment to God rather than compromise to a pagan society. God honored their obedience and, long story short, Daniel became a top advisor to the king.

The prophet Jeremiah had said Israel's exile in Babylon would last for 70 years (Jeremiah 25:11-12). By the time we get to Daniel chapter 9, the prophet is an elderly man. Through his study of Jeremiah's prophecy, he realizes Israel's 70-year captivity is almost over.

This moves Daniel to seek God in prayer, and he does so "with fasting and sackcloth and ashes" (Daniel 9:3). This reveals the intensity of Daniel's heart posture before God. He remembers it was the people's wickedness that led to this exile (Daniel 9:5-7). And he acknowledges the Lord as "the great and awesome God" who keeps His promises (verse 4). He knew that only God could make it possible for the Jews to return home to Jerusalem.

Daniel was compelled to pray because he knew a prophecy was about to be fulfilled. He wanted to be ready with a right heart before God. Likewise, when we read prophecies about Christ's soon return, we should be moved to prayer. We should approach God with a humble heart, asking Him to help prepare us for whatever He wants to do through us in these last days.

DOES GOD'S SOVEREIGNTY MAKE OUR PRAYERS MEANINGLESS?

I, Daniel, perceived in the books the number of years that...must pass before the end of the desolations of Jerusalem, namely, seventy years. Then I turned my face to the Lord God, seeking him by prayer (Daniel 9:2-3).

If God has already said what He will do in a certain situation, does that negate any prayers we might offer about the matter? Does His sovereignty make our prayers meaningless? The prophet Daniel didn't think so.

By the time we reach Daniel 9, Daniel and the Jewish people had been captives in Babylon for nearly 70 years. At this time, Daniel read the writings of the prophet Jeremiah—and noticed God's prophetic promise that the Jewish exile would last for 70 years (Jeremiah 25:11-12). Though Daniel knew God would keep His promise to let them return home soon, he still felt an overwhelming urge to pray. Baring his heart to God, he confessed the sins of the people of Israel, which was why they were in captivity. He also prayed for forgiveness and restoration.

Because God had already ordained what He would do, Daniel could have said, "Why bother praying?" But his response was the opposite. He chose to pray so he could acknowledge God's sovereignty, express gratitude for God's faithfulness, and put himself in a place of service.

God will carry out His plans, but that shouldn't keep us from praying. Prayer gives us the opportunity to tune our hearts to God's will. It helps us to see people and situations as He sees them. And it puts our heart in a posture of usefulness.

An awareness of God's sovereign plans should increase our enthusiasm for prayer, not diminish it. As we draw closer to the fulfillment of so many end-times prophecies, we find that we now have a wealth of opportunities to pray—in an informed way—for God's will to be done.

WHEN WE PRAY IN RESPONSE TO PROPHECY

I prayed to the LORD my God and made confession, saying,
"O Lord, the great and awesome God, Who keeps covenant
and steadfast love with those who love him...Delay not, for
your own sake, O my God" (Daniel 9:4, 19).

Daniel realized that the Jewish people's 70-year captivity in Babylon was about to end. Upon recognizing a prophetic promise was about to be fulfilled, he knelt in prayer and poured out his heart to God.

Daniel's prayer is instructive. It shows how we ought to pray in response to Bible prophecy. With the prophecies of Christ's second coming in mind, here is how we can pray:

Pray with a heart for holiness. Daniel began by confessing, "We have sinned and done wrong and acted wickedly" (Daniel 9:5). Most of his prayer was about turning away from sin, seeking forgiveness, and expressing a willingness to obey God. We should desire to be holy and right before God so that we are always ready for His use when He carries out His plans.

Pray with a desire for God's glory. Daniel concluded the prayer by saying, "Delay not, for *your own sake*, O my God, because your city and your people are called by your name" (verse 19). Daniel wasn't concerned about Israel's reputation, but God's. As God's children, we should want our lives to portray Him in positive ways to a godless world. In everything we do, we should ask, *Am I bringing honor to God?* Our uppermost concern should be what unbelievers think about God, not us. We are called to live for His sake, not ours.

When we read Bible prophecy, we should be spurred to holiness so that we are ready for God's use. And we should seek to honor God so that a watching world is able to see that He is good and worthy of their trust and devotion.

THREE GREAT TRUTHS ABOUT GOD

O Lord, the great and awesome God, who keeps covenant and steadfast love with those who love him and keep his commandments (Daniel 9:4).

When Daniel sought God's help for Israel's soon release from captivity, he lifted up a prayer that is a model for us. At the opening of the prayer, he proclaimed three important truths we should remember whenever we seek God's help.

God is great. Even though Jerusalem had been destroyed and the Jewish people taken captive to Babylon, God had enabled them not only to survive, but to prosper. He had also protected Daniel's friends from a fiery furnace and Daniel from hungry lions. So even when Israel was being punished for disobeying God, He showed Himself to be great on their behalf. In the times when we are tempted to question God about our negative circumstances, we need to recognize His greatness and infinite wisdom, and place our full trust in Him.

God is faithful. When God made His covenant promises to Israel, He made it clear they were *forever* promises. In the scriptures where God declared the extent of His commitment to His chosen people and their land, we see the words *everlasting* and *forever* used repeatedly. Even when God's people wander from Him, He will prove Himself loyal. Second Timothy 2:13 says that when "we are faithless, he remains faithful."

To love God is to obey Him. In Exodus 20:5-6, God told Israel He would show "steadfast love to...those who love me and keep my commandments." Jesus said, "If you love me, you will keep my commandments" (John 14:15). There is a link between love and obedience. We obey not to earn God's love, but to affirm our love for Him. The more we are willing to do God's will, the more gladly we will submit to it. That's the attitude we should have when we pray.

THE ESSENTIALS TO EFFECTIVE PRAYER

We have sinned and done wrong...We have not listened
to your servants the prophets (Daniel 9:5-6).

I f we want to have a right heart before God when we come to Him in prayer, it is vital that we include confession and humility in our appeals to Him. We see both exhibited in Daniel's prayer on behalf of the Israelites shortly before their captivity in Babylon came to an end.

Daniel sought God with "pleas for mercy with fasting and sackcloth and ashes" (verse 3). He prayed "and made confession" (verse 4). After acknowledging "the great and awesome God," Daniel's first words got straight to the point: "We have sinned and done wrong." He was heartbroken over the sins of God's people—sins that had led to their captivity. Notice that Daniel used the word "we," making sure to include himself in this confession.

Daniel was a righteous man and a zealous prayer warrior. But he didn't come before God and pat himself on the back for his seven decades of loyal service to the Lord. He didn't blame others for God's punishment and, out of pride, exclude himself. With a humble heart, he included himself in this prayer of confession.

To approach God humbly in prayer means recognizing we need His mercy just as much as everyone else. The closer we are to God, the more sensitive we will be to our sin. When we possess a deep love for God, our desire to honor Him will heighten our awareness of any sin present in us.

James 5:16 says, "Confess your sins...the prayer of a righteous person has great power." Only when we confess our sin and humble our hearts can we lift up effective prayers. This is true even for the most faithful of believers and the greatest of prayer warriors. When we pray, it is the state of our heart that God cares about, not our accomplishments.

SEEKING GOD'S GLORY IN OUR PRAYERS

*O Lord, hear; O Lord, forgive. O Lord, pay attention and
act. Delay not, for your own sake. O my God, because your city
and your people are called by your name (Daniel 9:19).*

When Daniel prayed for the Jewish captives in Babylon to be given permission to return to Jerusalem, he didn't say, "Time's up, Lord. We've been punished long enough. We deserve better treatment now."

Daniel wasn't concerned for the people's relief, but for God's reputation. He prayed, "Delay not, for *your* own sake...because *your* city and *your* people are called by *your* name." When God permitted the Jews to be taken captive because of their sins, the people of other nations concluded God was too weak to protect them. This reflected negatively on God and His name. Because of the people's sin, God's name was despised (Isaiah 52:5).

Also at stake was God's holy character. By choosing to remain in sin, the people of Israel had failed to reflect God's holiness to the nations. Daniel's desire was for the Israelites to exhibit genuine repentance and right behavior so that the nations could see God through them.

Also important was God's reputation as one who keeps His promises. He had said the captivity would last 70 years. Daniel knew God would follow through and keep His promise. But Daniel wanted his fellow Jews—and the nations—to realize that the release from captivity was due to God's faithfulness, and not anything the people had done.

From beginning to end, Daniel's prayer extolled God's greatness and sought His glory. The way in which Daniel approached God is rich with lessons for us. In all that we pray for, our ultimate desire should be God's exaltation so that a watching world will come to right conclusions about Him. It is for this reason that we pray, "Hallowed be your name."

70 WEEKS: GOD'S PLANS FOR ISRAEL

Seventy weeks are decreed about your people
and your holy city (Daniel 9:24).

D aniel 9:24-27 records one of the most profound prophecies in the entire Bible. In this passage, we are given God's prophetic timeline for history from 444 BC to Christ's millennial kingdom. This gives us a framework for understanding everything God's Word says about the future. In these verses are the keys needed to unlock the meaning of other prophecies in Scripture. A right understanding of Daniel 9:24-27 is essential if we want a clear picture of end-times events.

Many readers devote their attention to figuring out the "seventy weeks" math in this prophecy. Often overlooked is the angel's important declaration to Daniel at the start of the prophecy: These 70 weeks are "decreed about *your* people and *your* holy city." The prophecy is all about the future of the Jewish people *in* Jerusalem and Israel. If we miss this, we will mess up what God is revealing here. Nowhere in this passage do we see the future church.

When Daniel prayed to God for insight about the Jewish people's *near*-future return from Babylon to their homeland, God gave Daniel far more than he requested. He gave the prophet a glimpse of Israel's *distant*-future return to the land in anticipation of Jesus' millennial kingdom!

It is in Daniel 9:24-27 that we learn that the purpose of the seven-year tribulation—which is the seventieth week in the 70-weeks prophecy—is not only to bring judgment upon a wicked world, but also for God to call Israel back to Himself and fully restore the nation.

God has not forgotten or rejected His chosen people. Today, Israel is a nation again by God's design. He is preparing Israel as the stage for Christ's millennial kingdom. The many prophecies that promise a glorious future for Israel are on the way to being fulfilled, including Zechariah 8:3: "Thus says the LORD: I have returned to Zion and will dwell in the midst of Jerusalem, and Jerusalem shall be called the faithful city, and the mountain of the Lord of hosts."

70 WEEKS: WHAT ARE THESE WEEKS?

Seventy weeks are decreed (Daniel 9:24).

The 70-weeks prophecy in Daniel 9:24-27 is complex, yet rich with wonderful truths. It is helpful to keep in mind that in these verses, the Hebrew term "weeks" literally means "sevens." Many scholars agree that the clearest understanding of this passage occurs when these sevens, or weeks, are viewed as years. That gives us this general breakdown:

Verse 25: Seven weeks plus 62 weeks (for a total of 69 weeks of seven years) will pass from the day Cyrus issues the decree to rebuild Jerusalem in 444 BC to the day the anointed one, or Jesus, enters Jerusalem on a donkey in AD 33. This totals exactly 483 years to the day.[12] Then God's prophetic clock will stop for a gap between weeks 69 and 70.

Verse 26: During the gap, the anointed one, the Messiah, will be cut off or killed. Jerusalem and the temple will be destroyed (by Rome in AD 70). And the Jewish people, who will be pushed out of the land, will suffer hardship and persecution "to the end," or end times. This is why the clock will stop—because Daniel 9:24-27 is about Israel *in* the land, not outside.

Verse 27: Then will come one who signs a seven-year peace treaty with Israel. For this to happen, Israel must be in the land—as it is now. With the treaty signed, God's clock will start again and begin week 70— the seven-year tribulation. A comparison of Daniel 9:27 with other passages helps to identify the treaty maker as the antichrist, who will rise to power at this time.

The mathematical precision in Daniel 9:24-27 is stunning. Far in advance, God pinpointed the exact day the Messiah would present Himself to His people. This should not surprise us, for God created an entire universe that is governed by precise mathematical laws. The accurate fulfillment of the first 69 weeks of Daniel's 70-weeks prophecy is powerful evidence that the Bible came from God, for only He could know the future so perfectly.

70 WEEKS: GOD'S PURPOSES FOR ISRAEL

Seventy weeks are decreed about your people and your holy city, to finish...
to put an end...to atone...to bring...to seal...to anoint (Daniel 9:24).

Daniel asked God for insight about Israel's *near* future. God gave Daniel far more—He provided a glimpse of Israel's *distant* future. In Daniel 9:24, God said that at the end of the 490 years in Daniel's 70-weeks prophecy, these six purposes would be accomplished with Israel:

To finish the transgression. At the second coming, a surviving remnant of Jewish people will receive Christ as their Messiah (Zechariah 12:10).

To put an end to sin. Israel's repentance will remove her sin (Romans 11:25-27).

To atone for iniquity. When the people of Israel repent, Christ's atoning work at the cross will make it possible for them to receive the gift of salvation (Romans 3:24-26; 6:23).

To bring in everlasting righteousness. After receiving Christ as Savior, the Jewish remnant will enter the millennial kingdom and experience its righteousness (Jeremiah 23:5-6).

To seal both vision and prophet. Everything the prophets promised about Israel and the Messiah will be fully realized in the millennial kingdom.

To anoint a most holy place. Because of Christ's once-for-all sacrifice for sin, the holy place in the millennial temple will be anointed, or set apart (Zechariah 6:13).

After the 70 weeks concludes at the end of the tribulation, Christ's millennial kingdom will begin. The sin that had plagued Israel and brought punishment will be no more. The Jewish people will be restored and made righteous. God's forever promises to them will be fulfilled at last. It's as if God is saying in Daniel 9:24, "Everything I have promised you will come true."

Because God is able to perfectly keep all His promises, He is able to perfectly guarantee every believer's future glory. Whenever our hearts are weary, may this truth cause us to rejoice!

DANIEL SPEAKS TO US TODAY

The words are shut up and sealed until the time of the end (Daniel 12:9).

After the angel Gabriel revealed the future to Daniel, the prophet was so excited that he asked, "What shall be the outcome of these things?" (Daniel 12:8). Daniel wanted to know more! He was in awe of God's plans for Israel—plans that would have greatly encouraged him.

Gabriel answered, "Go your way, Daniel, for the words are shut up and sealed until the time of the end" (verse 9). The revelations to Daniel were complete. Once the prophecies were recorded, they would be sealed shut and saved "until the time of the end"—that is, for the generations alive during earth's last days and especially the tribulation. God also had additional details about the future that He wouldn't reveal until the New Testament was written.

For centuries, Daniel has been a sealed book. Many of the prophecies in it did not make sense to those who read them. That's because for nearly 2,000 years, the Jewish people were scattered worldwide, and the nation of Israel didn't exist. This made it difficult to figure out how a lot of the prophecies relating to Israel would be fulfilled.

But now that Israel has been reborn, the revived Roman Empire is taking shape, and New Testament prophecies are helping to fill in the blanks, today's believers are able to read Daniel with much greater clarity. We have the exciting privilege of being the generation that sees God setting the stage for the fulfillment of some of the most amazing prophecies in the Bible!

There are a number of prophecies in the Old Testament that God gave specifically with today's generations in mind. He knew what we would need to know so we could keep watch and exercise discernment as we approach the end times. He also provided these prophecies knowing that they would serve as helpful warnings and alerts for the Jewish people and tribulation-era believers who face the challenge of trying to survive during the tribulation.

HOPE IN THE MIDST OF JUDGMENT

I will return to Zion, and dwell in the midst
of Jerusalem (Zechariah 8:3).

Tragically, the Hebrew people refused to listen to the prophets. They paid no attention to the warnings of destruction and captivity. Wickedness spun out of control, going from bad to worse.

The northern kingdom was conquered by the powerful Assyrian Empire in 722 BC, and the people exiled to other lands. The southern kingdom suffered three invasions by the Babylonian army from 605 to 586 BC. All three times, captives were taken to Babylon.

As the storm clouds of wrath grew darker over the northern and southern kingdoms, God still sent rays of hope to His people. Every single prophet except Jonah spoke not only of impending judgment, but also future restoration.

Hope is a persistent theme in the prophets' messages. In Jeremiah 25:11-12, God promised the exiled Jews in Babylon that they would return home after 70 years of exile. In Ezekiel 36:10 is the promise of a different return to the land after the Jews were scattered worldwide. This pointed to Israel's rebirth in 1948, and it has flourished since. There are also many prophecies about a restored Israel and Jerusalem in Christ's future millennial kingdom. As God said in Zechariah 8:3, "I will return to Zion, and dwell in the midst of Jerusalem."

Punishment was necessary because of the hardness of people's hearts. Sin had to be dealt with, or God would not be righteous. But deliverance would come to future generations.

As we read about how God dealt with Israel in the Old Testament, we may think that because it all happened in the past, it's not relevant to us. But it's very relevant. God is the same yesterday, today, and forever. He does not change. Just as He offered hope alongside His warnings back then, He does the same today. If we listen to His rebukes, He will restore us. As we admire the grace God displayed in the past, we can know He still shows that same grace today.

CHRIST EVERYWHERE IN THE BIBLE

Behold, your king is coming to you (Zechariah 9:9).

Christ and the wonders of all that He has done and will do for us is the theme of the entire Bible. From Genesis to Revelation runs a continuous thread that foreshadows and proclaims Christ's first coming as Savior, His second coming as Conqueror, and His eternal reign as King. At the center of this epic love letter from God to man is the cross, where sin was forever defeated and redemption was forever secured.

The book of Zechariah is a great example of how richly Christ is portrayed across the pages of Scripture. Here is a sampling of the ways our Savior and Lord is prophetically depicted:

- He will bring comfort to His people (1:13, 17).
- He is the Savior who will remove our sins (3:9).
- He will be our priest and bring back true worship (6:13).
- He will lovingly restore His people and the land (8:3-8, 12-13).
- He is the servant who will come in humility, riding on a donkey (9:9).
- He will be the good and true shepherd who cares for His flock (11:8-17).
- He will come as the sacrificial lamb who is pierced for our transgressions (12:10).
- In grace and mercy, He will pour out the Holy Spirit upon His people (12:10).
- He is the all-sovereign Lord who will rule the entire earth (14:9).

As we read the Bible, one of the greatest pursuits we can engage in is to ask: What can I learn about Christ in this passage or book? The more we are diligent to ask this question, the more we'll discover the depths and riches and wonders of our Savior and Lord. The better we know Him, the more we will appreciate Him and draw closer to Him. And the more we will look eagerly toward the day when we are united with Him in eternal fellowship!

GOD DOES IT ALL FOR US

I will make them strong in the LORD, and they
shall walk in his name (Zechariah 10:12).

The one greatest question of all time about the nation of Israel appears in Romans 11:1: "Has God rejected His people?" The apostle Paul asks this after God's people have denied Him again and again—leading up to the ultimate refusal: sentencing Christ to death on a cross. Surely with such a long and persistent history of spurning God, the Lord would have cast off Israel!

But no. In Romans 11:2—the very next verse—Paul writes, "God has not rejected his people." Then later in Romans chapter 11, he makes this climactic declaration: "All Israel will be saved, as it is written, 'The Deliverer will come from Zion, he will banish ungodliness from Jacob'; and this will be my covenant with them when I take away their sins" (verses 26-27).

Who will remove Israel's ungodliness and sin? God! Notice the "I wills" in Zechariah 10:6: "*I will* strengthen the house of Judah, and *I will* save the house of Joseph. *I will* bring them back because I have compassion on them, and they shall be *as though I had not rejected them.*"

Just as God delivered His people from the perils of slavery in Egypt, the Red Sea, the Jordan River, the ruthless Canaanites, and captivity and exile, He will deliver them from their sin. A day is coming when He will "make them strong in the LORD" (Zechariah 10:12).

We cannot take any credit for the salvation God has given us and the incredible inheritance that awaits us in heaven. God does it all for us. "It is the gift of God...so that no one may boast" (Ephesian 2:8-9). "Because of him you are in Christ Jesus" (1 Corinthians 1:30). How should we respond? "Let the one who boasts, boast in the Lord" (verse 31). May we boast in the Lord at every opportunity we have, for this will be our primary occupation in heaven. Let's rehearse and prepare our hearts for an eternity of gratitude and worship to our great God!

FROM ARMAGEDDON TO GLORY

On that day I will seek to destroy all the nations that
come against Jerusalem (Zechariah 12:9).

In Zechariah chapters 12–14, we go from Israel's darkest moment to Israel's brightest hope. Zechariah 12 opens with the antichrist bringing the armies of the world against Jerusalem to destroy the Jewish people once and for all. This is popularly known as the campaign of Armageddon. But God will push back against this siege: "I will make Jerusalem a heavy stone for all the peoples. All who lift it will surely hurt themselves" (verse 3). God will "destroy all the nations that come against Jerusalem" (verse 9).

When all looks hopeless for Israel, God will "pour out on the house of David and the inhabitants of Jerusalem a spirit of grace and pleas for mercy." He will pour out the Holy Spirit, and in response, the Jews will look "on him whom they have pierced, [and] they shall mourn for him" (verse 10). In this glorious moment, the "partial hardening" on Israel will be lifted (Romans 11:25). The Jewish people's spiritual eyes will be opened. They will recognize—and receive—their Messiah. And "all Israel will be saved" (verse 26).

At the end of His first coming, Jesus ascended to heaven from the Mount of Olives (Acts 1:9-10). Zechariah tells us that when Christ returns, He will come to the Mount of Olives (14:4). This will end Armageddon—the nations will fall, and Christ will become sole ruler of the earth.

God has promised that a day of deliverance is coming. The Savior who first came to save us from our sins will return as Judge and King to take back the world and reign over it forever. The hope of Israel and the hope of the church will fulfill every promise He has made to establish a kingdom in which we will dwell with our King. In His presence, we will know fullness of joy and pleasures forevermore (Psalm 16:11).

GOD REMEMBERS

On that day living waters shall flow out from Jerusalem (Zechariah 14:8).

The journey from Babylon back to Jerusalem was a long one. When the Jewish exiles finally arrived, they were greeted by ruins. Their future looked bleak. Rebuilding the city and their lives would be a monumental task. This destruction happened because they had abandoned God. As they surveyed the grim scene, they couldn't help but wonder: Had God forever abandoned them?

The prophet Zechariah's name means "God remembers." How fitting it is that the book that bears his name repeatedly trumpets the truth that God will never forget His people!

I will return. God said, "I have returned to Zion and will dwell in the midst of Jerusalem" (Zechariah 8:3). Here, God declared His absolute commitment to the people.

I will bring revenge. Looking to the end times and His second coming, the Lord said, "On that day I will seek to destroy all the nations that come against Jerusalem" (Zechariah 12:9). God had preserved His people in the past. He will do the same when Armageddon's armies descend upon Jerusalem to destroy it. He will avenge Israel's enemies, and save His people.

I will restore. "I will pour out on the house of David…a spirit of grace and pleas for mercy, so that, when they look on me…they shall mourn" (Zechariah 12:10). God will send the Holy Spirit, and Israel will repent and receive Christ as Messiah. Spiritual restoration is coming.

I will reign. "On that day living waters shall flow out from Jerusalem" (Zechariah 14:8). When Jesus returns, He will establish His promised throne in Jerusalem, from where living waters will flow. And Israel will "blossom as the rose" (Isaiah 35:1 NKJV).

When life looks bleak and you're surrounded by ruins of your own doing, do not despair. Though you may have forgotten God, He will never forget you. God remembers. With your repentance comes His restoration. Seek Him, and He will deliver you.

BEHOLD, OUR KING!

The LORD will be king over all the earth (Zechariah 14:9).

The book of Zechariah is too often underappreciated. Its 14 chapters are rich with prophecies. In the final six chapters, the prophet Zechariah reveals the grand sweep of both Gentile and Jewish history, taking us all the way to eternity. Chapters 9 to 11 reveal how God will bring an end to Gentile rule and kingdoms, and chapters 12 to 14 look ahead to the end times, when God will purge Israel of the rebellious and restore a Jewish remnant who welcomes Jesus as their Messiah.

For this reason, Zechariah is often called the apocalypse of the Old Testament. It's like a preview to the book of Revelation, written nearly 600 years before Revelation was penned. In Zechariah we see the tribulation, the second coming, the millennial kingdom, and eternity.

In the final chapter of Zechariah, we read the final chapter of history. God will "gather all the nations against Jerusalem to battle" (14:2). Christ will return to "fight against those nations," and "his feet shall stand on the Mount of Olives" (verses 3-4). Every believer who was raptured prior to the tribulation will return with Him! (verse 5). "On that day, living waters shall flow out from Jerusalem…And the LORD will be king over all the earth" (verses 8-9).

The Lord will be king over all the earth! Human rulers will forever be silenced, and the one true sovereign in all the universe will reign. Zechariah 14:9 goes on to say, "On that day the LORD will be one and his name one." The Lord stands alone above all. As King without compare, He alone can bring forth a kingdom without compare. When Christ arrives, He will become the only King, His will be the only kingdom, and it is He alone whom all will worship.

Ultimately, every prophecy in the Bible points to these truths: God's will *will* be done. He will reign. He will restore paradise. All through time, He will redeem both Jews and Gentiles to be a people who are holy and set apart for Him for all eternity. Behold, our King!

A HUMBLE BIRTHPLACE
FOR THE KING OF KINGS

*You, O Bethlehem Ephrathah, who are too little to be
among the clans of Judah, from you shall come forth for
me one who is to be the ruler of Israel (Micah 5:2).*

Bethlehem. Little would anyone have expected that God would choose this tiny town as the birthplace of the Messiah. "You...who are too little" tells us Bethlehem had no stature "among the clans of Judah." Had humans written the script, a "better" place would have been chosen.

But this is how the Lord works. God delights in using the obscure and the insignificant to accomplish His purposes. Just as David was the least of his brothers yet became Israel's greatest king, Bethlehem was the least among the towns of Judah yet has been widely immortalized as the birthplace of Immanuel, God with us. God's use of lowly vessels like Mary and Joseph and unnoticed places like Bethlehem demonstrates that He has no need of worldly significance to help further His plans for the ages. For God, the humble and the ordinary are His instruments of choice for doing His most glorious achievements.

God pinpointed the Messiah's birthplace more than 700 years in advance. The inclusion of "Ephrathah" in Micah 5:2 helped to distinguish this Bethlehem from a Galilean town of the same name. It's also fitting that the Lord Jesus Christ, who will someday rule on King David's throne, was born in the same town as David.

As Joseph, Mary, and the shepherds set their eyes on the baby Jesus that night long ago, they were looking at the one who would become "ruler in Israel, whose coming forth is from old, from ancient days" (Micah 5:2). As the Hebrew text literally says, they were looking upon the one from "days of immeasurable time." This newborn child had always existed in eternity past and will rule over everything in eternity future. This was their beloved Savior and King.

THE LAST PROPHECY
IN THE OLD TESTAMENT

Behold, I will send you Elijah the prophet before the great
and awesome day of the LORD comes (Malachi 4:5).

In the final prophecy in the Old Testament, Malachi takes us to "the great and awesome day of the LORD." This phrase is used in many Bible passages to describe a time when God will pour out supernatural judgment upon the earth. That will happen during the tribulation. But "the day of the Lord" can also refer to the millennium (Joel 3:14-18) and eternity (2 Peter 3:10-13). This means the day of the Lord stretches from the tribulation into eternity. This makes sense because during the tribulation, God will wrest control of the world back from sinful humanity. And from the second coming onward, Christ's rule will be everlasting. During the tribulation portion of the "day of the LORD," God will take direct control of history, never to let it go.

In Malachi 4:5, we can safely conclude "the day of the LORD" refers to the tribulation because verse 6 ends with the Lord coming to "strike the land" in judgment. During the tribulation, this Elijah—either the literal Elijah or someone in the spirit and power of Elijah—will "turn the hearts of fathers to their children and the hearts of children to their fathers" (Malachi 4:5). This speaks of repentance and turning to God. Without this repentance, God would be forced to bring destruction upon His people.

In the Hebrew text of Micah 4:5, the final word of the Old Testament translates to "curse." With humanity's fall into sin in Genesis 3:15 came the curse. Its deadly effects are visible all through the Old Testament, which ends with the tragic word "curse." The next time we hear from God, He sends angels to announce that the cure is about to be born. It is because of this cure's triumph at the cross that the final chapter of the New Testament is able to end on an entirely different note, and declare, "There will no longer be any curse" (Revelation 22:3 NASB).

IN GOD'S PERFECT TIMING

When the fullness of time had come, God
sent forth his Son (Galatians 4:4).

The greatest event in all human history took place at the right time. God, who never errs in His ways and possesses perfect wisdom, appointed the date of Jesus' birth with precision. All the participants and circumstances on the world stage were in place just as God had willed.

What made conditions so ideal for the time of Christ's birth? Thanks to the conquests of Alexander the Great, Greek was the commonly spoken language by most people in the known world. Thanks to the later conquests of Rome, peace was widespread and there was economic and political stability. Rome's armies had built a massive road system that enabled people to travel far and wide. Synagogues, which served as meeting places for the Jewish people, had been built in many towns, enabling contact and communication. All these factors helped to make it possible for the gospel to spread rapidly when it came time for Jesus' followers to be His witnesses "in Jerusalem and in all Judea and Samaria, and to the end of the earth" (Acts 1:8).

When we consider the millions and billions of details God had to orchestrate to fulfill all the prophecies about Christ's first coming so perfectly, and when we realize these details have ripple effects that require additional orchestration going backward and forward in time, there is only one possible conclusion for us to arrive at: All of time is in God's hands. Nothing happens randomly or by chance. There is no overlooked moment in the big picture of God's plans. God is able to synchronize all things according to His sovereign design.

Jesus was born at the fullness of time. Conditions were right for His arrival because God had made them so. Likewise, God is sovereign over all that happens around us today. Ephesians 1:11 says that He "works *all* things according to the counsel of his will." Though we won't always understand how this is so, we can be assured our lives and times are fully in His hands.

A MOST PRECIOUS PROPHECY

He will save his people from their sins (Matthew 1:21).

As the angel announced Jesus' coming birth to Joseph, he gave a simple yet profound prophecy about what Jesus would do: "He will save his people from their sins."

This is why Jesus was born. He came to die. Jesus' birth makes no sense apart from His crucifixion and resurrection. At the cross, this Lamb of God "offered for all time a single sacrifice for sins" (Hebrews 10:12). He has delivered us from the penalty of sin and opened for us "a new and living way" (verse 20). At one time we were separated from God, and now we are "fellow citizens with the saints and members of the household of God" (Ephesians 2:19).

When it comes to sin and all that it encompasses, there is much we have been saved from. This includes everything from the misery and bondage caused by possessing a sin nature, to the emptiness that results from living in sin, which can never satisfy, to the spiritual and physical deaths that are the ultimate consequence of sin.

In Jesus, we are able to be forgiven and cleansed of our sins, and we will one day be perfectly and entirely freed from our sins. When the angel said, "He will save his people from their sins," he spoke of an all-encompassing deliverance. Hebrews 7:25 puts it this way: Jesus "is able to save to the uttermost those who draw near to God through him." Christ's saving power is complete and eternal. He has done all the work. There is nothing left for us to do. We will never perish. Our salvation is secure and our destiny is sure. As we await heaven, He intercedes for us, enables us, and preserves us. In these ways, we have been saved to the uttermost.

Among the most precious prophecies in Scripture are those that speak to the purpose of Christ's first coming—to save His people from their sins. These prophecies affirm the greatness of God's love for us, and the extent to which He would go to bring us back to Him.

GOD WITH US, PART 1

They shall call his name Immanuel
(which means, God with us) (Matthew 1:23).

In this devotion and the next two, we'll unpack the riches of the name *Immanuel*, taking a closer look at the significance of *God* with us, God *with* us, and God with *us*.

The name *Immanuel* communicates a profound truth about our Lord Jesus Christ: He is *God* with us! Jesus is God Himself, and He came in human flesh to dwell among us. "He is the image of the invisible God... for in him the whole fullness of deity dwells bodily" (Colossians 1:15; 2:9).

Because the name Immanuel is most famously connected with Isaiah's prophecy about the virgin giving birth to a son, we usually think of "God with us" in connection with Jesus' earthly ministry. But "God with us" did not end when Jesus departed for heaven; He lives right now in everyone who has received Him as Savior and Lord, and He will be with them always (Galatians 2:20; Matthew 28:20).

Here is what it means to have God with us: The one who is preeminent, infinite, eternal, sovereign, perfect, almighty, holy, righteous, glorious, unchanging, incomprehensible, all-powerful, all-wise, all-knowing, everywhere present, true, faithful, trustworthy, compassionate, merciful, gracious, loving, patient, generous, good, just, creator, Lord, Savior, redeemer, king, Shepherd, sanctifier, light, and life dwells in us and with us.

In Immanuel, we have at our disposal all that God is and offers. It is God Himself who watches over us, walks with us, and lives in us. It is because of God with us that we have been "blessed...with *every* spiritual blessing" (Ephesians 1:3). We are experiencing those blessings now, and they will continue into eternity. He has given His all, and in Him we have all we need.

GOD *WITH* US, PART 2

They shall call his name Immanuel
(which means, God with us) (Matthew 1:23).

W e've looked at the rich meaning behind *God* with us. Now, let's consider God *with* us.

In the phrase "God with us," the little word *with* carries far more meaning than is apparent at first glance. C.H. Spurgeon observed, "This glorious word Emmanuel means, first, that God in Christ is with us in very near association. The Greek particle used here is very forcible, and expresses the strongest form of 'with.'...This preposition is a close rivet, a firm bond, implying, if not declaring, close fellowship. God is peculiarly and closely 'with us.'"[13]

In God *with* us, the brief word *with* covers a broad expanse. Our connection with God is not a casual one. God's "with-ness" involves a closeness that is real, continuous, inseparable, and eternal. There are no boundaries to the extent of His "with-ness"!

God's presence with us is real. Romans 8:9 says, "The Spirit of God dwells in you." God's Spirit makes His home in us. That's how near He is.

God's presence with us is continuous. "I am with you always" (Matthew 28:20). He stays with us constantly. We never need to be afraid He might abandon us for some reason or other.

God's presence with us is inseparable. "Neither death, nor life, nor angels, nor principalities, nor things present, nor things to come, nor powers, nor height, nor depth, nor any other created thing will be able to separate us from the love of God that is in Christ Jesus our Lord" (Romans 8:38-39). God with us is an unbreakable bond.

God's presence with us is eternal. Revelation 21:3-4 describes heaven as a place where God will dwell with us, and we will be His people—forever.

God *with* us begins at salvation and has no end. It is the ultimate kind of with!

GOD WITH *US*, PART 3

*They shall call his name Immanuel
(which means, God with us) (Matthew 1:23).*

As if it weren't enough to be overwhelmed by the riches of *God* with us and God *with* us, we also have God with *us*.

When God took on human flesh, He departed the glories of heaven, where He was exalted, and came to a corrupt world, where He was despised. He went from His place of honor to a place of humility. He descended from His throne, surrounded by worshipping angels, to walk among people who would doubt, mock, and kill Him.

As Philippians 2:5-8 says, "Christ Jesus...though he was in the form of God, did not count equality with God a thing to be grasped, but emptied himself by becoming obedient to the point of death, even death on a cross."

As the incarnate one, Jesus experienced the frailties of being clothed in a mortal human body—tiredness, thirst, hunger, temptation. As Hebrews 4:15 points out, He is not "unable to sympathize with our weaknesses, but...in every respect has been tempted as we are."

In becoming God with us, the Lord Jesus Christ performed the greatest act of condescension ever. In fulfilling His purpose for the incarnation, He made the greatest sacrifice ever. In giving up all that He did, He paid the highest price ever.

The consequences of becoming God with *us* were profound. He went from being the undisputed sovereign over all to being rejected, betrayed, and crucified. He went from being loved and adored to hated and reviled. From the heights of holiness to the depths of evil.

When Christ became God with us, He did so not reluctantly, but willingly. He loved us so greatly that He endured the cross with joy, knowing the outcome was worth it.

THE MYSTERY OF GOD WITH US

They shall call his name Immanuel
(which means, God with us) (Matthew 1:23).

When God came to earth and took on human flesh, He did what man could not do: He bridged the chasm between Himself and us. In the Garden of Eden, mankind was banished from the presence of God and had no way back. Dead in sin, man was utterly lost and could do nothing to rescue himself. So God "became flesh and dwelt among us" (John 1:14). By dying on the cross, Jesus removed the barrier that sin imposed and gave us a way back to the Father.

That Jesus was "God with us" means He was fully God and fully man. How God and man could possibly be united perfectly in one person is a mystery that has puzzled many through the ages. But Scripture clearly states Jesus was both divine and human. It also tells us we are finite and God is infinite. Rather than be unsettled by what we don't understand, we should rejoice that God is beyond our comprehension—otherwise, He wouldn't be God.

Job 11:7 asks, "Can you find out the deep things of God? Can you find out the limits of the Almighty?" We cannot. Job 36:26 proclaims, "Behold, God is great, and we know him not."

In Isaiah 55:9, God says, "As the heavens are higher than the earth, so are my ways higher than your ways and my thoughts than your thoughts." In the book of Romans, after writing 11 chapters of profound truths about how God made salvation possible for us, Paul wrote, "Oh, the depth of the riches and wisdom and knowledge of God! How unsearchable are his judgments and how inscrutable his ways!" (Romans 11:33).

"God with us" is among the deep things of God we cannot fully understand on this side of heaven. But this much we do know: It is because of "God with us" that we will enjoy the deep things of God and His goodness for all eternity!

GOD WITH US EVERY STEP OF THE WAY

They shall call his name Immanuel
(which means, God with us) (Matthew 1:23).

The promise of "God with us" began at Christ's birth. For every believer, this promise becomes a powerful reality from the moment of salvation onward. When we respond with belief to the gospel, the Lord comes to reside in us, and He walks with us every step of the way during our journey as pilgrims here on earth.

As believers, it is no longer us who lives, but Christ who lives in us (Galatians 2:20). He will never abandon us—He has said, "I will never leave you nor forsake you" (Hebrews 13:5). We have the assurance that "he who began a good work in [us] will bring it to completion at the day of Christ" (Philippians 1:6). Before Jesus ascended to heaven, He gave this promise to His disciples and all who would follow Him: "I am with you always, to the end of the age" (Matthew 28:20). That word "always" means exactly that: every one of our days.

One of the most beautiful pictures of "God with us" appears in Psalm 23. Here, we read of how dearly our Lord cares for us. The Great Shepherd's eyes are on us at all times. He gives us rest, restores us, and leads us in the ways of righteousness. He nourishes and provides for us. We have no reason to fear evil—His protective care secures and comforts us. He attends to our needs when we are surrounded by enemies. He anoints us so that we might be renewed and revived. Because His faithfulness never ceases, we lack nothing.

Because God is with us here on earth, we can say, "Surely goodness and mercy shall follow me all the days of my life." And because He will be with us in heaven, we can say, "I shall dwell in the house of the LORD forever" (Psalm 23:6). Every step of the way, He is with us. And He will personally call us home to stay in His presence evermore.

GOD WITH US IN LIFE'S DARKEST MOMENTS

Fear not, for I am with you. Be not dismayed (Isaiah 41:10).

Even with the many assurances we have of Christ's constant presence with us, there are times when doubt strikes. A prayer is not answered, a difficult circumstance arises, or we are unable to see any light at the end of the tunnel. Temptations overwhelm us, loved ones abandon us, life veers wildly out of control. With the psalmist, we feel like saying, "Will the Lord spurn forever, and never again be favorable? Has his steadfast love forever ceased?…Has he in anger shut up his compassion?" (Psalm 77:7-9).

When doubt comes, we can find comfort in knowing Jesus endured the sorrows, hurts, and pain we face. He knew what it was to be hungry, thirsty, and have no place to lay His head. He faced temptation. He knew the grief caused by death and wept. He was slandered for doing right. He was abandoned and betrayed. He knew what it was to die a horrible death. He was touched by our infirmities and faced far worse: He bore the fullness of God's wrath upon sin. His darkest moment was greater than any we will ever face.

No matter what our all-too-human feelings tell us, we can count on the enduring truth that God is with us in every one of life's dark moments. In Isaiah 41:10, He declared, "Fear not, for I am with you; be not dismayed, for I am your God; I will strengthen you, I will help you, I will uphold you with my righteous right hand."

The same psalmist who asked, "Has his steadfast love forever ceased?" went on to say, "I will remember your wonders of old…You with your arm redeemed your people" (Psalm 77:11, 15). God's past faithfulness is evidence that His faithfulness will continue in the present and the future. In the times when God seems absent from your life, He isn't. "The word of the Lord is right and true; he is faithful in all he does" (Psalm 33:4 NIV).

FROM IMPOSSIBLE TO POSSIBLE

I bring you news of great joy (Luke 2:10).

If Christ had not taken on human flesh, descended to earth, died on the cross, and risen victorious, we would have no hope of ever escaping the bondage of sin and the penalty of death. The total and irreversible separation from God that began in Eden would still be in force today. Our wanderings in spiritual darkness and blindness would continue without end. Despair and futility would be all that our hearts and minds would know. Our vocabulary would lack beautiful words like *salvation, justification, sanctification*, and *glorification*. The joys of fellowship with fellow believers and church life would be nonexistent. Not a single hymn of worship, praise, or gratitude would ever have been written. We would have no awareness of the glories of relationship with God, heaven, and eternal life.

It is only because Christ descended to earth that we are able to ascend to heaven. He took on our sin so that we could take on His righteousness. He humiliated Himself so that we could be exalted. Because God came to be with us, we can go to be with Him. Because of what Christ has done, the impossible became possible.

No wonder the angel, on that night in Bethlehem, told the shepherds, "I bring you news of great joy." He brought the greatest and sweetest news mankind could ever hear. Apart from the incarnation, there would be no other good news for us at all. In the manger was the one who would deliver us from the depths of sin and carry us to the heights of glory.

So wonderful is this news of great joy that we should never let it grow old. As we continue to grow in our awareness of all that Christ's birth means to us, our hearts should fill up more and more with thanks and rejoicing. That night long ago, the baby Jesus brought to us the gift of eternal life. And the best gift we can give to Him in return is our eternal praise.

A BABY LIKE NO OTHER

Unto you is born this day in the city of David
a Savior, who is Christ the Lord (Luke 2:11).

The baby Jesus was like no other baby. The angels made that clear when they announced His birth to the shepherds. They called Him by three of His exalted titles: Savior, Christ, and Lord.

The shepherds understood the significance of these titles. They recognized the angelic host for who they were. They knew it was God who had sent these messengers. And after they had seen the infant, they glorified and praised God for what they had heard and seen.

When the angels called this newborn the *Savior*, they were declaring the long-awaited Redeemer had arrived—the one who would bring salvation. In the Old Testament, God tells His people He is their Redeemer and Savior (Isaiah 43:1-3). He then adds, "Besides me there is no savior" (verse 11). Surely the shepherds realized the one whom the angels called "Savior" was the prophesied Immanuel, which means "God with us" (Isaiah 7:14). Yes, the Savior had come!

The name *Christ*—and its Old Testament equivalent *Messiah*—means "anointed one." This title designated the child as the descendant who would sit on David's throne forever (2 Samuel 7:12-16). He is the appointed "King of kings" (Revelation 19:16).

For the angels to call this infant *Lord* was to say He is God. This divine title declared His authority to reign over all.

The shepherds were amazed by what they heard from the angels. They realized who this child was. "Let us go and see!" they exclaimed. And "they went with haste" (Luke 2:16).

Anytime we ponder the baby in the manger, may we be filled with awe. May the full force of His titles—Savior, Christ, and Lord—cause us to fall to our knees in reverent worship. In this tiny package was God. He came to bring us home. Oh come let us adore Him!

READY FOR CHRIST'S ARRIVAL

There was a man in Jerusalem, whose name was Simeon, and
this man was righteous and devout...And it had been
revealed to him by the Holy Spirit that he would not see death
before he had seen the Lord's Christ (Luke 2:25-26).

All through the Old Testament are a wealth of prophecies about a
coming Messiah, a Savior who would set people free from their
sins. With this abundance of advance notices, you would think many
of the people of Israel would have been on the lookout for His arrival.

Yet in the days before Jesus' birth, very few were watching for Him.
Simeon, a righteous man, was among them. The Spirit had revealed
that he would not die before seeing the Christ. While this information was revealed to Simeon by the Spirit, we can safely conclude
Simeon was already aware of God's many promises of Christ's coming. Simeon was described as "devout," which tells us he was reverent toward God. Such love and devotion would have driven him to
be familiar with the Scriptures, and caused him to long for Christ's
first advent. Most likely, this is the reason that God was pleased to let
Simeon know Jesus' arrival was near.

Just as Christ's first coming was preceded by widespread apathy and
spiritual darkness, the same will happen again before His return. There
are eight times as many prophecies about His second coming as there
were for His first, yet few are watching. Jesus Himself warned about those
who would not be ready for Him (Matthew 25:1-12). Second Peter 3:4
speaks of scoffers who, in the last days, will doubt and mock teachings
about Christ's return.

Simeon was righteous, devout, and waiting. We can be sure it was
Old Testament prophecies that spurred his readiness. May the many
promises of Christ's return give us a similar devotion—a zeal that we
nurture by staying constantly in the Scriptures.

LIVING EXPECTANTLY FOR CHRIST

Simeon…[was] waiting (Luke 2:25).

Typically, we think of the word *wait* in a negative sense. We don't like to be kept waiting. Time that is spent "on hold" is usually seen as time lost, as an inconvenience that delays a desired result. To have to wait for something often discourages us. Such waiting is often accompanied by uncertainty. We're unsure of what will happen, and when.

Yet there is a positive kind of waiting that fills us with hope. When Luke 2:25 describes Simeon as waiting, it does so in a positive way in the present tense—he looked forward to Jesus' arrival with constant expectation. He delighted in watching for the Messiah. He had his eyes fixed on God's promises about the future. This shaped his thoughts and actions about the present. Simeon's waiting was also based on certainty. He knew he could trust God to follow through on His prophetic promise, and this made him alert.

Simeon is not mentioned anywhere else in the New Testament. His appearance in Luke 2:25-35 is so brief it's easy for us to miss what is said about him. He appears in the shadow of the amazing account of Christ's birth. But what little we are told about Simeon reveals him to be a godly person who serves as an example of how we ought to live.

Simeon is famous not only because he was righteous and devout, but because he lived in anticipation of Christ's first coming. So noteworthy is this fact about him that it's recorded on the pages of Scripture for all to see through the ages.

Can it be said of us that we live with an ongoing excitement about Christ's return? Is our yearning strong enough that we don't allow it to be derailed by the interruptions of daily life? Titus 2:12-13 calls us to "live…godly lives in the present age, waiting for our blessed hope, the appearing of the glory of our great God and Savior Jesus Christ."

THE CONSOLATION OF ISRAEL

...waiting for the consolation of Israel (Luke 2:25).

Every one of Christ's titles or names is rich with meaning. In Luke's account about Simeon is one that had to be especially meaningful to the aged man: Jesus as "the consolation of Israel."

In Simeon's day, the people who professed to follow God had strayed far from Him. Though they had the prophecies they needed to identify the Messiah, they were blinded by their human expectations of Him. They wanted a conqueror who would overthrow Rome and bring earthly freedom. Instead, God provided them with a consoler—a comforter—who would overcome sin and offer spiritual freedom.

Charles Wesley captured the essence of what is meant by "the consolation of Israel" in his 1744 hymn "Come, Thou Long Expected Jesus":

> Come, thou long expected Jesus, born to set thy people free;
> From our fears and sins release us, let us find our rest in Thee.
>
> Israel's strength and consolation, hope of all the earth Thou art;
> Dear desire of ev'ry nation, joy of ev'ry longing heart.

Simeon was likely familiar with the promise in Isaiah 25:9 of a Messiah who would bring true deliverance: "This is our God; we have waited for him, that he might save us. This is the LORD; we have waited for him; let us be glad and rejoice in his salvation." No wonder he was so excited upon seeing the infant Jesus. The consolation that Israel needed had arrived! This consolation is ours as well. He alone is able to provide the joy our hearts long for.

SIMEON'S PSALM

[Simeon] took [Jesus] up in his arms and blessed God and said,
"Lord, now you are letting your servant depart in peace...
For my eyes have seen your salvation...A light for revelation to the
Gentiles, And for glory to your people Israel" (Luke 2:28-32).

Simeon was overwhelmed with awe as he held the infant Jesus in his arms. Here was the consolation of Israel, the Messiah! Salvation had come at last. God had given him the honor of seeing the Savior with his own eyes. So complete was Simeon's joy that he felt ready to die.

His heart full of praise and gratitude, Simeon proclaimed, "My eyes have seen your salvation." This was true not only physically, but spiritually. Simeon was one of the rare few who understood the prophecies about Christ's coming and purpose. He knew Jesus was "a light for revelation to the Gentiles," and not the Jews only. Most of Simeon's fellow Jews wouldn't have agreed. Even after the resurrection, Jesus' own disciples lacked understanding on this. They assumed Jesus' earthly kingdom was for Israel alone (Acts 1:6). Simeon may have been familiar with Isaiah 42:6, which says the Messiah would be "a light for the nations"— for *all* peoples.

Earlier, the shepherds who visited the newborn Jesus had told Mary what the angels said about Him: He was the "Savior, who is Christ the Lord." Now, Simeon further confirmed Jesus' identity and deity. Joseph and Mary "marveled at what was said about him" (verse 33).

With Jesus' birth, a divine light shone into the world. It pierced the thick and suffocating darkness caused by sin. The dawn of redeeming grace was here, but many missed it. The few who understood Jesus' arrival were greatly blessed as they saw God's prophetic promises being fulfilled. Likewise, blessings await those who are watchful for Christ's second coming!

SIMEON'S PROPHECY

Behold, this child is appointed for the fall and rising of
many in Israel, and for a sign that is opposed (and a sword
will pierce through your own soul also), so that thoughts
from many hearts may be revealed (Luke 2:34-35).

After Simeon poured out praise to God for allowing him to live long enough to see the birth of the Savior, he uttered a prophecy of warning to Mary. This was God's way of alerting her—well in advance—of the hostility Jesus would face someday. Simeon's words are haunting but necessary, for the motherly pain she would experience would be great.

This child is appointed for the fall and rising of many. In Jesus, all are called to account before God. The way people respond to Jesus determines their destiny—their condemnation or salvation. In unbelief they fall and perish; in belief, they rise and are promised resurrection.

For a sign that is opposed. During His earthly ministry, Jesus faced intense opposition. As He announced the arrival of God's kingdom and pointed the way to God, He was rejected, reviled, and hated. He had many enemies and still does—the chief one being Satan, who will inspire all the world's armies to war against Christ at His second coming (Revelation 19:19).

So that thoughts from many hearts may be revealed. A person's thoughts are concealed in their heart, but their reaction to Christ reveals those thoughts. As John 3:19 says, "This is the judgment: the light has come into the world, and people loved the darkness rather than the light." Jesus exposes the truth about what is hidden in one's heart. No one can escape the all-important question, "What do you think about the Christ?" (Matthew 22:42).

So fierce would be the enmity against Jesus that Mary would be pierced with great pain—especially when her Son was nailed to the cross. Blessed to have given birth to Jesus, she would know great agony as well. With tender care, God prepared her for what was to come.

THE RESPONSE OF A DEVOTED HEART

Anna...was advanced in years...as a widow to the age of eight-four.
She did not leave the temple grounds, serving night and day with fasts
and prayers. And at that very moment she came up and began giving
thanks to God, and continued to speak about Him to all those who were
looking forward to the redemption of Jerusalem (Luke 2:36-38 NASB).

Anna was another of the rare and precious souls who lived in the expectation of Messiah's arrival. While carrying out her service at the temple, she came up to Simeon. There's no doubt these dear and aged servants were longtime friends. The fact Anna was a prophetess is noteworthy. She may have been called this because she was intimately familiar with the prophecies about Christ's first coming and spoke of them. She and Simeon had surely talked many times about their anticipation for the promised Messiah.

As Anna came up to Simeon, Joseph, Mary, and the infant Jesus, she probably overheard Simeon's words of praise, "My eyes have seen your salvation" (Luke 2:30). She immediately recognized Simeon was talking about Jesus. In response, she burst forth with gratitude.

From that day onward, Anna "continued to speak about Him to all those who were looking forward to the redemption of Jerusalem." Evidently there were others in her realm of influence—right at the temple itself—whose hearts eagerly awaited the Redeemer. Like Simeon and Anna, they were true seekers who held to the same hope.

Because we live in a dark world that has no care for the things of God, we will often feel alone in our love for Christ. The hope we have in Jesus and His coming is meant to be shared with others of like mind. As we do this, we are reminded that we're not by ourselves in the faith, and we bring much-needed encouragement to one another.

A LOWLY AND
UNEXPECTED APPEARANCE

*Behold, I send my messenger, and he will prepare the way before me. And
the Lord whom you seek will suddenly come to his temple (Malachi 3:1).*

Joseph and Mary brought baby Jesus to the temple because it was
time for Mary's "purification according to the Law of Moses," and
for Jesus to be presented "to the Lord" (Luke 2:22-23).

In Malachi 3:1 is a prophecy that foretells Jesus' visit to the temple.
In this prophecy, and in Joseph and Mary's encounter with Simeon and
Anna, we see God announce the news of Jesus' arrival to those at the
temple in a way we would never expect.

Malachi's prophecy first introduces us to a messenger who will "prepare the way" for Jesus—John the Baptist. Isaiah spoke of John 700 years
earlier when he said, "A voice cries: 'In the wilderness prepare the way of
the LORD'" (Isaiah 40:3). The fact John the Baptist fulfills these prophecies is confirmed in Matthew 3:3, Mark 1:2, Luke 1:17, and John 1:23.

The prophet Malachi then says, "The Lord whom you seek will suddenly come to his temple." The word "suddenly" here suggests a lowly
and unexpected appearance. Jesus' first arrival at the temple—the center of Jewish worship and life—was not trumpeted with fanfare. He
did not get the attention of those in positions of power and prestige.
No, God chose to reveal the Savior of the world quietly to two humble,
elderly, and faithful souls.

God orchestrated Joseph and Mary's encounter with Simeon and
Anna before He created the world. He planned for all their paths to cross
in this seemingly random moment to achieve His purposes. Simeon's
words would affirm Jesus' deity and prepare Mary for the opposition
Jesus would face. The widow Anna would go on to share the news of
Messiah's arrival with other genuine seekers at the temple. Today, God
continues to work in lowly and unexpected ways through the humble and willing. Never underestimate what He might do through you.

THE PEOPLE GOD CHOOSES

The LORD looks on the heart (1 Samuel 16:7).

As the Gospels of Matthew and Luke describe the men and women who had key roles in welcoming Jesus to earth, we cannot help but notice they all exhibited character traits that showed their love and reverence for God. Here is what Scripture reveals about them:

We are told that the priest Zechariah and his wife, Elizabeth, who were the parents of John the Baptist, "were both righteous before God, walking blamelessly" (Luke 1:6).

When the angel told Mary she would bear a child, she responded, "Behold, I am the servant of the Lord; let it be to me according to your word" (Luke 1:38).

When Joseph was unsure of what to do when he was told Mary was pregnant, we are told he was "a just man" (Matthew 1:19).

Simeon was "righteous and devout" (Luke 2:25).

Anna "did not depart from the temple, worshiping with fasting and prayer night and day" (Luke 2:37).

Every one of these people were devoted to God. All were fervent in their desire to honor the Lord and do what was right. None were prominent by earthly standards. None were picked for their stature or position in life. God entrusted them with their roles not because of their accomplishments, but their hearts. "The LORD sees not as man sees; man looks on the outward appearance, but the LORD looks on the heart" (1 Samuel 16:7).

God seeks hearts that are fully yielded to Him. When we live in total surrender, we are saying to the Lord, "Your will, not mine." When we set ourselves apart for His use, we become vessels through which He can work mightily.

WHAT JESUS MEANS TO US

You shall call his name Jesus (Matthew 1:21; Luke 1:31).

When messenger angels announced to Joseph and Mary on separate occasions that Mary would conceive and bear a son, both of them were told, "You shall call his name Jesus." At the time, little did they know what Jesus would be like in person and action. Never had anyone encountered a human who was without sin. Never had there been someone who could say, "Whoever has seen me has seen the Father" (John 14:9).

All that changed during Jesus' ministry on earth. And ever since Christ's resurrection, everyone who has believed what Jesus said about Himself and received Him as Lord and Savior has found the name *Jesus* to be special. Upon hearing or reading His name, our hearts are moved to reverence, affection, and gratitude.

In Jesus, we see a compassion that genuinely cares for those in need. In Him, we see a righteousness that is pure and just. In Him, we see a power that evidences true sovereignty and makes victory over sin and the restoration of all things possible. In Him, we see grace and mercy extended even to the most undeserving. In Him, we see knowledge and wisdom that guides us well and seeks our best. In Him, we have a shepherd who protects and provides. In Him, we have an intercessor who acts on our behalf. In Him, we see a love that is perfect and willing to die for its enemies. In Him, we have the promise of resurrection, heaven, and eternal life. No wonder the name Jesus is so endearing!

It's sobering to think of where we would be if Jesus had never come. Thankfully, He *did* come. It would be impossible for us to exhaust all of what that means for us. In Jesus alone we find the difference between despair and hope, pointlessness and purpose, deprivation and abundance, death and life, hell and heaven. Truly, Jesus is the name above all names!

MISUNDERSTANDING THE MESSIAH

When Herod the king heard this, he was troubled,
and all Jerusalem with him (Matthew 2:3).

When the angelic host announced, "Unto you is born this day in the city of David a Savior, who is Christ the Lord," the shepherds immediately knew the identity of this newborn. And they were quick to go visit Him in the manger.

But when the magi from the East arrived in Jerusalem and inquired about where they could find this child, the reaction they received from many in Jerusalem was the opposite. The magi asked, "Where is he who has been born king of the Jews? For we saw his star when it rose and have come to worship him" (Matthew 2:2). Their question caused a stir. King Herod "was troubled, and all Jerusalem with him" (verse 3).

Herod then turned to the chief priests and the scribes for an answer. These were the most learned Jewish religious scholars of the day. They provided the answer from Micah 5:2: "You, O Bethlehem…from you shall come forth for me one who is to be ruler in Israel."

The teachers and caretakers of Scripture correctly cited the 700-year-old prophecy about Bethlehem as the birthplace for their long-awaited ruler. But they expressed no enthusiasm for joining the magi to find this child "who is to be ruler in Israel." They had the information, but they showed an astounding lack of interest.

Tragically, they had wrongly interpreted the prophecies about their coming King. They were expecting a conquering hero, not a baby, who would overthrow their Roman oppressors and restore Israel to her former glory. They failed to realize their King would first come as a Savior to deal with their sin problem. They knew much yet understood none of it. So they entirely missed God's presence among them. And they serve as a warning to us to not do the same.

JESUS PROPHESIES HIS RESURRECTION

Destroy this temple, and in three days I will raise it up (John 2:19).

In righteous anger, Jesus turned over the tables of the moneychangers. The Jewish religious leaders had made the Passover—a time of repentance and worship—into a moneymaking operation that took advantage of people. Outraged by Jesus' actions, the Jewish leaders demanded, "What sign do you show us for doing these things?" They challenged His authority and wanted immediate confirmation of it. In reply, Jesus gave a prophecy that stated He would verify His authority after His death: "Destroy this temple, and in three days I will raise it up."

Jesus' response confused His listeners. They said, "It has taken forty-six years to build this temple, and will you raise it up in three days?" (verse 20). They thought Jesus was speaking about the temple buildings and complex. Even the disciples thought the same, for it wasn't until after Jesus' resurrection that they "remembered that he had said this, and they believed the Scripture and the word that Jesus had spoken" (verse 22). But John 2:21 makes it clear Jesus "was speaking about the temple of his body." Three days after He was killed, He would rise.

When the religious leaders confronted Jesus about His authority, little did they know they would play a role in confirming that very authority! Later, they demanded Jesus be crucified. By putting Him to death, they put into motion His ensuing resurrection, a miracle that proved He was God, the supreme authority. Their question was answered, but not in the way they expected.

When Jesus gave the prophecy that He would raise up the temple, He not only predicted His resurrection, He also proclaimed this truth: Soon, a physical temple would no longer be needed. We who serve a risen Lord have been made a church, a spiritual temple that replaces the physical one (Ephesians 2:19-22). No longer do we need a building in which to meet God; we who comprise the church are the temple in which God's Spirit dwells! (1 Corinthians 3:16-17).

JESUS FULFILLED THE PROPHETS

Do not think that I have come to abolish the Law or the Prophets;
I have not come to abolish them but to fulfill them (Matthew 5:17).

At the cross, Christ fulfilled the demands of the law for us. In our fallen state as sinners, the law sentenced us to death and eternal separation from God. But thankfully, God sent His Son to pay that penalty. As 2 Corinthians 5:21 says, "For our sake he made him to be sin who knew no sin, so that in him we might become the righteousness of God." This is frequently called the great exchange: Christ took our sins upon Himself so His righteousness could be placed upon us.

Jesus not only fulfilled the law, but the prophets as well. Everything the Old Testament prophets said about our Lord's first coming came to pass with perfect accuracy. Even more amazing is that every one of those prophecies was recorded hundreds to thousands of years before His birth. The human impossibility of one person fulfilling so many prophecies made so far in advance serves as powerful evidence that Scripture was divinely inspired by God Himself. He alone knows all, including the future. There simply is no other alternative.

Typically, we think of the New Testament as providing an account of Jesus' life and imparting instructions about how we are to live. Yes, it does that, but it also does much more. Every truth communicated in the New Testament is upheld by the fact Jesus truly was the Messiah predicted by the prophets. It is Jesus' fulfillment of Old Testament prophecies that confirms the supernatural nature and absolute credibility of the New Testament.

Fulfilled prophecies serve as proof of the truthfulness and reliability of God's Word. Taken together, they invite all people to examine the evidence and conclude that yes, the Bible is true, and yes, Jesus really is Savior and Lord.

JESUS, THE GREAT PROPHET

A great prophet has risen among us! (Luke 7:16).

When Jesus and His disciples visited the town of Nain, they encountered a large funeral procession. The only son of a widow had died, and pallbearers were carrying his casket to his grave. With great compassion for the woman, Jesus said, "Do not weep" (Luke 7:13). He then turned to the casket and commanded, "Young man, I say to you, arise" (verse 14).

When the man came to life, fear filled the crowd. They exclaimed, "A great prophet has arisen among us!" and "God has visited his people!" (verse 16). Jesus was hailed as a prophet sent by God Himself.

Jesus was again recognized as a prophet on Palm Sunday as He entered Jerusalem on a donkey. The crowd cried, "Hosanna to the Son of David! Blessed is he who comes in the name of the Lord!" (Matthew 21:9). When some bystanders asked, "Who is this?" the crowd answered, "This is the prophet Jesus" (verse 11).

Prophet is yet another of Jesus' exalted titles, yet it's often overlooked. Jesus even called Himself a prophet when He said, "A prophet is not without honor except in his hometown and in his own household" (Matthew 13:57).

Like the Old Testament prophets, Jesus was both a messenger and a revealer of the future. Yet He superseded them all as the greatest prophet because He was the one to whom they had pointed. More importantly, He Himself was God. He spoke with ultimate divine authority. He didn't say, "Thus says the LORD…" Rather, He said, "I say to you…"

God's people were commanded to listen to the prophets, who revealed God's truth. Jesus said, "Whoever has seen me has seen the Father" (John 14:9). Because as prophet Jesus not only spoke God's truth but revealed God Himself, how much more eagerly should we listen to Him!

PARABLES ABOUT THE
KINGDOM OF HEAVEN, PART 1

*Great crowds gathered about him...and he told them
many things in parables (Matthew 13:2-3).*

The day Jesus first spoke in parables marked a pivotal turning point in His ministry. In Matthew chapter 13, in front of a large crowd, Jesus shared eight parables.[14] Up to this time, He had never spoken one. But from this day onward, all that changed. Jesus would go on to teach about 40 of them. In Matthew 13, it's clear that many who heard these parables did not understand them, for the disciples asked Jesus, "Why do you speak to them in parables?" (verse 10).

Jesus answered, "To you it has been given to know the secrets of the kingdom of heaven, but to them it has not been given" (verse 11). He then added, "This people's heart has grown dull, and with their ears they can barely hear, and their eyes they have closed" (verse 15). In saying this, Jesus pointed out a major transition was taking place in how people responded to Him. From here onward, they would either reject His words or receive them. They would harden their hearts or open them. Those who opposed Him would close their ears and reject the truth, and those who listened would have their ears opened and welcome the truth.

Jesus had two reasons for speaking in parables: to *reveal* the truth, and to *conceal* the truth. He told the disciples, "To you has been given the secret of the kingdom of God, but for those outside everything is in parables" (Mark 4:11).

When Jesus described the parables as "the *secrets* of the kingdom of heaven," He confirmed that those who receive Him will be given more light, and those who reject Him will remain in darkness. Apart from God's help, we cannot understand His truth. That's why it is vital that we have the heart of the psalmist, who wrote, "Open my eyes, that I may behold wondrous things out of your law" (Psalm 119:18). God reveals His truth to those with open ears and hearts.

PARABLES ABOUT THE
KINGDOM OF HEAVEN, PART 2

The kingdom of heaven is like…
(Matthew 13:31, 33, 44, 45, 47, 52).

What exactly is a parable? Very simply, it's a word picture, or a metaphor. One popular definition is that a parable is an earthly story with a heavenly meaning. Another is that a parable is a spiritual truth illustrated by a familiar everyday object or practice.

Six out of the eight parables in Matthew 13 begin with the words, "The kingdom of heaven is like…" This tells us these parables have to do with the kingdom of heaven. When we read them more closely, we come to realize that the topic of every parable is the gospel and salvation. Without salvation, people cannot have part in God's kingdom—either spiritually here on earth now in their hearts, or physically in the Lord's future millennial kingdom and heaven.

For example, the parable of the sower teaches that some with soft hearts will receive the gospel, but many with hardened hearts won't. The parable of the wheat and tares reveals that at the same time the true gospel is sown, the enemy will sow weeds that aren't the gospel. In the end, the good will be separated from the bad, and the bad will be sent to judgment.

Through the parables in Matthew 13, Jesus explained that during the time between His first and second comings—that is, the church age—the gospel would spread and bear fruit. And He warned that condemnation awaited those who rejected the gospel. He used illustrations from everyday life to urge people to receive the gospel so they will go to heaven and not hell.

As believers, we bear the kingdom of God spiritually in our hearts as we submit to Him and do His will. Our purpose here on earth is to share the gospel so people may enter Christ's future and physical kingdom on earth and in heaven. Christ's mission is our mission. Now is the time of harvest, and the time that remains for pointing people to salvation is becoming shorter with each passing day.

THE KIND OF DEATH JESUS WOULD DIE

I, when I am lifted up from the earth,
will draw all people to myself (John 12:32).

In Psalm 22:16, David prophesied the kind of death Jesus would die: "A company of evildoers encircles me; they have pierced my hands and feet." In Isaiah 53:5, we read, "He was pierced for our transgressions." In Numbers 21, when serpents bit the rebellious Israelites, killing them, Moses made "a fiery serpent and set it on a pole" (verse 8), and told the people that any bitten person who looked upon it would live. John 3:14 tells us this was a foreshadow of Jesus on the cross: "As Moses lifted up the serpent in the wilderness, so must the Son of Man be lifted up."

In all those passages, we see prophecies about the kind of death Jesus would die: He would be raised up and pierced. In John 12:32, Jesus Himself confirmed these prophecies, saying, "I, when I am lifted up from the earth, will draw all people to myself." Why is this important? Had the Jewish religious authorities killed Jesus, He would have been stoned to death. That was their means of execution. Only the Romans did crucifixions.

When Pontius Pilate told the Jewish religious leaders, "Take him yourselves and judge him by your own law," they responded, "It is not lawful for us to put anyone to death" (John 18:31). They refused to execute Jesus. Why? John tells us: "This was to fulfill the word that Jesus had spoken to show by what kind of death he was going to die" (verse 32). This refers to what Jesus said earlier in John 12:32 about being "lifted up from the earth."

Had the Jewish authorities killed Jesus by stoning, God and all the prophecies about the crucifixion would have been wrong. But as it turned out, Jesus died the way Scripture said He would. In Jesus' final 24 hours, 33 prophecies were fulfilled with precision—unintentionally by people, and very intentionally by God. No matter how people oppose God, He is able to orchestrate and override their evil so that His prophetic plans come to pass.

A PROPHECY ON THE NECESSITY OF THE CRUCIFIXION

Jesus began to show his disciples that he must go to Jerusalem and suffer many things from the elders and chief priests and scribes, and be killed, and on the third day be raised (Matthew 16:21).

In this prophecy given by Jesus Himself, notice the words "he must." Jesus' suffering, death, and resurrection were necessary. Many prophecies in the Old Testament declare to us that God's plan of salvation required the Messiah to suffer and die.

God's plan was for Jesus to go to Jerusalem. That's where the temple stood and sacrifices were offered to God. It's where God told Abraham to offer Isaac as a sacrifice (Genesis 22:2). In Luke 13:33, Jesus prophesied, "It cannot be that a prophet should perish outside of Jerusalem."

The next part of God's plan was for Jesus to "suffer many things." The chief priests and elders would arrest Him, hold mock trials with false witnesses, and hand Him over to the Roman authorities to be beaten. In all this, Israel's rejection of Christ would become official.

Next, Jesus was to "be killed." Why was this necessary? Hebrews 9:22 tells us that "without the shedding of blood there is no forgiveness of sins." Romans 6:23 says, "The wages of sin is death."

And finally, Jesus would "be raised." As the firstfruits of the resurrection, He would conquer death, making resurrection possible for all believers as well (1 Corinthians 15:20-23).

It was God's will for Jesus to die and rise again on our behalf. Only then could prophecies be fulfilled, and salvation become possible. That's why Jesus had to go to Jerusalem, endure abuse, and die. There was no other alternative. Yet for Jesus, this was not a mission of forced compliance. He gave His life willingly—it wasn't taken from Him (John 10:17-18). So great was His love for us that He was pleased to do God's will.

JESUS' FIRST PROMISE OF THE SECOND COMING

The Son of Man is going to come with his angels
in the glory of his Father (Matthew 16:27).

The disciples were stunned. Jesus had just told them "he must go to Jerusalem and suffer many things from the elders and chief priests and scribes, and be killed, and on the third day be raised" (Matthew 16:21).

Suffer? Be killed? This didn't make sense. Many Old Testament prophecies had promised a Messiah who would come as the conquering King to rule forever. Persecution and martyrdom didn't fit with their understanding of what the Messiah would do. They didn't realize He would come twice, not once. First, Jesus had to die as a sacrifice for sin. Then in a separate event, He would return to establish His eternal rule. God's plan to rescue mankind and restore creation required the cross to come before the crown. Sacrificial Savior, then sovereign Lord.

In anger, Peter rebuked Jesus: "Far be it from you, Lord! This shall never happen to you" (verse 22). This reveals how greatly the disciples misunderstood the purpose of Jesus' ministry.

It got worse. Next, Jesus said, "If anyone would come after me, let him deny himself and take up his cross" (verse 24). The disciples got the point clearly. The cross was an instrument of execution. It represented a horrible, violent death. To follow Christ is to deny self and suffer.

The disciples wanted Christ as king immediately. Jesus said, "That comes later." After He warned of hardship and death, He gave a prophecy they could cling to: "The Son of Man is going to come with his angels in the glory of his Father." This was His first clear promise of the second coming. In the end, all will be made right. Christ will return in glory and majesty, and He will reward His followers. But first would come suffering—for Him, and for us. A willingness to take up our cross and share with Jesus in His sufferings assures we will share with Him in His glory.

A PROPHECY ABOUT
JESUS' TRANSFIGURATION

I say to you, there are some standing here who will not taste death until
they see the Son of Man coming in his kingdom (Matthew 16:28).

After Jesus told the disciples He must die, He promised He would later return in glory. Then He spoke another prophecy that has confused many through the ages: "I say to you, there are some standing here who will not taste death until they see the Son of Man coming in his kingdom."

But Christ didn't come and set up His kingdom while the disciples were still alive. Does this mean He was wrong?

Because Jesus is God, and because He is perfect and all-knowing, we can be certain He didn't make a mistake here. Our first step toward a clear understanding of Matthew 16:28 is to know that "kingdom" is the Greek term *basileia*, which can be taken to refer to Jesus' "kingly splendor," and not a literal kingdom. Also, as we look at the context provided in the next few verses, we're given a valuable clue that enables us to better understand what Jesus meant.

Matthew 17:1-2 goes on to tell us that six days later, Jesus took Peter, James, and John up a mountain, where He "was transfigured before them, and his face shone like the sun, and his clothes became white as light." Here, Jesus gave a preview of His glory at His second coming!

Jesus' transfiguration was not a random event without reason. It had a specific purpose: to give a glimpse of His future return in glory. Discouraged by the news that their beloved Lord would die, the disciples needed their confidence restored. This spectacular display of Jesus in full glory confirmed His deity and backed up His promise of a future kingdom.

We have no reason to doubt Jesus' promise that He will return. The victory Christ secured at His first coming guarantees His second coming. We are destined for future glory and blessing. Because our Lord has already been raised up in full splendor, we will be too.

THE ARRIVAL OF THE KING

You will find a donkey tied, and a colt with her (Matthew 21:1).

Jesus' triumphal entry into Jerusalem on the colt of a donkey took place at the beginning of His final week on earth. This event had been planned in eternity past, and 550 years before it took place, God revealed these details through His prophet Zechariah: "Rejoice greatly, O daughter of Zion! Shout aloud, O daughter of Jerusalem! Behold, your king is coming to you; righteous and having salvation is he, humble and mounted on a donkey, on a colt, the foal of a donkey" (9:9).

In this prophecy, we read about the loud and joyful crowds who would welcome King Jesus as He rode into Jerusalem on a humble beast of burden. The fulfillment of this prophecy is so significant that it's reported in all four Gospels.

Jesus' omniscience is on bright display in two ways as He prepares to enter Jerusalem. First, He knows that now is the time for Him to fulfill the prophecy given by Zechariah. Second, with prophetic precision, He tells the disciples, "Go into the village...and immediately you will find a donkey tied, and a colt with her. Untie them and bring them to me" (Matthew 21:2). Jesus specified exactly what the disciples would find, and where.

Zechariah's announcement that Israel's king would arrive on the colt of a donkey likely puzzled all who read the prophecy. Why would a king ride on such a lowly creature? But this is in line with the purpose of Jesus' first coming: to be a servant, save the lost, and sacrifice His life. It was not yet time for Him to sit on His throne in glory and rule the earth.

Little did the crowds who shouted with adoration for their king realize that, just a few days later, they would shout with anger for Him to be crucified. But Jesus knew. Yet He was not deterred. He knew the wonderful outcome that awaited Him beyond the cross, He was resolved to carry out His Father's will. Let the prophecies about the future give you a similar resolve!

JESUS: GOD AND PROPHET

This is the prophet Jesus, from Nazareth of Galilee (Matthew 21:11).

How can we know Jesus really is God? One major evidence of His deity is that He gave many prophecies that came to pass. Only God can tell the future in advance, which confirms Jesus is God. Here are some examples of prophecies He gave that were and are still being fulfilled:

- *Growth of the church.* "On this rock I will build my church" (Matthew 16:18).
- *Coming of the Spirit.* "The Helper, the Holy Spirit, whom the Father will send...he will teach you all things" (John 14:26).
- *Betrayal.* "He said, 'Truly, I say to you, one of you will betray me'" (Matthew 26:21).
- *Abandonment by disciples.* "You will all fall away because of me" (Matthew 26:31).
- *Denial by Peter.* "Before the rooster crows, you will deny me three times" (Matthew 26:34).
- *Crucifixion.* "The Son of Man will be delivered up to be crucified" (Matthew 26:2).
- *Resurrection.* "Destroy this temple, and in three days I will raise it up" (John 2:19).

Every prophecy Jesus gave about His earthly life was fulfilled perfectly. He also spoke extensively about the end times and His return. We can be certain that if all His first-coming prophecies came to pass, then all His second-coming prophecies will come to pass as well.

Not only was Jesus a prophet, but He was the greatest of all the prophets. He did more than foretell the future; He planned and orchestrated it. All the prophets who preceded Him merely *spoke* about what would happen; Jesus was able to *fulfill* what was to happen. They had limited knowledge and power; Jesus was all-knowing and all-powerful. They spoke *for* God; Jesus *was* and *is* God. Most wonderful of all, the earthly prophets *pointed* to the salvation that was to come; the heavenly prophet *was* that salvation who came...and He made us right before God.

JESUS ON THE END
TIMES #1: BE READY

Be ready (Matthew 24:44 NIV).

E very prophecy in the Bible was breathed by God and revealed to those who penned the Scriptures so that we could know what God says about the future. But there is one prophetic passage in the Bible, Matthew chapters 24–25, that is especially noteworthy because in it, we find Jesus' own words to us about the end times.[15] These words were spoken directly by God in human flesh and not through a human prophet. They were spoken by the one who knows all things and holds the future in His hands.

Jesus' teachings on the end times were prompted by a question the disciples asked: "What will be the sign of your coming and of the end of the age?" (Matthew 24:3). Jesus' answer is the longest that He gives in response to any question recorded in the Gospels. That's because He *wanted* all people to know about the signs that will precede His second coming.

A careful look at the context of Matthew 24–25 reveals these signs take place during the tribulation. This means the warnings given by Jesus are primarily for Jewish and Gentile believers alive on earth during that age. However, the events that occur during the tribulation won't suddenly arise out of nowhere. *Before* the tribulation begins, and *before* the rapture occurs, events that lead to the signs in Matthew 24–25 will already start building up. They will cast their shadows into our day and serve as early indicators that the tribulation and Christ's return are near.

Every warning Christ gives for tribulation-era believers about His second coming should be of interest to believers today, *before* the tribulation. No matter how we view Matthew 24–25, *all* believers are called to live in a constant state of readiness. Today's believers are to be just as ready for the rapture as tribulation-era believers are to be ready for the second coming. The reason Christ explained the signs of His coming so far in advance was so we would be ready.

JESUS ON THE END TIMES #2: THE BIRTH PAINS

All these are but the beginning of the birth pains (Matthew 24:8).

Right now, there are wars taking place around the world. Do these wars have anything to do with Jesus' warning in Matthew 24:6 about "wars and rumors of wars"?

Among trusted Bible prophecy experts, some say yes, these wars and other signs listed in Matthew 24 will occur during the church age. Others say the signs apply only to the tribulation period, after the church has been raptured from the earth to heaven. Why the different views?

Those who say the "birth pains" in Matthew 24:4-14 will occur all through the span of time between Christ's first and second comings reason that the birth pains are already happening now and will continue to increase in intensity as we approach the tribulation.

Others say the birth pains in Matthew 24:4-14 are specific to the tribulation. They reason that if verse 15 describes the midpoint of the seven-year time of wrath—when the antichrist enters the temple and says he is God—then it makes sense for verses 4-14 to describe the first half. They also say that nowhere in Matthew 24:4-14 does Jesus mention the rapture or the church. This seems to indicate the rapture has already happened, and the church is no longer on earth. Finally, a careful comparison of the events in Matthew 24:4-14 with those in Revelation 6:2-12 (the seal judgments) shows they are parallel. But even if we believe the birth pains occur only during the tribulation, we can correctly say they will cast foreshadows that reach into our day. Even now, we are ramping up toward the tribulation.

Today, God is setting the stage for Christ's return. Planet Earth may seem to be spiraling out of control, but it's not. Jesus said, "See that you are not alarmed, for this must take place" (Matthew 24:6). As we witness events that make it seem as if the world is falling apart, we are actually seeing God's sovereignty in action, bringing His plans to completion.

JESUS ON THE END TIMES #3:
BE ALERT FOR DECEPTION

See that no one leads you astray (Matthew 24:4).

In Matthew 24–25, Jesus reveals to His disciples—and to believers of all ages—the signs that will precede His second coming. The very first sign He mentions is that of spiritual deception. This is an alarming sign for two reasons: First, because deception is Satan's primary weapon for drawing people away from the truth into error; and second, because deception is what will pave the way for the antichrist to become powerful and convince people to worship him. Deception is deadly because it turns people away from the truth and persuades them to embrace lies.

Jesus warned, "See that no one leads you astray. For many will come in my name, saying, 'I am the Christ,' and they will lead many astray... many false prophets will arise" (24:4, 11). What's frightening is that these deceptions will come not only from outside of Christianity, but also from those who claim to represent Christ Himself! Paul spoke of this when he wrote, "In the last days there will come times of difficulty. For people will be...lovers of pleasure rather than lovers of God, having the *appearance of godliness*, but denying its power" (2 Timothy 3:1-2, 4-5). Those who deceive will appear to be godly on the outside, yet on the inside will be ungodly.

The most dangerous deceptions are ideas that appear to be true but are mixed with lies. The intent of deception is to get people to think they are following the truth when, in reality, they aren't. This is what makes deception so perilous. People are deceived without being aware of it.

During the tribulation, deception will be rampant. It's already a serious problem now. How can we protect ourselves from spiritual deceit? Scripture urges us to "contend for the faith that was once for all delivered to the saints. For certain people have crept in unnoticed" (Jude 3-4). We are to guard the truth and watch out for those who sneak lies into the church. When we devote ourselves to knowing and protecting the truth, we equip ourselves to detect error.

JESUS ON THE END TIMES #4:
WARS, DISASTERS, DEATH

You will hear of wars and rumors of wars...there will
be famines and earthquakes...they will deliver you
up...and put you to death (Matthew 24:6-7, 9).

In Matthew 24:4-14, as Jesus unveils the signs that will precede His return, we notice stunning parallels between these signs and the seal judgments that occur at the beginning of the tribulation (Revelation 6:2-12). The first sign, about false Christs and deception, corresponds with the first seal judgment, which depicts the arrival of the antichrist on a white horse to conquer the world by promising peace. From there we go to the next several parallels between signs and seals:

Wars and rumors of wars/second seal (Matthew 24:6-7; Revelation 6:3-4). War and slaughter will be everywhere. Nation will rise against nation, and people will slay one another.

Famines and earthquakes/third seal (Matthew 24:7; Revelation 6:5-6). One tragic side effect of war is food shortages, or famines. Large numbers of people will die of starvation.

Persecution and death/fourth seal (Matthew 24:9; Revelation 6:7-8). One-fourth of the world's population will be killed by the antichrist, by war and famine, and by other causes.

Martyrdom/fifth seal (Matthew 24:9; Revelation 6:9-11). Jesus said those who become Christians during the tribulation will be hated "for my name's sake." They will be "slain for the word of God and for the witness they had borne." The antichrist will kill all who follow Christ.

Today's believers have no reason to fear the tribulation because we will be raptured beforehand (1 Thessalonians 1:10; 5:9). Though it is sobering to know many Christians will be killed by the antichrist in the end times, it is encouraging to realize they will prefer death over submission to this evil ruler. They will view martyrdom as their gateway to eternity in Christ's presence. Like Paul, they will say, "To live is Christ, and to die is gain" (Philippians 1:21).

JESUS ON THE END TIMES #5: THE ABOMINATION OF DESOLATION

When you see the abomination of desolation spoken of by the prophet Daniel, standing in the holy place...(Matthew 24:15).

The most blasphemous moment of the seven-year tribulation will occur when the antichrist enters the temple in Jerusalem and proclaims himself to be God. There's a sinister name for this event: the abomination of desolation.

We first read about the antichrist's despicable deed in Daniel 9:27. There, we are told he will make a treaty with Israel for seven years. Then at the midpoint of that period, he will "put an end to sacrifice and offering." He will shut down all Jewish worship activity. Second Thessalonians 2:4 says that when this happens, the antichrist will take "his seat in the temple of God, proclaiming himself to be God."

Jesus warns about the abomination of desolation in Matthew 24:15. This will mark a horrifying turning point—the world dictator who promised peace to Israel will turn on the nation. Jesus urges that all Jews at the time should "flee to the mountains" and "not turn back" (verses 16, 18). During the tribulation, the antichrist will unleash unimaginable persecution on the Jews. His hatred and genocidal rampage will eclipse even the evils carried out during the Holocaust.

Why will the antichrist declare himself to be God? Scripture tells us that long ago, Satan became so prideful that he wanted to rise above God and receive worship, which belongs to God alone (Isaiah 14:13-14; Ezekiel 28:12, 15, 17). For this sin, he was punished and cast to earth. Satan's craving to usurp God has never waned. One of the ways he tempted Jesus was to offer Him "all the kingdoms of the world" in exchange for worship (Matthew 4:8-9). During the tribulation, Satan will use the antichrist to exalt himself as God. But when Christ returns, the devil will be crushed, bound, and eventually, banished to the lake of fire for all eternity.

JESUS ON THE END TIMES #6: THE GREAT TRIBULATION

When you see the abomination of desolation...there will be
great tribulation, such as has not been from the beginning of the
world until now, no, and never will be (Matthew 24:15, 21).

We know from Daniel 9:27 that the abomination of desolation will take place at the midpoint of the seven-year tribulation. At that time, the antichrist will stand in the holy place in the temple in Jerusalem and desecrate it, declaring himself to be God (2 Thessalonians 2:3-4). Here in Matthew 24, Jesus said this blasphemous event will unleash the "great tribulation."

The magnitude of the horrors that will engulf planet Earth during the last three-and-a-half years of the tribulation will far exceed any other cataclysmic time in history. With the antichrist—the man of lawlessness—ruling the world, wickedness and evil will explode. God's divine wrath upon rebellious mankind will escalate to apocalyptic proportions. The book of Revelation tells us hundreds of millions will die. And countless Jewish people and Christians will face brutal persecution and be slaughtered.

In Matthew 24:21, the term "tribulation" comes from the Greek word *thlipsis*, which means "to crush or place under great pressure"—as happens to grapes under a heavy millstone. Jesus' use of the word "great" before "tribulation" warns of just how severe this time will be.

During the great tribulation, humanity will be at its absolute worst. The corruption and depravity that abounds will reveal the shocking depths to which the human heart can descend. All the worst manifestations of wickedness throughout human history will pale by comparison.

So bad will the great tribulation be that it will appear as though the forces of darkness will never be defeated. But even with the antichrist at peak power and Satan bringing about the worst of deception and destruction, God will still be in control—and He will prevail in the end.

JESUS ON THE END
TIMES #7: OUR MISSION

*There will be great tribulation, such as has not been from the beginning
of the world until now, no, and never will be (Matthew 24:21).*

Scripture tells us the tribulation will last seven years. On the timeline of human history from start to finish, it will be a tiny dot at
the very end. But what an emphatic dot it will be!

When Jesus described the last half of this period, He said, "There
will be great tribulation, such as has not been from the beginning of the
world until now, no, and never will be" (Matthew 24:21). Absolutely
nothing in mankind's past compares to what will happen during earth's
final days. Note our Lord's triple use of negatives here—*not, no, never.*
Things will get bad—worse than we can ever imagine.

It's not easy to read about the tsunami of wickedness that will drown
the world and the cascade of divine judgments that will come in response.
But God gave an abundance of details about what is to come. Clearly,
He intended for us to know what will happen.

Why is this? God surely has His reasons, and we can safely guess
these are among them: (1) He wants us to know that in the end, evil
will be defeated and righteousness will prevail. (2) He wants to affirm
His sovereignty over all things and the futility of rebelling against Him.
(3) He wants the warnings about the future to stir within us a sense of
urgency for sharing the gospel with unbelievers.

The knowledge of God's coming judgment should spur us to stay
focused on His final command: "Go therefore and make disciples of all
nations" (Matthew 28:19). We're to point the unsaved to Him while
there is still time. The cataclysmic events of the future are meant to evoke
compassion in our hearts today.

The tribulation is a reminder that we've been given a mission. May
we stay on task!

JESUS ON THE END TIMES #8:
HIS GLORIOUS RETURN

They will see the Son of Man coming on the clouds of
heaven with power and great glory (Matthew 24:30).

A t Christ's first coming, very few people realized who He was. He arrived quietly, without fanfare. Tragically, many were not ready for Him, and "did not receive him" (John 1:11).

Yet when Christ returns, people will recognize Him instantly. No one will miss His grand appearance—"every eye will see him" (Revelation 1:7). In fact, at the end of the tribulation, all the heavenly bodies that give or reflect light will go dark (Matthew 24:29). Christ and His great glory will be the source of illumination. It will be impossible to miss Him!

However, just as happened at Jesus' first coming, there will be many who are not ready for Him. That's why, in the latter verses of Matthew 24 and all of chapter 25, our Lord repeatedly calls for people to keep watch and be ready. Sadly, even with these warnings, and even after the many judgments poured out during the tribulation, people will still be unprepared. And their fate will be sealed.

When the King of kings and Lord of lords returns, He will radiate with brilliant splendor and majesty. He will come "on the clouds of heaven with power and great glory." This will be a truly awesome and spectacular event. Every saint, angel, and creature in heaven and all believers on earth who survive to the end of the tribulation will burst forth with rejoicing.

The King is coming. We will be with Him, "arrayed in fine linen, white and pure…following him on white horses" (Revelation 19:14). Together with the angels, we will witness that incredible moment when He "will sit on his glorious throne" (Matthew 25:31). When Christ comes, we will see, with our own eyes, the fullness of His sovereign authority on display over all His creation. And our hearts will be filled to overflowing with endless praise.

JESUS ON THE END TIMES #9:
REACTIONS TO HIS RETURN

All the tribes of the earth will mourn (Matthew 24:30).

When they look on me, on him whom they have pierced,
they shall mourn for him (Zechariah 12:10).

U p until now, the high point of all human history has been Christ's crucifixion and resurrection. If it were not for our Lord's victory over sin and death, the destiny of every person who ever lived would be the same. Heaven would be empty, and hell would be full.

Christ's second coming will mark the peak—and the end—of human history. In that moment, the kingdom of the world will "become the kingdom of our Lord and of his Christ, and he shall reign forever and ever" (Revelation 11:15). When that happens, there will be three reactions from those still alive on planet Earth.

The rejoicing of believers. Those who become Christians during the tribulation will have instant death sentences put upon them by the antichrist. Few will survive. Imagine their relief when Christ returns and destroys the antichrist!

The mourning of the unrepentant world. When Christ comes, "all the tribes of the earth will mourn" (Matthew 24:30). Those who rebelled against God during the tribulation will mourn not out of regret, but because they will now face judgment and the consequences of their sin.

The mourning of repentant Jews. When Christ returns, those Jews who cry out to God for deliverance from the antichrist's persecution will finally realize Jesus is their Messiah. They will mourn with a genuine sorrow that leads to repentance (Zechariah 12:10). This is the great moment Paul wrote of when he said, "All Israel will be saved" (Romans 11:26). At the second coming, the descendants of Abraham will come full circle and embrace the one they rejected at His first coming. In bringing about this miracle, God will prove His faithfulness to His people.

JESUS ON THE END TIMES #10: KEEP WATCH

Keep watch (Matthew 24:42; 25:13 NIV).

When Jesus taught about the end times and His return in Matthew 24–25, the disciples clung to every word. They were eager to know the signs that would precede the arrival of His kingdom. They couldn't wait for Jesus to conquer their oppressive Roman rulers and return Israel to her former glory. But in their preoccupation to know the signs, did the disciples overlook what Jesus emphasized most in His message?

Many people today are equally eager to know the signs, yet they overlook the fact Jesus spent much of His time making this simple point: Be ready. That's the theme of portions of Matthew 24 and all of Matthew 25. In the latter chapter, when Jesus taught the parable of the ten virgins, the parable of the talents, and warned about end-times judgment, He was saying, "Be on high alert for my arrival. If you're not ready, you'll face consequences."

Note also these repeated commands from Jesus in Matthew 24 and 25:

- "*Keep watch*, because you do not know on what day your Lord will come" (24:42 NIV).
- "*Be ready*...the Son of Man will come...when you do not expect him" (verse 44 NIV).
- "*Keep watch*, because you do not know the day or the hour" (Matthew 25:13 NIV).

The phrases "keep watch" and "be ready" are calls for us to live with *continual expectancy*. Though these commands are directed to those on earth during the tribulation in anticipation of the second coming, we who are waiting for the rapture should heed them too.

Every believer should be ready for Christ—whether before the rapture or the second coming. This requires that we be familiar with what the Bible teaches about the end times. When we are aware and alert, we'll be motivated to readiness. Scripture even promises that the Lord will reward "the crown of righteousness...to all who have loved his appearing" (2 Timothy 4:8).

JESUS ON THE END TIMES #11:
SHEEP AND GOATS JUDGMENT

He will separate them from one another, just as the shepherd
separates the sheep from the goats (Matthew 25:32 NASB).

Many people hold to the common misperception that everyone who has ever lived will be judged at the same time. They envision every person standing before God's throne, awaiting His verdict.

But the Bible informs us there will be multiple judgments. All church-age Christians will be taken up to heaven at the rapture—first dead believers, then those who are alive. While the tribulation is taking place on earth, we will come before Christ's judgment seat in heaven. Because Jesus has already taken God's wrath on our behalf, our salvation is secure, and our judgment has to do with rewards. As 1 Corinthians 3:11-15 says, our works will be tested by fire, and we will be given rewards—or deprived of them—based on our service to Christ.

At the end of the tribulation, Christ will return and judge all who are still alive on earth. The sheep, or believers, will be ushered directly into His millennial kingdom. The goats, or unbelievers, will be sent away into eternal punishment (Matthew 25:31-46). This judgment will involve *only* those who survive to the end of this seven-year period of God's wrath.

All other unbelievers from throughout history will not be resurrected for judgment until 1,000 years later, at the end of Christ's millennial kingdom. They will face the Lord at what is known as the great white throne judgment (Revelation 20:11-12). Only unbelievers will be present, and the fate of every single one will be the lake of fire.

As a Christian, are you anxious about giving an account of your service to the Lord? Remember the depth of His love for you, which cannot be broken and is everlasting. Such great love calls for grateful love in return, which is expressed through wholehearted service to Him. As you serve Christ with gladness, you'll want to give your best, which will be well rewarded.

THE FIRST PROMISE OF
THE RAPTURE, PART 1

*Let not your hearts be troubled. Believe in
God; believe also in me (John 14:1).*

The disciples were at a total loss. Earlier that week, Jesus had entered Jerusalem surrounded by huge crowds welcoming Him and saying, "Hosanna to the Son of David! Blessed is he who comes in the name of the Lord! Hosanna in the highest!" For the people to call Jesus the Son of David was to recognize Him as Messiah and King. At the time, the disciples' excitement had reached fever pitch. *Surely the Lord is about to overthrow our Roman oppressors and set up His kingdom*, they thought. They had assumed Jesus was on the verge of taking His rightful place on the throne of David and establishing His sovereignty over all the earth.

But now, as they sat together observing Passover in the upper room, Jesus had told them He was about to be betrayed, and He would soon leave them: "Little children, yet a little while I am with you. You will seek me, and just as I said to the Jews, so now I also say to you, 'Where I am going you cannot come'" (John 13:33). Shortly before that, Jesus had told the disciples He would soon be put to death.

None of this fit with the disciples' expectations. If He was the Messiah, why did He have to die? What was this about Him being with them for only a little while longer? Was their Lord about to abandon them?

In response to their fear and inner turmoil, our Lord gently urged, "Let not your hearts be troubled. Believe in God; believe also in me." With tenderness and compassion, Jesus told them that in the same way they could trust God, they could trust Him. As their faith wavered, Jesus told them a promise that He wanted them to cling to for the rest of their lives—a promise we can cling to as well: This separation would be temporary!

THE FIRST PROMISE OF
THE RAPTURE, PART 2

*In my Father's house are many rooms. If it were not so, would I have
told you that I go to prepare a place for you?...I will come again and
will take you to myself, that where I am you may be also (John 14:2-3).*

J esus knew exactly what His beloved disciples needed to hear in this
moment of great distress. They were filled with grief over the news
that He would soon leave them. Like the news of His upcoming death,
this did not fit in with their expectations. They still didn't understand
what God's perfect plan of salvation required of Jesus.

As the Lord sought to comfort the disciples, He immediately assured
them that their separation from Him would be temporary. "In my Father's
house are many rooms...I go to prepare a place for you." Then came this
promise: "I will come again and will take you to myself, that where I am
you may be also." There was coming a day when they would be reunited!

The personal nature of Jesus' promise is what makes it so powerful. Note the intimacy of His words. He made it clear He *wanted* to be
together with the disciples again. The fact He would spend their time
of separation "to prepare a place for you" revealed they would be on
His mind the entire time. And the assurance that He was coming again
made it clear He would follow through. They could count on it.

In Jesus' words "I will come again and will take you to myself," we
see His deep affection for His disciples—and for all His children, including us. We see His *initiative*—He is preparing heaven for us. We see His
eagerness—He will come again. And we see that *we* are the reason He
is coming. He longs for us to be *with* Him, never to be separated again.

THE FIRST PROMISE OF
THE RAPTURE, PART 3

*I will come again and will take you to myself, that
where I am you may be also (John 14:3).*

The disciples still hadn't figured it all out yet. When Jesus gave His promise that He would come again and they would be reunited with Him, He was saying, "Trust Me." That's all He was asking them to comprehend at the time. God's divine plan would continue to unfold exactly as it should, and they were still very much a part of it, even though that didn't seem to be the case.

In John 14:1-3, for the first time, Jesus reveals the promise of a rapture—a catching up of all believers in the air to meet Him. This promise of His coming is not to be confused with His future return to the earth in judgment and to set up His kingdom. In John 14:1-3, Jesus does not say He will come all the way to the earth. Instead, He will take His own up to Himself. He makes it clear that together, our immediate destination will be the Father's house, or heaven, and we will dwell there together. The rapture is only the first phase of Christ's return. Not until the second phase will our Lord descend all the way to earth—along with us!—to conquer His enemies and establish His earthly throne.

Jesus' promise in John 14:1-3 lines up with Paul's teaching in 1 Thessalonians 4:13-18, which is clearly a rapture passage. There, Paul wrote that at the appointed moment, "the dead in Christ will rise first. Then we who are alive...will be caught up together with them in the clouds to meet the Lord in the air, and so we will always be with the Lord" (verses 16-17). This meeting will take place *in the air*, after which we will *always* be with our Lord.

According to Romans 8:35-39, *nothing* can separate us from the love of Christ. If we die before the rapture, we will be "at home with the Lord" (2 Corinthians 5:8). And if we're still alive at the rapture, we will be taken up to His presence instantly. Either way, we are with Him!

A WARNING FOLLOWED
BY A PROMISE

*In the world you will have tribulation. But take
heart; I have overcome the world (John 16:33).*

Little did the disciples know that soon, their lives would be turned
upside down. Never could they have envisioned the horror of what
Jesus was about to face. Nor did they anticipate their fear would cause
them to abandon Him. The Lord they loved would soon be crucified, and
the persecution they were about to face would be intense for a long time
to come. They would face threats against their lives and imprisonment.

It was in this dark hour that our Lord said to the disciples: "In the
world you will have tribulation. But take heart; I have overcome the
world" (John 16:33).

Jesus' warning and promise in John 16:33 apply to all believers today
as well. Because of our beliefs, we are at odds with the world. We're misunderstood, mocked, criticized, and wrongly accused. As we struggle
with such opposition, we're reminded of Jesus' words, "You will have
tribulation." But we also need to remember the second half of what Jesus
said: "Take heart; I have overcome the world."

After the crucifixion, the disciples hid behind locked doors, fearing that those who put Jesus to death would come after them next.
But when the risen Christ appeared to them, they were radically transformed—they became men of great courage. A short time later, when
Peter and John were arrested, they unashamedly proclaimed the gospel
to their captors, who "saw the boldness of Peter and John, and...were
astonished" (Acts 4:13).

When opposition arises, we can respond with supernatural boldness.
We can take courage in the truth that yes, Christ *has* overcome the world.
We have no reason to be afraid. Our "faith and hope are in God" (1 Peter
1:21), who protects us and has already won the victory.

NOTHING HAPPENS OUTSIDE
OF GOD'S SOVEREIGNTY

You would have no authority over me at all unless it
had been given you from above (John 19:11).

I s God truly sovereign over all things? Sometimes we may find ourselves asking that question because events happen in ways that make
it appear God isn't always in control.

But Scripture makes it clear that God's sovereignty is total. We find
a powerful affirmation of this in John 19:10-11.

In a dramatic exchange that took place between Pontius Pilate and the
Lord Jesus Christ, we see man's authority stand face to face with God's
authority. Pilate said, "Do you not know that I have authority to release
you and authority to crucify you?" And Jesus responded, "You would
have no authority over me at all unless it had been *given you from above.*"

This reveals that even Pilate's power to condemn God's Son to death
was not outside the sovereignty of God. Even in the crucifixion, God
was supremely in control. In Acts 2:23, we read that Jesus was "delivered
up according to the definite plan and foreknowledge of God." The fact
that God's authority supersedes man's at all times is confirmed by the
end result of Christ's death and resurrection. Paul wrote in 1 Corinthians 15 that "death is swallowed up in victory…Thanks be to God, who
gives us the victory through our Lord Jesus Christ."

We will have times when we struggle because people act in ways that
make it appear as though God isn't sovereign. We will wonder why God
permits evil to go seemingly unchecked. We may not understand why
God allows certain things to happen, but Scripture repeatedly confirms
that what people mean for evil, God can use for good (Genesis 50:20).
Nothing can happen apart from God's sovereignty. Though we might
not see God's sovereign design evident in a situation, we can know it is
present and will prevail.

JESUS, THE BRIDGE BUILDER

Let us not tear it, but cast lots for it to see whose it shall be (John 19:24).

What's amazing about many Bible prophecies is that even the smallest details within them are rich with meaningful truths. This is true about Psalm 22:18, where King David prophesied, "They divide my garments among them, and for my clothing they cast lots." At first glance, this might seem a minor subplot in the epic drama that is the crucifixion. But it's not.

John 19:23 says, "When the soldiers had crucified Jesus, they took his garments and divided them into four parts, one part for each soldier; also his tunic." Typically, four soldiers were assigned to crucifixion detail. Jesus evidently had five articles of clothing, four of which were divided evenly. The fifth item was a seamless tunic, which led the soldiers to say, "Let us not tear it, but cast lots for it."

Here is what's significant about the seamless tunic: it was the garment worn by Israel's high priest. When the soldiers gambled for Jesus' tunic, they called attention to the fact Jesus was the perfect and final high priest who offered Himself as the sacrifice who could pay for our sins, once and for all. Hebrews 4:14 calls Jesus our "great high priest," and Hebrews 10:14 says that "by a single offering he has perfected for all time those who are being sanctified."

In the Old Testament, the high priest was a mediator between God and people. In Jesus, we have a high priest who is the ultimate mediator. The Latin word for priest, which is *pontifex*, is informative here. It means "bridge builder." A priest's primary duty was to serve as a bridge between God and people.

At the cross, Jesus built a bridge that spanned the uncrossable chasm between God and mankind. He wore the garment of a high priest and fulfilled the duty of a high priest. A selfish deed by unbelieving soldiers was used to fulfill a seemingly minor yet very important prophecy.

A PROPHECY FROM THE CROSS

Truly, I say to you, today you will be with me in paradise (Luke 23:43).

One of the most profound—and unexpected—professions of saving faith in the entire Bible came from the repentant thief who was crucified next to Jesus.

As the thief hung in agony, he cried out, "Jesus, remember me when you come into your kingdom" (Luke 23:42). Moments earlier, he had heard Jesus say, "Father, forgive them for they know not what they do" (verse 34). The thief, fully aware that he was "receiving the due reward" of his deeds, wanted this forgiveness (verse 41).

A close look at the thief's words reveals an amazing depth of belief packed into them. His plea "Remember me when you come into your kingdom" shows he believed Jesus was the promised Messiah who would someday rule over a kingdom, as stated in many Old Testament prophecies. It also shows he believed Jesus would rise from the dead, for no one survived a crucifixion. Surely he had heard the news about the recent resurrection of Lazarus, which confirmed Jesus' power over death.

Jesus knew this man's repentance was genuine. "Truly, I say to you, today you will be with me in paradise," He said. That word "truly" is significant for two reasons: It emphasizes that even a person who seems unworthy of salvation can receive forgiveness. And it reinforces the truth that the moment we die, spiritually, we are immediately taken into the Lord's presence. When we are "away from the body," we are "at home with the Lord" (2 Corinthians 5:8).

From the cross, Jesus forgave a thief and gave powerful words of comfort to someone about to die: You will be in my presence immediately. He replaced the fear of death with the promise of life—in His presence! That same promise is true for every one of us who has placed our faith in Christ. Death is not the end, but is the entrance to life forever with our Lord.

A PERFECT STORM

*There was darkness over all the land until
the ninth hour (Matthew 27:45).*

At the cross, Satan and humanity gave their worst. And God gave His best. On the hill where Jesus died, a perfect storm took place between the hatred of Satan, the hostility of mankind, and the love of God.

The hatred of Satan. In Genesis 3:15, the first messianic prophecy in the Bible, God said there would be enmity between Satan and Jesus. He said that the serpent would bruise the heel of the woman's offspring. All through the Old Testament, Satan tried to destroy Israel so the Messiah couldn't be born. After Jesus' birth, Satan did all he could to keep Jesus from fulfilling His mission. And at the cross, Satan poured out all his fury, knowing it was his last chance.

The hostility of mankind. Romans 5:10 tells us that before salvation, we were enemies of God. Hebrews 12:3 describes the intense opposition and hostility Jesus faced from sinners. It was this hostility that shouted, "Crucify, crucify Him!"

The love of God. Isaiah 53:10 (NASB) says, "The LORD desired to crush Him, causing Him grief." He was pleased to send Jesus to die because it would bring salvation to the lost.

At the cross, God poured out all His love, overruling both Satan and humanity. He took the ultimate act of evil and turned it around into the ultimate act of good. Supreme wretchedness and supreme love clashed in a perfect storm, and God won out.

God's victory at the cross is the ultimate confirmation of His sovereignty. This was peak evil defeated by peak righteousness. Whenever we find ourselves affected by evil and we wonder whether God can ultimately use the situation for His good purposes, we need only to look to the cross. If God could overrule the magnitude of hatred and hostility hurled against Him there, He can overrule them anywhere.

JESUS CONNECTS THE DOTS, PART 1

He interpreted to them in all the Scriptures the
things concerning himself (Luke 24:27).

Shortly after His death and resurrection, Jesus appeared to two of
His followers on the road to Emmaus. They were sad, and at first,
they didn't recognize Him. When Jesus asked what they were talking
about, they said, "Are you the only visitor to Jerusalem who does not
know the things that have happened there in these days?" (Luke 24:18).

"What things?" Jesus asked.

"Concerning Jesus of Nazareth," they replied. "Our chief priests and
rulers delivered him up to be condemned to death, and crucified him.
But we had hoped that he was the one to redeem Israel" (verses 19-21).

These two men were struggling with doubt. They were sad because
Jesus had been crucified. They weren't sure how to respond to the news
they had just heard about His empty grave. Was it possible He wasn't
the Messiah after all?

"Oh foolish ones," said Jesus. "Was it not necessary that the Christ
should suffer these things and enter into his glory?" Then "beginning
with Moses and all the Prophets, [Jesus] interpreted to them in all the
Scriptures the things concerning himself" (verses 25-27).

Jesus took them through God's Word and connected all the dots
between the Old Testament prophecies about Him and how He fulfilled them. In this way, He built an irrefutable case for the fact that He
was the very redeemer they had been waiting for.

Their eyes were opened—and they were amazed. Then Jesus vanished. The two men immediately went to Jerusalem to find Jesus' disciples. They declared, "The Lord has risen indeed!" The many prophecies
Christ had fulfilled convinced them of this truth.

JESUS CONNECTS THE DOTS, PART 2

Everything written about me in the Law of Moses and the
Prophets and the Psalms must be fulfilled (Luke 24:44).

After appearing to the two men on the way to Emmaus, Jesus next
visited the 11 disciples. He told them, "Everything written about
me in the Law of Moses and the Prophets and the Psalms must be fulfilled." Then "He opened their minds to understand the Scriptures"
(Luke 24:44-45).

Once again, Jesus confirmed all that the prophets had said about
Him. He connected the dots. He explained how He had fulfilled everything the Scriptures said He would do.

In two separate encounters, when Jesus wanted to prove His identity, He did so by appealing to Bible prophecy. In this way, He was saying, "Here are my credentials. Here is the proof I really am your Messiah.
Here is the evidence I am your Savior and Lord."

Jesus so perfectly fulfilled every single prophecy about His first coming that there was only one possible conclusion: He was the Savior, Messiah, and Lord predicted in the Law, the Prophets, and the Psalms—all
three major parts of the Old Testament.

When Jesus declared, "Everything written about me...must be fulfilled," He did two things: He confirmed His identity as the long-awaited
Savior in His first coming, and He stated the absolute certainty that all
the remaining prophecies about Him would go on to be fulfilled. He
had accomplished all that the prophets had said He would do up to this
point, and He will fulfill all the future prophecies about Him.

Are the claims Scripture makes about Jesus credible? Hundreds of
fulfilled prophecies shout, "Yes!" Jesus Himself appealed to those very
prophecies as trustworthy evidence. Fulfilled prophecy serves as proof
that He is the Messiah and that our faith is built on a strong foundation that can be trusted. Jesus really is who He says He is!

WAIT, ANTICIPATE, AND TRUST

Lord, will you at this time restore the kingdom to Israel? (Acts 1:6).

On that final Sunday when Jesus entered Jerusalem prior to His death, the crowds shouted, "Hosanna to the Son of David!" (Matthew 21:9). They acknowledged He was King and Messiah. This led the disciples to think Jesus was about to set up His kingdom and rule on David's throne.

That's why, later that week, the disciples asked Jesus, "What will be the sign of your coming and of the end of the age?" (Matthew 24:3). They thought the time for His earthly kingdom had arrived. Instead, a few days later, Jesus was put to death on a cross. The disciples hadn't expected this. They were sad and confused. Later, when the risen Lord appeared to them, "they were startled and frightened and thought they saw a spirit" (Luke 24:37).

Then Jesus "opened their minds to understand the Scriptures" (verse 45). He explained "everything written about [Him] in the Law of Moses and the Prophets and the Psalms" (verse 44). At last, they realized Jesus had done exactly what Bible prophecy had said He would do. Finally, they understood—to a point. They still didn't realize it was not yet time for Christ to set up His kingdom. That's why, when Jesus prepared to ascend to heaven, they asked, "Lord, will you at this time restore the kingdom to Israel?" Jesus said no, but didn't rebuke their anticipation of a literal kingdom. Their expectation was correct! Only their guess about the timing wasn't.

When Jesus said, "It is not for you to know times or seasons that the Father has fixed by his own authority" (Acts 1:7), He affirmed three great truths: First, His kingdom *will* come—we just don't know when. Second, because we don't know when, we should always be ready. Third, though we should never try to guess the *when* of His coming, we can know God's timing will be perfect. We are called to wait, anticipate, and trust. As we do so, we will find ourselves motivated to make every moment count and minister to others while there is still time.

JESUS' FINAL PROPHECY ON EARTH

You will receive power when the Holy Spirit has come upon you (Acts 1:8).

If the disciples had been in charge of Jesus' plans for the future, they would have skipped the church age entirely and gone directly to setting up Christ's earthly kingdom. Because He had risen from the grave, they assumed it was time for Him to ascend David's throne and rule the world. They asked, "Lord, will you at this time restore the kingdom to Israel?" (Acts 1:6).

But Jesus had better plans. Far better. It wasn't time to bring His kingdom to earth—not yet. Rather, it was time to fill His kingdom with more people. Before He departed for heaven, He proclaimed one last prophecy meant not only for the disciples, but for every believer since, including us: "You will receive power when the Holy Spirit has come upon you, and you will be my witnesses in Jerusalem and in all Judea and Samaria, and to the end of the earth" (Acts 1:8).

The presence of the Spirit within every believer is among God's greatest miracles. It is the Spirit within us who supernaturally enables us to proclaim the gospel for the purpose of adding people to Christ's kingdom. As Christians, we have been given the honor of taking part in the greatest construction project ever during this time in history: building Christ's church!

It is the Spirit who enables the building of the church (Ephesians 2:21-22), convicts people of sin (John 16:7-9), transforms believers into the image of Christ (2 Corinthians 3:18), and guides and teaches them in all truth (John 14:26; 16:13). He supernaturally brings about new life (John 3:3-7; Titus 3:5), baptizes us into the body of Christ (1 Corinthians 12:13), and indwells us and empowers us for service (Romans 8:9; 1 Corinthians 12:4-11). How amazing that the Spirit does all this in and through us!

Not only do we have the privilege of living in Christ's future kingdom, but of helping to fill it. This gives us great purpose. May this be our passion and joy as we are active till He returns!

THE POWER OF PROPHECY
WHEN SHARING THE GOSPEL

[David] foresaw and spoke about the
resurrection of the Christ (Acts 2:31).

On the road to Emmaus, Jesus explained to His followers how the messianic prophecies in the Old Testament all pointed to Him. He connected the dots between the prophecies and Himself. All this served as confirmation that He was their Savior, Messiah, and Lord.

So powerful was the evidence of fulfilled prophecy that from then onward, the disciples also appealed to it when they preached the gospel. On the day of Pentecost, Peter quoted a prophecy from King David in a sermon that led 3,000 people to salvation: "I saw the Lord always before me, for he is at my right hand that I may not be shaken; therefore my heart was glad, and my tongue rejoiced; my flesh also will dwell in hope. For you will not abandon my soul to Hades, or let your Holy One see corruption. You have made known to me the paths of life; you will make me full of gladness with your presence" (Acts 2:25-28). Peter then explained that in these words, David "foresaw and spoke about the resurrection of the Christ" (verse 31).

Jesus Himself is our example for turning to fulfilled Bible prophecies as a means of proving He truly is Savior and Lord. His companions on the road to Emmaus picked up on that, and from the day the church was born, fulfilled prophecies have had an important role in helping people to realize and confirm Christ's identity.

While it is the gospel alone that has the power to save (Romans 1:16), we can reason with people from all the Scriptures, as God did with the people of Judah in Isaiah 1:18: "Come now, let us reason together." The context here speaks of settling a dispute. When it comes to settling differences of opinion about Jesus' identity and people's need for a Savior, the Bible is our most powerful ally—and that includes fulfilled prophecies. Knowing these prophecies and their fulfillments can serve as valuable reinforcements when we share the gospel with others.

HOW PROPHECY
CONFIRMS THE GOSPEL

...in accordance with the Scriptures (1 Corinthians 15:3-4).

How do we know the gospel message is trustworthy? Before we can answer that, first we must ask: What *is* the gospel? A simple definition is this: It's the good news of salvation made available to those who put their faith in Christ.

The apostle Paul gave a wonderful summary of the gospel in 1 Corinthians 15:3-4: "Christ died for our sins in accordance with the Scriptures...he was buried...he was raised on the third day in accordance with the Scriptures." Here, we can see in outline form that the gospel includes these four points: (1) All people are sinners; (2) Christ is the Savior; (3) Christ died in our place and paid the penalty for our sins; (4) Christ rose and defeated death.

As Paul presented these core truths of the gospel, notice what he said not once, but twice: "in accordance with the Scriptures."

What "Scriptures" was Paul talking about? The Old Testament prophecies that declared what Christ would do at His first coming.

When Paul stood on trial before King Agrippa, he shared about how he had become saved. Then he said, "I stand here testifying both to small and great, saying nothing but what the prophets and Moses said would come to pass" (Acts 26:22). *Nothing but what the prophets and Moses said would come to pass!* And what was that? "The Christ must suffer," and He would be "the first to rise from the dead" (verse 23).

The gospel wasn't something new. It had already been proclaimed by the Old Testament prophets many times: Jesus was ordained to die for our sins. By rising from the grave, He conquered death. This made salvation possible. Every single prophecy that proclaimed these truths came to pass, exactly as foretold by the prophets. That is why the gospel can be trusted!

THE MYSTERY OF THE RAPTURE

*Behold! I tell you a mystery. We shall not all sleep, but
we shall all be changed (1 Corinthians 15:51).*

First Corinthians chapter 15 presents one of the grandest themes in all the New Testament letters: the hope we possess because of Christ's resurrection. Because Christ rose from the dead, we too will rise from the dead. As 2 Corinthians 4:14 so wonderfully proclaims, "He who raised the Lord Jesus will raise us also with Jesus." Christ's resurrection guarantees ours.

All through 1 Corinthians 15, Paul presents one powerful truth after another. He explains the proof of the resurrection (verses 4-8), why it's essential to our faith (verses 12-19), the order of the resurrections (verses 20-28), and the nature of the resurrection body (verses 35-50). Then the chapter comes to a climax when he writes, "Behold! I tell you a mystery."

"Behold!" alerts us that Paul wants our attention. "Here is something important!" he exclaims. What is it? He continues, "I tell you a mystery." In the New Testament, a mystery refers to a truth previously hidden and now revealed. What is this truth? Not all believers must die to receive their resurrection bodies. Those who are alive at the rapture will receive their changed bodies instantaneously! A moment ago in verse 50, Paul had said that the perishable (our present bodies) cannot inherit the imperishable (our glorified bodies). But that won't hinder God at the rapture. By God's power, we will be miraculously transformed.

All who are taken up at the rapture will experience one of God's most astounding miracles. The corrupt and mortal bodies of millions of believers will instantly become perfect and immortal. Imagine the power required to make this happen. Some find it hard to believe God could do a miracle of this magnitude. Because God is all-powerful, He can, and He will. "With man it is impossible, but not with God. For all things are possible with God" (Mark 10:27).

THE SWIFTNESS OF THE RAPTURE

In a moment, in the twinkling of an eye, at the
last trumpet (1 Corinthians 15:52).

Every single statement that Scripture makes about the rapture reveals this will be an astounding event. Every aspect of what will happen challenges our imagination. Through the rapture, God's power will be displayed on a scale that we cannot fathom. Consider the greatness of what happened at creation: All God had to do was speak, and a magnificent, complex, and intricate universe was born. At the rapture, God will put His powers of creation to work again, transforming millions of corrupt and mortal bodies into incorrupt and immortal ones.

The enormity of what God will do to us when we go from *before* to *after* is astounding. Also breathtaking is the fact this change will take place instantly. We are told it will occur "in a moment, in the twinkling of an eye." The language Scripture uses here is colorful and captivating. The rapture will not only demonstrate the magnitude of God's power, but how swiftly He is able to express it.

The word translated "moment" comes from the Greek term *atomos*, which gives us the English word *atom*. It speaks of a span of time so small it cannot be divided. "The twinkling of an eye" refers to how quickly the eye can move—it has the fastest muscles in the body.

Our change will be instantaneous. In the briefest amount of time possible, our earthly bodies will become heavenly bodies. So quickly will we be changed that we won't even be aware of it until after it has already taken place.

In the twinkling of an eye, we will depart earth and enter heaven. One moment we will be mortal, then in the next, we will be immortal. The best part? We will *stay* immortal forever—and live in the presence of the one who made our transformation possible.

THE RESULT OF THE RAPTURE

This perishable body must put on the imperishable, and this
mortal body must put on immortality (1 Corinthians 15:53).

As finite and fallen creatures, we are unable to comprehend just how much of a transformation we will experience when we are resurrected in the rapture. From birth, we are trapped in fleshly bodies that are enslaved to sin. Our bent is to rebel against God, not seek Him. And the effects of sin have left us in a damaged world filled with strife, disappointment, hurt, and pain. All of this impairs our ability to understand the greatness of what is to come.

Scripture gives us a glimpse of just how big a change will occur at the rapture, and it's mind-boggling. Here's what we know:

We will go from perishable to imperishable. Due to the corrupting effects of sin, our bodies are subject to aging, decay, and death. At the rapture, we will be given a body that never ages, never decays, and never dies. No longer will our days come to an end; they will be endless!

We will go from mortal to immortal. Scripture describes our earthly bodies as temporary tents (2 Corinthians 5:1, 4). At the rapture, we will be given permanent heavenly bodies. We will experience a total makeover!

Paul was so excited by these truths that he exclaimed, "Death [will be] swallowed up in victory" (1 Corinthians 15:54). In this statement about our bodily resurrection, Paul was quoting a prophecy in Isaiah 25:8: "He will swallow up death forever."

At the rapture, we will experience a spectacular change. Every imperfection our bodies know here on earth will disappear. Our new bodies will be perfect and eternal, enabling us to live in heaven and dwell with God forever. That is why every Bible passage that speaks about the rapture radiates with so much hope!

THE VICTORY OF THE RAPTURE

When the perishable puts on the imperishable, and the mortal puts on immortality, then shall come to pass the saying that is written: "Death is swallowed up in victory" (1 Corinthians 15:54).

While no two people experience the exact same struggles and trials that come with living in a fallen and sin-cursed world, there is one common and dreaded enemy that every single person throughout history has had to face: death.

Death is often called the great equalizer. There is nothing we can do to avoid it. In our younger years, we usually don't give much thought to our mortality. But as we age, we become more mindful of the fact we won't live forever. We grapple with the sobering reality that, apart from Christ, death brings a cold, hard end to all the wonders that are associated with being alive.

For unbelievers, a fear of death is understandable because of their uncertainty about what happens beyond the grave. But for believers, there is no reason for fear because of the certainty of our future destiny. The resurrection of Christ has given us the absolute assurance that we, too, will be resurrected. So certain is our future that we can proclaim, "Death is swallowed up in victory." Because Christ has conquered death, we who are in Christ will conquer it as well!

As believers, physical death brings us spiritually into the presence of Christ (2 Corinthians 5:8), while our bodies are put to rest in a grave. At the rapture, whatever remains of our perishable beings will be raised and made imperishable. Those of us who are still alive when the rapture happens will experience this same miracle and put on immortality. For this reason, we can all proclaim, "Thanks be to God, who gives us the victory through our Lord Jesus Christ" (1 Corinthians 15:57).

A COMPLETE AND FOREVER VICTORY

Death is swallowed up in victory (1 Corinthians 15:54).

Apart from Christ, death reigns over mankind. There is no avoiding it. As Romans 6:23 says, "The wages of sin is death." Romans 5:12 further informs us, "Sin came into the world through one man, and death through sin, and so death spread to all men because all sinned." Adam's transgression against God plunged the entire human race into sin against God. In case anyone should attempt to argue that they are exempt from the sin nature, the apostle Paul wrote, "None is righteous, no, not one...no one seeks for God. All have turned aside...no one does good, not even one" (Romans 3:10-12).

Where there is sin, there is death. And because all have sinned, all must die. Only with the removal of sin can death be removed. That's exactly what God made possible through what Christ accomplished at the cross—the removal of sin. Second Corinthians 5:21 explains this glorious truth in these words: "[God] made him to be sin who knew no sin, so that in him we might become the righteousness of God."

Because of the cross, we can be cleansed of our unrighteousness. While we must still face death physically, it no longer has power over us. Christ has defeated death—so much so that it is not we who die, but death that dies! On the other side of the grave, a glorious future awaits us—one that is securely ours and cannot be taken away.

"Death is swallowed up in victory" is among the most triumphant statements in Scripture. In swallowing up death, Christ has given us a complete and eternal victory. For the believer, death's effects have been entirely extinguished.

Swallowed up in victory—what powerful imagery! In these picturesque words, Paul conveys the totality of Christ's triumph on our behalf.

GREAT TRUTHS ABOUT THE RAPTURE #1: DON'T BE IGNORANT

We do not want you to be uninformed, brothers, about
those who are asleep, that you may not grieve as others
do, who have no hope (1 Thessalonians 4:13).

We do not want you to be uninformed" are the opening words to the most detailed New Testament passage about the rapture. With this declaration, the apostle Paul alerts us he is about to address an important subject—so much so, that he says it's not good for believers to be ignorant about it.

Some Christians today are dismissive toward end-time topics, saying they're not relevant. Yet Paul tells us we should be informed. And as we read the words that follow, we discover his instruction is not only doctrinal, but pastoral. He wants to bring comfort to brokenhearted Christians who had two concerns: First, because they were experiencing persecution (1 Thessalonians 3:3-4), they thought they had entered the tribulation and missed the rapture. And second, because some of their brothers and sisters in Christ had already died, they feared their deceased brethren would not be reunited with them at the rapture, but rather, at some later time.

For these reasons, Paul offers words of hope. As he does, he calls attention to a powerful difference between believers and unbelievers. Christians have no reason for sorrow because death immediately ushers us into Jesus' presence—our souls are "away from the body and at home with the Lord" (2 Corinthians 5:8). It is only our bodies that are asleep, awaiting the rapture, at which time our earthly vessels will instantly be raised up, glorified, and reunited with our souls (1 Corinthians 15:51-53). In contrast, for unbelievers, death brings inconsolable and permanent grief. There is no prospect of a happy reunion with loved ones.

God's purposes for informing us about the rapture are to fill us with comfort and anticipation. To be uninformed is to forego the hope meant to sustain and encourage us!

GREAT TRUTHS ABOUT THE RAPTURE #2: WE *WILL* BE RESURRECTED

Since we believe that Jesus died and rose again, even
so, through Jesus, God will bring with him those who
have fallen asleep (1 Thessalonians 4:14).

In these words, the apostle Paul declares an incredible truth: We know with absolute certainty that Christ was resurrected from the dead. And we can know with *equal* certainty that we, too, will be resurrected from the dead. Because Christ arose, we who are in Him will also arise.

Christ's resurrection was the turning point of all human history. Before the cross, mankind had no hope, no way of ever coming back into relationship with God. Christ's sacrifice—His atoning work—changed all that. With the resurrection, God the Father was saying, "Through My Son, the penalty for sin has been paid in full. The righteous demands of the law have been fulfilled." On the cross, God "made him to be sin who knew no sin, so that in him we might become the righteousness of God" (2 Corinthians 5:21). And because of the cross, when we place our belief in Christ as Savior and Lord, we are clothed in His righteousness, which permits us to enter God's presence. In Christ, we have been made acceptable to God.

For these reasons, we are thoroughly assured of our future resurrection!

At death, our soul immediately goes to be with the Lord, and our bodies return to the earth. Then in that great moment known as the rapture, we're told that "God will bring with him those who have fallen asleep" (1 Thessalonians 4:14).

With these very words, the Christians in Thessalonica must have wept tears of great joy. Just as they could have full confidence in Christ's resurrection, they could know their deceased fellow believers would be resurrected. In the rapture, God will bring their souls from heaven to be reunited with their bodies "to meet the Lord in the air" (1 Thessalonians 4:17). Then we who are still alive on earth will be taken up to join them. What a wonderful day that will be!

GREAT TRUTHS ABOUT THE RAPTURE #3: IT IS IMMINENT

We…who are left until the coming of the Lord, will not precede
those who have fallen asleep (1 Thessalonians 4:15).

In 1 Thessalonians 4:15, the little word "we" is loaded with meaning. But before we explore why, let's celebrate what Paul affirms here: *All* Christians from throughout the entire church age will participate in the rapture. No one will be left out!

Paul wrote this to encourage grieving believers in the church at Thessalonica. They feared either that they themselves had missed the rapture, or that their deceased fellow believers would. They thought they might not be immediately reunited with their loved ones at the rapture, and that those who had "fallen asleep" would miss it and thus end up being inferior in some way to those who were alive at the time of the rapture. But Paul put those worries to rest by saying *all* believers will be taken up. In fact, the dead in Christ will arise first!

Here's what is so important about the word "we": It reveals Paul believed the rapture could happen during his lifetime. He had taken to heart Christ's exhortation, "Keep watch, because you do not know on what day your Lord will come" (Matthew 24:42 NIV). That's why he admonished all believers to live with this mindset: "The hour has already come for you to wake up from your slumber, because our salvation is nearer now than when we first believed. The night is nearly over; the day is almost here" (Romans 13:11-12 NIV).

Scripture consistently affirms the rapture is imminent. Because we don't know when it will happen, we should live in full expectation of it at any time. Biblically, there are no events that must occur before the rapture; it is the next prophetic event on God's calendar.

Just as we shouldn't set dates for the rapture, we shouldn't assume it's in the far future. The possibility the rapture could occur at any time should profoundly influence how we live.

GREAT TRUTHS ABOUT THE RAPTURE #4: THE ORDER OF EVENTS

The Lord himself will descend from heaven with a cry of command, with the voice of an archangel, and with the sound of the trumpet of God. And the dead will rise first. Then we who are alive...will be caught up (1 Thessalonians 4:16-17).

Christians have always been fascinated about the rapture and wondered: *When will it take place, and how will it happen?*

Jesus Himself made it clear we cannot know the timing. Repeatedly in the New Testament, we're simply urged to live with a constant sense of expectation. But Paul does describe how the rapture will unfold. Here's the sequence:

Christ will descend from heaven with a shout of command. He will come from heaven, but not all the way to earth, as He does at the second coming. The rapture and return are two separate events. As He descends, He will shout with authority—just as He did when He declared, "Lazarus, come out." All He needs to do is speak, and all dead believers will arise.

The voice of an archangel will go forth. We're not told which archangel, but apparently this angel's voice will accompany or follow Christ's shout.

The trumpet of God will sound. This trumpet appears in 1 Corinthians 15:52, another rapture passage. This is not a trumpet of judgment; no rapture passage includes judgment in it. In Numbers 10:2, we see trumpets were sounded to gather God's people, as will happen here.

The dead in Christ will arise first. They will burst forth from their graves!

Then we who are alive will follow. The wonderful assurance that all dead and living believers will be taken up at the rapture is yet another affirmation that nothing—not even death—can separate us from the love Christ has for us! (Romans 8:38-39).

GREAT TRUTHS ABOUT THE RAPTURE #5:
AN INSTANT TRANSFORMATION

We…will be caught up together (1 Thessalonians 4:17).

The rapture of those who are dead and alive in Christ will be a miraculous event of colossal proportions. Imagine the extent of the power God will express as He suddenly empties the graves of many millions of deceased believers, snatches up millions more who are alive in Christ all over the globe, *and* gives all those people glorified bodies! When we wonder how God will make this happen, we need only to remember: "All things are possible with God" (Mark 10:27). This is the same God who, merely by speaking, called the entire universe into existence.

Some people wonder: Where does the word *rapture* come from? It's not in the Bible—is it scriptural? The answer is yes. In the original Greek text of the New Testament, the phrase "caught up" is the word *harpazo*. When Jerome translated the Bible into Latin around AD 400, the Greek *harpazo* became the Latin *raptus*—the origin of our English term *rapture*.

"Caught up" speaks of a strong, sudden, forceful act. In some other places where *harpazo* is used in the New Testament, here are the meanings:

- John 6:15—"take him by force"
- Acts 8:39—"suddenly took…away" (NIV), or "snatched" (NASB)
- Acts 23:10—"take him away…by force" for the purpose of rescue
- 2 Corinthians 12:2, 4—"caught up" to a new location

Our transformation from mortality to immortality will occur "in a moment, in the twinkling of an eye" (1 Corinthians 15:51-52). Remember, "moment" refers to a unit of time so small it cannot be divided. In a literal instant, God will resurrect the dead in Christ, rapture the living in Christ, *and* we all will be given imperishable bodies. How spectacular! May we marvel at God's inexhaustible power every time we think about the rapture!

GREAT TRUTHS ABOUT THE RAPTURE #6: WITH THE LORD FOREVER

...to meet the Lord in the air, and so we will always
be with the Lord (1 Thessalonians 4:17).

The rapture will be an incredible experience for us on so many levels: We will meet, for the first time, countless believers from ages past, including those we read about on the pages of the New Testament. We will be reunited with brothers and sisters in Christ who preceded us in death. We will see once again dear brethren from whom we were separated on earth by distance and circumstances. Our bodies will be unshackled of every earthly imperfection and we will experience complete heavenly perfection. And sweetest of all will be our first face-to-face encounter with the Lord Jesus Christ in the air.

Can you imagine the emotions you'll feel as you are brought into the presence of the one who made possible every wonderful benefit you know as a believer? At last, you will see the Lord Jesus Christ with your own eyes. Imagine the thrill! And your excitement will be accompanied by a deep humility that comes from recognizing you could never exalt Him enough for all He has done for you.

With the rapture, for the first time ever, our perception of Jesus will not be impaired by flesh-tainted lenses. How often have we underestimated Him, misjudged Him, made Him into someone He is not! We will see Him as He truly is; we will be stunned by how infinitely glorious and perfect and majestic He is.

Scripture says that from the moment of the rapture onward, "we will always be with the Lord." Never again will we be separated. The promises "I am with you always" and "I will never leave you nor forsake you" took effect at the moment of salvation. We are already secure. Now we are waiting to enter His presence. How marvelous that day will be!

GREAT TRUTHS ABOUT THE RAPTURE #7: A SOURCE OF HOPE

Encourage one another with these words (1 Thessalonians 4:18).

Every rich truth that Paul proclaims about the rapture in 1 Thessalonians 4:13-18 is meant to encourage us. God wants us to know about the rapture so that we look forward to it with hope.

While it's natural for us to be curious about the rapture, sometimes we allow ourselves to become so preoccupied with certain details of the event that we fail to rejoice in what the rapture means to us. We get caught up in debate with fellow believers about the specifics. Yet in spite of the different views Christians have about the rapture, pretty much all agree on these truths:

1. The dead in Christ will be resurrected.
2. Those who are raptured alive in Christ will never experience death.
3. The dead and living in Christ will be reunited.
4. We will instantly be given glorified bodies.
5. We will dwell with Christ forever!

How many times have we longed to be freed of temptation's unrelenting assaults and sin's devastating effects upon us? How deeply have our hearts ached with the passing of a loved one in Christ? How often have we agonized over our lack of consistency in prayer and personal holiness? How frustrated have we gotten because, in our fallen humanness, we found it difficult to understand or pursue God's designs and purposes for us? The rapture will change all that.

When the dead in Christ are taken up first and we immediately follow, *everything* will change. Sin will no longer affect us. Mortal will become immortal. The threshold we will cross in the instant that the rapture happens will bring about a complete and eternal transformation.

In so many ways, what Scripture teaches about the rapture can fill us with encouragement. May we be faithful to remind one another of the hope that is before us!

WHAT IS THE DAY OF THE LORD?

You yourselves are fully aware that the day of the Lord will
come like a thief in the night (1 Thessalonians 5:2).

After Paul comforted the Christians in Thessalonica by affirming that the rapture would reunite them with their deceased fellow believers, he then wrote about "the day of the Lord." This day will come "like a thief in the night"—it will arrive unexpectedly, without warning. Because no one knows when the rapture will happen, those who remain on earth will likewise have no warning about this subsequent day of the Lord.

What is this day of the Lord? Isaiah 13:9, 34:8, and Joel 1:15 describe it as a time during which God will pour out supernatural judgment against sin. The term "the day of the Lord" also appears in 2 Thessalonians 2:2 in reference to the rise of the antichrist, which will occur during the tribulation. Revelation 6:17 describes the tribulation as "the great day of...wrath." So, the seven-year tribulation is part of the day of the Lord.

Other passages reveal the day of the Lord will extend beyond the tribulation and include the second coming (Matthew 24:43-44), the millennium and restoration (Joel 3:14-18), the destruction of the old heavens and earth, and the creation of the new heavens and earth (2 Peter 3:10-13). So the day of the Lord will begin with the start of the tribulation, when God intervenes in human history to take back the earth, and it will never end because Christ's reign will never end. It will have two phases: a time of judgment, followed by a time of blessing.

For believers, the day of the Lord is no reason for alarm because we will be taken up in the rapture, which will occur before that day. And after God has completed the pouring out of His wrath will come a time of unparalleled blessings that continues forever. Imagine the joy of living in a paradise in which God directly rules over His creation and His will is always done!

WHEN THE THIEF COMES

*Sudden destruction will come upon them...and
they will not escape (1 Thessalonians 5:3).*

When Paul wrote about the day of the Lord, he said it would arrive like "a thief in the night" (1 Thessalonians 5:2). A thief does not give advance warning of when he will strike. Similarly, the day of the Lord will descend quickly and take the whole world by surprise.

Paul said this will happen at a time when people are saying, "There is peace and security" (verse 3). The world will delude itself into believing that all is well. Leaders will proclaim that a global utopia is around the corner. In mockery, scoffers will declare, "Where is the promise of his coming?" (2 Peter 3:4).

The fact the tribulation will arrive unexpected will make its onset all the more terrifying. God will begin pouring out His wrath quickly and globally, and no one will be able to escape. His judgments will affect everyone, and they will have no place to hide.

Before the tribulation, the world will already have become engulfed in wickedness and darkness. But the chaos and damage that occurs will all be of human origin. With the day of the Lord, however, the wrath and havoc will be of divine origin. It will come from above and be supernatural. The devastation and carnage will far exceed anything that has ever happened before.

A world that will have deceived itself by saying "There is peace and security" and "There is no God" will suddenly find itself convulsing with turmoil that can only be explained as coming from God. The fact so many people will be taken by surprise is sobering evidence of the powerful grip of spiritual blindness. During the tribulation, every unbelieving soul will be held accountable by God. He sees all, and He will judge all.

NO FEAR

*You are not in darkness, brothers, for that day to
surprise you like a thief (1 Thessalonians 5:4).*

After Paul described what would happen to unbelievers when the
day of the Lord arrives, he turned his attention to his fellow believers—to those who "are not in darkness." He addressed them with tender affection, calling them "brothers." In the next verse, he goes on to call them "children of light" (1 Thessalonians 5:5).

Ultimately, there are only two types of people in the world: those who are in the light, and those who are in the darkness. Spiritually, mentally, and morally, we are one or the other. Those who live in spiritual darkness are ignorant of the truth and are morally bankrupt. Those who possess spiritual light are able to understand and discern God's truth with the help of the illuminating ministry of the Holy Spirit (1 Corinthians 2:14-16). As they yield to the Spirit, they are mentally and morally enabled to live in the light, producing spiritual fruit that is pleasing to God (Galatians 5:22-23).

Spiritual darkness results in an ignorance that puts people on the path to judgment. Because of their blindness, they will be taken by surprise on the day of the Lord.

Within the words of 1 Thessalonians 5:4 is a wonderful promise: We who are not in the darkness will not face the day of the Lord. There is no surprise in store for us. We will not be caught off guard. As children of the light, we will be delivered from this day. That guarantee is given to every person in Christ. As Paul wrote a few verses earlier in 1 Thessalonians 4:16-18, we will be taken up to heaven in the rapture, never to face God's impending judgment.

Repeatedly, Scripture assures us we are not destined for God's wrath. The Lord made this truth clear so that as we keep watch for Him, hope will be our constant companion.

WALKING AS CHILDREN OF LIGHT

You are all children of light, children of the day. We are not
of the night or of the darkness (1 Thessalonians 5:5).

In both the ancient Hebrew and Greek cultures, to be referred to as "children of _____" was a way of describing a person's dominant characteristics and influence. Those who are of the darkness are negative, rebellious, ignorant, wicked, and opposed to God. Those who are of the light "walk in newness of life" (Romans 6:4). They are "a new creation" (2 Corinthians 5:17), whom God desires "to be conformed to the image of his Son" (Romans 8:29).

Because the timing of the rapture and the beginning of the tribulation are unknown, we are urged to live in a state of readiness. We are to live as those who are awake in the daytime morally and spiritually, not as those who are asleep in the dark or hiding evil under the cover of nighttime.

Our attractiveness as bearers of light is what calls the attention of those who are trapped in darkness. Jesus said, "Let your light shine before others, so that they may see your good works and give glory to your Father in heaven" (Matthew 5:16).

To live as children of light means living in a way that is consistent with our identity as new creatures *in Christ*. Can others see our Lord based on what they see in us? Or are we allowing lapses into darkness to eclipse our light? As those who belong to the Lord, it doesn't make sense for us to live as those in the night because God "has delivered us from the domain of darkness and transferred us to the kingdom of his beloved Son" (Colossians 1:13).

In 1 Thessalonians 5:5, the present tense form of the phrase "you are" speaks of habitually walking in the light. For the believer, consistency in character is vital because we are in Christ, and because time could be short. May we always shine boldly!

THE POWER OF FAITH, HOPE, AND LOVE

Since we belong to the day, let us be sober, having put
on the breastplate of faith and love, and for a helmet
the hope of salvation (1 Thessalonians 5:8).

Here, we are given some insight into what it looks like to live as children of the day. With the mention of a breastplate and a helmet, we are reminded that in Scripture, our calling as Christians is often compared to the duties of a soldier. In 2 Timothy 2:3-4, we read that "a good soldier of Jesus Christ" does not "get entangled in civilian pursuits, since his aim is to please the one who enlisted him."

Soldiers are always ready for duty, and that's how we ought to approach our service to Christ. "Let us be sober" speaks of constant alertness. Key to our success in spiritual battle are "the breastplate of faith and love," and the "helmet [of] the hope of salvation."

A breastplate protects a soldier's greatest vulnerability, the vital organs. And it is our faith and love that supplies this breastplate. Our faith includes our wholehearted trust and belief in God, His Word, and His promises to us. As we place our trust in God, we shield ourselves from temptation. It is when we lack faith that our breastplate falls and we are susceptible to sin.

Our love for God—our total devotion to Him—is another form of protection. The more fervent our love for the Lord, the less enticing the things of this world become.

A helmet's purpose is to protect our head from dangerous blows. The hope of our salvation is the certainty that we will one day be glorified. As we walk through life with our eyes fixed on this hope, we are motivated to keep ourselves pure (1 John 3:2-3) and to "take every thought captive to obey Christ" (2 Corinthians 10:5). As we fill our minds with thoughts of obedience, we displace wrongful thoughts that can do great harm to us.

When we exercise faith, hope, and love, we are able to stand strong and serve well.

READY FOR THE END TIMES #1:
EXPECTING THE RAPTURE

*Concerning the coming of our Lord Jesus Christ and being
gathered together to him…(2 Thessalonians 2:1).*

By the time we reach 2 Thessalonians chapter 2, this is the *sixth* time
in 1 and 2 Thessalonians that Paul mentions the first phase of our
Lord's coming, or the rapture. In none of these instances does he refer to
the second phase, or Christ's return to earth. This repetition reveals just
how important it is for us to have a clear and correct understanding of our
rapture to heaven, and to not confuse it with the Lord's return to earth.

As we continue our way through 2 Thessalonians 2 over the next
few devotions, we'll see why Paul devoted so much space to the rapture
in these two epistles. Amazingly, his instructions are just as timeless for
us today as they were for the Christians of his era.

A key reason God wants us to be informed about the rapture is so
we will always be ready for it. This makes sense because of the fact we
cannot know the day or hour of Christ's coming. Our *awareness* of the
rapture is meant to stir our *anticipation* for it.

For some believers, the knowledge the rapture could happen at any
moment creates trepidation rather than anticipation. They hope the Lord
doesn't come anytime soon because they're either ashamed of their spiritual condition, or they're having a hard time letting go of worldly pursuits.

One reason the New Testament frequently reminds us that the rapture could happen at any time is so that we'll deal with sin quickly and
ruthlessly. The knowledge that the rapture is imminent ought to motivate us to holy living and keeping a clear conscience. Doing this will
result in joy, and allow us to cheerfully say, "I always take pains to have
a clear conscience toward both God and man" (Acts 24:16).

READY FOR THE END TIMES #2: DON'T BE DECEIVED

We ask you, brothers, not to be quickly shaken in mind or alarmed...
to the effect that the day of the Lord has come (2 Thessalonians 2:1-2).

False teachings have existed in the church from the very beginning. Paul warned his fellow church leaders, "After my departure fierce wolves will come in among you, not sparing the flock; and from among your own selves will arise men speaking twisted things" (Acts 20:29-30).

When false teachers were promoting errors about the end times to the believers in Thessalonica, Paul said they were doing this "either by a spirit or a spoken word, or a letter seeming to be from us" (2 Thessalonians 2:2). These deceivers had gone so far as to forge a letter that appeared to be from Paul himself. Their message seemed authentic but was not.

What were they saying? "That the day of the Lord has come." They misled people to think the tribulation was here. The Christians in Thessalonica panicked. How had they missed the rapture? Did this mean they now had to face the tribulation and God's wrath?

Earlier, Paul had twice told these believers they were not destined for the tribulation (1 Thessalonians 1:10; 5:9). Rather, all who are in Christ will be taken up at the rapture. In Paul's words here we sense a loving urgency: He wanted to bring comfort through correction.

There is an abundance of wrong teachings about the end times in the church today. Often it is "backed" by seemingly authoritative or authentic "evidence." Paul's words about "rightly handling the word of truth" (2 Timothy 2:15) apply just as much to Bible prophecy as to any other topic in Scripture. To avoid being misled or alarmed by sensational or incorrect teachings about the last days, we should carefully examine what the Bible says. Making the effort to do this will protect us from confusion and fear.

READY FOR THE END TIMES #3:
KNOW THE ORDER OF EVENTS

*Let no one deceive you in any way. For that day will
not come, unless the rebellion comes first, and the man
of lawlessness is revealed (2 Thessalonians 2:3).*

Our understanding of Bible prophecy can mean the difference between facing the future with fear or with hope. That's very true when it comes to the timing of the antichrist's arrival on the world scene. If we believe we will someday face the antichrist and the horrors of the tribulation, we will live in fear. But if we interpret God's promises about the rapture to mean that we will be taken to heaven before the antichrist and tribulation arise, we will live with hope.

In 2 Thessalonians 2:3, "that day" refers to the Lord's second coming. Paul had to warn, "Let no one deceive you" because false teachers were spreading untruths about this event. Paul's purpose in this passage was to assure people Christ's return couldn't happen yet because "the rebellion" had to come first, in which "the man of lawlessness is revealed."

In other words, the antichrist must first rise to power and do his act of rebellion—that is, desecrate the temple (verse 4), before Christ will return.

Christians in the early church were being deceived because some teachers were giving a wrong chronology of the end times. By distorting the order of events, they were leading people to live in fear rather than hope.

While Scripture doesn't give us every detail about the chronology of the last days, we can still determine the general order. That includes 100 percent certainty about the fact no believer will face persecution from the antichrist or suffer during the tribulation. The promise that we will be removed from earth before the tribulation is sure. We are destined for bliss in heaven, not hell on earth. That assurance comes from knowing a right chronology of end-time events.

READY FOR THE END TIMES #4: REMEMBER WHAT YOU'VE LEARNED

Do you not remember that when I was still with you I told you these things? (2 Thessalonians 2:5).

Truth is our greatest defense against deception.

Paul's question "Do you not remember…?" was written in response to the news that certain teachers were spreading errors about the end times. Earlier, Paul had spoken to the believers in Thessalonica about the rapture, tribulation, and second coming. After his departure, others arose who contradicted what Paul had said. That's why the apostle found it necessary to repeat what he had taught.

The context of Paul's question is significant—he's dealing with the subject of Bible prophecy. For him to admonish his audience on this matter affirms the importance of a correct understanding of what God has revealed about the last days, including the order of events. Our views about the future have a definite impact on how we live today. They can determine whether we have uncertainty or confidence about what lies ahead.

God gave us Bible prophecy to encourage us about what is to come. His promises about the *salvation* that would be made possible at the first coming, the *glorification* that will occur at the second coming, and the *restoration* that will take place in eternity were all given to fill us with peace, hope, and anticipation.

When it comes to Bible prophecy, it's worthwhile for us to earnestly study God's Word so we can discern truth from error. In this way, we protect ourselves from being misled. May we never tire of revisiting the prophetic truths meant to bless us. Doing so will help guard us against deceptions that can undermine the ways God intends to build and encourage us through Bible prophecy.

SELF-LOVE IN THE LAST DAYS

In the last days...people will be lovers of self (2 Timothy 3:1-2).

On the surface, for a person to be a lover of self might not seem all that dangerous. But it was a love of self that led Adam and Eve to spurn God and choose sin. When it came to eating the forbidden fruit, the first couple had a choice: love God or love self. Their decision had deadly consequences and ended up putting them on the path to sin and destruction. That's how devastating self-love can be.

Every choice we make in life can be viewed through this lens: Will I choose to love God, or will I choose to love self?

James 3:16 warns that "where...selfish ambition exist[s], there is disorder and every evil thing" (NASB). To love self is to be selfish, and where there is selfishness, we will find evil. Scripture makes it clear that life's choices are a matter of either selflessly seeking to please God or selfishly seeking to please self.

The closer we come to the last days, the more we can expect people to be lovers of self. We see abundant evidence of this all around us in today's culture. The preoccupation with seeking personal happiness—which amounts to pleasing self—is so great that it has even overtaken many in the church. Second Timothy 3 tells us that these people who are "lovers of pleasure rather than lovers of God" will have "the appearance of godliness" (verses 4-5). If we're not careful, we can easily be fooled by those who appear to be godly but in reality are lovers of self.

As we walk through each day and seek to make good decisions and exercise godly discernment, we will find it helpful to ask: Does this encourage love of God, or love of self?

HOW SELF-LOVE
AFFECTS OUR VIEW OF SIN

In the last days...people will be...lovers of pleasure
rather than lovers of God (2 Timothy 3:1, 4).

Self-love is dangerous because it leads us to take sin lightly and no longer view it as God does.

Self-love causes us to rationalize sin. Because we want to nurse a grudge, we refuse to forgive someone. Because we're upset that God didn't answer a prayer the way we wanted, we strike back at God by justifying our indulgence in some sin or other. Because we want to satisfy a momentary urge, we think, *Just once, and I won't do it again.* Because we want to take vengeance on someone, we refuse to talk to them. Because we think we deserve more, we give ourselves reasons to put self before others. Because we believe God wants us to be happy, we pursue personal fulfillment in the wrong ways.

Self-love causes us to redefine sin. Because we are enjoying a particular sin too much to let it go, we tell ourselves it's not so bad. Because we're too proud to admit we're wrong, we resort to illogical thinking to convince ourselves that we're right. Because a child we love dearly has chosen to participate in sinful behavior, we change our view of what the Bible says about such behavior. Because we don't want to face offense from unbelievers when we share the gospel, we soften or even omit what the Bible says about God and sin.

Self-love is dangerous because inevitably, it leads us to rationalize or redefine sin. Though seemingly harmless, it is a cancer that destroys. We need to arm ourselves against its contaminating influence by seeking to put our love of God first in all things.

As Christians, our love for God should be our highest priority and greatest joy. This is evident in 2 Corinthians 5:15, which says Christ died "that those who live might no longer live for themselves but for him."

THE WHERE, HOW, WHY, AND WHEN OF THE RAPTURE

Waiting for our blessed hope, the appearing of the glory of our great God and Savior Jesus Christ (Titus 2:13).

Scripture tells us *where* we will be taken at the rapture, *how* it will happen, and *why*. Yet we don't know *when*. Through the ages, many have tried to figure that out. But not only was it wise for God to keep that information hidden, the fact it's a mystery has been good for us!

Let's start with *where* we will be taken, and *how*. Shortly before Jesus was crucified, He told the disciples He was leaving them. They became distressed. That's when He promised, "I will come again and will take you to myself, that where I am you may be also" (John 14:1-3).

Later, Paul echoed this, giving more details: "The Lord himself will descend from heaven with a cry of command...And the dead in Christ will rise first. Then we who are alive, who are left, will be caught up together with them in the clouds to meet the Lord in the air" (1 Thessalonians 4:16-17). All this was communicated to give us hope—the assurance that one day, "we will always be with the Lord" (verse 17). That should be our greatest hope of all!

And *why* will we be raptured? To be delivered "from the wrath to come" (1 Thessalonians 1:10). "For God has not destined us for wrath" (5:9). These, too, are words of hope. As forgiven people made righteous in Christ, there is no reason for us to face God's judgments. We will be taken up before the tribulation to be in heaven with Jesus.

For these reasons, the rapture is rightly called "our blessed hope"! (Titus 2:13). That brings us to *when*. Not knowing the time of the rapture encourages us to live in constant anticipation, filling us with a spirit of hope. It also spurs us to share the gospel with the lost now rather than later, thus spreading the hope within us. In every way, what we know and don't know about the rapture is designed to fill us with hope and bring hope to others!

REVELATION WAS WRITTEN TO BE READ

The revelation of Jesus Christ, which God gave him to show his
servants the things that must soon take place (Revelation 1:1).

Many people view the book of Revelation as being difficult to understand. But in the very first verse, God immediately makes it clear His intent is to *reveal* the truth—about Jesus Christ and about what is to come. The Greek term translated "revelation" means "to become visible." The 22 chapters in this final book of the Bible were given to us for a reason: They abound with important truths for us to know.

Think about it: Why would God speak plainly from Genesis to Jude, then suddenly become indecipherable in the end? Much of what appears to be confusing at first glance becomes clear when we take the time to read carefully and compare the text with other Bible passages. An estimated 278 of the 404 verses in Revelation point or allude to truths from the Old Testament, and the New Testament books have parallel passages. With thoughtful study, we can gain clarity.

While there are some passages that are hard to understand, there is much in the book that is straightforward. We are given many details about Christ in His exalted state, the characteristics of a healthy church, the rise of the antichrist and his one-world order, God's final judgments upon mankind, Christ's earthly kingdom, and the new heavens and new earth.

As Revelation 1:1 says, God gave this book "to show his servants the things that must soon take place." This is information God *wants* us to know.

In Revelation, we see Christ in all His majesty and glory. We see Him worshipped and feared. And we see His triumphant return as King of kings and Lord of lords. Revelation is rich with truths that help us to gain a higher view of Christ. For that reason alone it is well worth reading! There is much we can learn from its pages, and God delighted to share it all with us.

A SENSE OF URGENCY

The time is near (Revelation 1:1).

After the apostle John says that those who read, hear, and keep the book of Revelation will be blessed, we are told that the reason it's so urgent for us to know what this book teaches is because "the time is near." With each passing day, the events described in Revelation are closer than ever. We are to live in continual anticipation of the rapture, tribulation, and Christ's return.

The fact the time is near should affect us in two ways: (1) spur us to use our days well, and (2) motivate us to bring the gospel to unbelievers before time runs out.

The term translated "near" doesn't refer to time in the sense of a clock, but to seasons or epochs. We are now in the church age, between Christ's first and second comings. Next will come the tribulation, then Christ's kingdom, followed by eternity.

Some people interpret "near" as meaning soon or right away. But Scripture reveals the wait will be long enough that scoffers will say, "Where is the promise of his coming? For ever since the fathers fell asleep, all things are continuing as they were" (2 Peter 3:4). We also want to keep in mind that for the Lord, "one day is as a thousand years" (verse 8). He is patiently waiting, "not wishing that any should perish, but that all should reach repentance" (verse 9).

Still, we are to be alert. Jesus said, "Stay dressed for action and keep your lamps burning, and be like men who are waiting for their master" (Luke 12:35-36). James wrote, "The coming of the Lord is at hand...the Judge is standing at the door" (James 5:8-9).

We are called to live with a sense of urgency and expectation. And during this wait, we are commanded "to meet together...encouraging one another...all the more as you see the Day drawing near" (Hebrews 10:25).

May the exhortation that "the time is near" motivate us to make sure every day counts.

LETTING REVELATION
INFLUENCE HOW WE LIVE TODAY

Blessed are those who…keep what is written in it (Revelation 1:3).

There are many who assume that because so much of the book of Revelation is about the future, it has very little application to us today. But Revelation 1:3 promises blessing to those who "keep what is written" in this book, which can powerfully shape four areas of our lives right now:

Our worship. In Revelation 1:12-20, the apostle John sees Christ in a vision—a Christ very different from the one he knew prior to the cross. Jesus' eyes are like a flame of fire, His feet like burnished bronze, and His voice like the roar of many waters. Here, we see Jesus in all the fullness of His authority and majesty. *This* is the Christ we follow. He is ever diligent for purity and truth to be the hallmarks of His church, and He stands ready to execute justice against evil. This should inspire our everyday worship of Him to be wholehearted and reverent.

Our lifestyle. In Revelation chapters 2–3, Jesus walks among His churches, urging His people to be steadfast in truth, faithful in purity, and to avoid compromise, sin, and falsehood. His admonishments are meant for all who belong to the church in all ages, including us. May we earnestly take to heart His desire for us to be holy!

Our witness. Revelation chapters 4–19 are an ever-present reminder that "now is the day of salvation" (2 Corinthians 6:2), before time runs out for the lost. Praying for unbelievers and sharing the gospel with them should be an ever-present part of our lives.

Our outlook. The immediate future of this world looks grim, and the end times will be the worst era ever in human history. But after the tribulation comes the millennial kingdom, then the new heavens and new earth. The glories that await us are real—they will happen! Soon, the temporal will give way to the eternal. Keeping our eyes on the finish line and living with a constant awareness of what is to come will fill us with a hope that keeps us moving onward.

PROPHECY AS A SOURCE OF BLESSING

*Blessed is the one who reads aloud the words of this prophecy,
and blessed are those who hear, and who keep what is
written in it, for the time is near (Revelation 1:3).*

The book of Revelation opens with a profound promise to everyone who reads, hears, and obeys it: They will be blessed! This promise alerts us to two facts: (1) This book is meant for our benefit, and (2) we need to pay close attention to it.

The word *blessed* is so widely misused today that it's easy for us to miss what is being promised here. It's the same word Jesus used when He taught the beatitudes in Matthew 5, where multiple times, He said, "Blessed are the…" and "Blessed are those…" This blessedness speaks of a genuine happiness that is deep, supernatural, and satisfying—it is an internal contentment that only God can provide. This contrasts with the superficial happiness the world offers, which is based on positive external circumstances that are fleeting and temporary.

God promises a true and lasting happiness to those who read the book of Revelation. As we learn about Christ's exalted state, the church's need for purity, the eradication of worldly kingdoms, the establishment of Christ's kingdom, and heaven and eternity, we will be blessed.

If we want to experience God's kind of happiness, the book of Revelation offers it to us in these ways:

1. It assures us God is sovereign and His plans for the future will unfold as He ordained.

2. It calls the church to purity so that we honor Christ and represent Him well to the lost.

3. It makes clear that the world we live in is temporary and encourages us to live with an eternal perspective.

4. It reminds us that in the end, Christ will triumph, and we will be victorious with Him.

SEVEN WAYS REVELATION IS RELEVANT FOR US TODAY

"Blessed are those…who keep what is written in it" (Revelation 1:3).

Because Revelation includes details about the future, many dismiss its relevance for today. Yet it offers an abundance of wisdom and guidance for us right now. Right at the start, we are encouraged by the promise that we who "keep what is written in it" will be blessed.

"To keep" refers to obedience. James 1:22 says to "be doers of the word, and not hearers only." If we're to obey what is in Revelation, that means the book is practical.

Christ Himself provides many instructions and rebukes in Revelation 2–3. In His letters to the seven churches in Asia are praises and reproofs written to today's churches as well. Because every believer is part of the church, we should take these seven letters to heart.

The prophetic content of Revelation is relevant to us in these ways:

1. Our confidence in God grows as we realize His ability to keep His promises.

2. Our trust in Scripture is strengthened by fulfilled prophecy.

3. We gain an eternal perspective as we realize the world is temporary and heaven is forever.

4. We are motivated to purity as we recognize God's hatred for sin.

5. We are compelled to share the gospel with the lost before time runs out.

6. The worsening of evil in the future helps us see the need to live as salt and light now.

7. Our reverent worship of God deepens as we see His power and wisdom on display.

The more we realize that Revelation is practical for today, the more excited we'll be as we read it. As you do so, make a deliberate effort to "keep what is written in it." You'll find this a worthwhile pursuit, for it comes with the promise that you will be blessed!

THE GOOD NEWS OF REVELATION: GRACE AND PEACE

Grace to you and peace from him who is and who
was and who is to come (Revelation 1:4).

*G*race. And *peace*. These two words in the opening of the book of Revelation rarely get the attention they deserve. They provide much-needed perspective for the entire book, reminding us that our eternal God—"who is and who was and who is to come"—is a God of grace and peace.

It may seem strange for Revelation to begin with wishes of grace and peace to its readers because the book is famously known for describing the opposite. It is filled with prophecies about wrath and war, punishment and destruction. It portrays a massive outpouring of God's judgment and fury in a time when people have descended into the darkest depths of evil ever.

Yet it is because of humanity's rejection of God that He has found it necessary to bring judgment. God's original design for those made in His image was a glorious world in which we dwelled with Him in grace and peace. That's what made Eden such a perfect paradise.

For the book of Revelation to open with wishes of grace and peace reminds us that God is the origin and provider of all grace and peace. It is humanity that ushered sin into the world and brought forth the curse that has resulted in decay and death. Nothing less than a complete eradication of sin and evil will make it possible for God's creation to be restored to the state He intended for it. After God's wrath has run its course and Satan and sin have been banished, we will once again live in God's presence and experience His perfect grace and peace.

The good news of Revelation is this: Even in a time of great judgment, His offer of grace and peace will continue to be proclaimed to people everywhere through vessels He has appointed for that purpose. His love for the lost is steadfast, and His character unchanging. And after the storm of His wrath has passed, His grace and peace will prevail—for all eternity.

JESUS: THE ULTIMATE PROPHET, PRIEST, AND KING

*Jesus Christ the faithful witness, the firstborn of the dead,
and the ruler of kings on earth (Revelation 1:5).*

At the beginning of Revelation, Jesus is introduced as Prophet, Priest, and King. In the Bible, those who held these offices were anointed—they were specially chosen by God for these responsibilities. Jesus' title *Messiah* means "anointed one." As God in human flesh, He is the ultimate Anointed One—the ultimate Prophet, Priest, and King.

As "the faithful witness," Jesus fulfilled the role of Prophet. In Scripture, a prophet is one who speaks for God. Luke 4:18 tells us Jesus was anointed to "proclaim good news." All through His ministry, He carried out the work of a prophet by pointing people back to the Father, revealing the truth, and foretelling the future. In these ways Jesus was the ultimate Prophet.

As "the firstborn of the dead," Jesus fulfilled the role of Priest. Representing us before the Father, He gave Himself as the sacrifice necessary to wash away our sins and restore us spiritually. Because He rose from the dead, we're guaranteed to rise from the dead too. As the ultimate High Priest, He shed His blood for us (Hebrews 7:27) and He prays for us (verse 25).

As "the ruler of kings on earth," Jesus will fulfill the role of King. All through the Old Testament, the prophets said the Messiah would one day reign as king (Genesis 49:10; 2 Samuel 7:16; Psalm 2:6). Daniel 7:13-14 tells us He will have "an everlasting dominion." As the "King of kings and Lord of lords" (Revelation 19:16), Jesus will be the ultimate King.

When sin separated us from God, we needed a prophet who would reveal the truth to us, a priest who could offer a sacrifice that cleansed us, and a king who would guide and care for us. In the Messiah, the ultimate Anointed One, we have all three. He is our Prophet, our Priest, and our King. In Jesus, we have everything we need.

REVEALING WHAT
CHRIST HAS DONE FOR US

*To him who loves us and has freed us from our sins by his blood
and made us a kingdom, priests to his God and Father, to him be
glory and dominion forever and ever. Amen (Revelation 1:5-6).*

I t is fitting that a book that begins with the words "the revelation of
Jesus Christ" would immediately start by revealing what Christ has
done for us, as stated in Revelation 1:5-6:

He loved us. God reached down to show His love for us even "while
we were still sinners" (Romans 5:8). So great is this love that He sent
His Son, who humbled Himself and died for us. And this love is eternal—*nothing* can separate us from Him! (Romans 8:37-39).

He freed us. Christ released us from our sins—forever. We are no longer in bondage, and no one can condemn us. In Him, we are righteous.
Our assurance of heaven is guaranteed!

He made us to be a kingdom. Christ dwells in us, which makes it possible for us to experience His loving rule in and through us, even while
we are still here on earth.

He made us priests to His God and Father. Because we are forgiven and
Christ's righteousness has been granted to us, we can enter God's presence.
We can approach His throne of grace in time of need (Hebrews 4:16).

Within the first few verses of Revelation, we see the incredible depth
of Christ's love, forgiveness, and provision for us. He loved us and freed
us from sin so we can enter heaven. Through us He rules, and He has
given us direct access to the Father!

The eternal benefits we enjoy as believers were prompted by Christ's
love for us. Only He could gift us with such wonderful blessings. In
light of what Christ has done for us, the appropriate response is this:
"To him be glory and dominion forever and ever" (Revelation 1:6). The
greatness of Christ's love for us should inspire us to exalt Him in praise.

ABSOLUTELY, CHRIST IS COMING!

Behold, he is coming with the clouds, and every eye will see
him, even those who pierced him, and all the tribes of the earth
will wail on account of him. Even so. Amen (Revelation 1:7).

Revelation 1:7 opens with the exclamation "Behold." The apostle John says this to get our attention. He doesn't want us to miss this announcement. Sure enough, the declaration that follows sets the stage for the entire rest of the book: Jesus is coming!

The absolute certainty of Christ's return is proclaimed all through the Bible. For every prophecy in Scripture about the first coming of our Lord Jesus, there are eight prophecies about His second coming. We have an incredible abundance of proof that Christ's first advent really happened and was fulfilled literally. And we have enormous prophetic evidence that His second advent will take place as promised. The God who brought about the first coming will bring about the second.

Jesus will return gloriously "with the clouds," and "every eye will see him." No one will miss this spectacular event. His descent from heaven will be seen by all, perhaps as He circles the globe, and because advanced technology will broadcast His dramatic arrival everywhere.

Zechariah 12:10 informs us that on this day, God will "pour out" upon the Jews (represented by "those who pierced him") "a spirit of grace." Many will genuinely repent. As for "the tribes of the earth," they "will wail" mostly in unrepentant terror.

John ends with two powerful affirmations: "Even so. Amen." The first is in Greek and is like saying, "This will be!" The second is in Hebrew, "amen," which is also a strong assurance.

He is coming. Every eye will see Him. Even so. Amen. In no uncertain terms, God makes it clear that Christ's return is a fixed event on His calendar. *It will happen!*

JESUS' FIRST WORDS IN THE BOOK OF REVELATION

"I am the Alpha and the Omega," says the Lord God, "who is and who was and who is to come, the Almighty" (Revelation 1:8).

This is the first prophetic declaration that Christ Himself gives in the book of Revelation. What an incredible way to usher us into the final book of the Bible—with a triumphant and absolute promise that yes, He *will* return!

In those few words, our Lord reveals the very reasons He is able to keep the promise of His second coming: He is the Alpha and Omega. He is eternal, He is transcendent, and He is omnipotent. *Nothing* can prevent His glorious and promised return!

These characteristics have always been true about Him and always will be. Nothing can supersede or diminish Christ's eternality, transcendence, or power.

He is coming back to reign forever.

He will transform our mortal bodies into immortal.

He will banish Satan and sin.

He will restore the heavens and earth and will dwell together with us.

Just as Christ fulfilled every prophecy about His first coming, He will fulfill every prophecy about His second coming.

Christ's first words to us in the book of Revelation are unequivocal. We are not left hanging with even the tiniest bit of uncertainty about His return and all that follows afterward. Because He is eternal, transcendent, and omnipotent, He *will* bring every single prophecy in the book of Revelation to pass—and He *will* reign supreme forever.

No wonder the apostle John ended the book of Revelation with this enthusiastic declaration: "Amen. Come, Lord Jesus!" (22:20).

THE LAMB AND THE LION

I saw...one like a son of man, clothed with a long robe and with
a golden sash...The hairs of his head were white...His eyes were
like a flame of fire, his feet were like burnished bronze...and his
voice was like the roar of many waters (Revelation 1:12-15).

In a vision, the apostle John saw his Lord again after more than 50 years—and what a contrast! His memories of Jesus hanging on the cross, bloodied and beaten, had to have been vivid. His last glimpse of Christ was when the risen Savior was taken up to heaven. And now, many years later, John saw Christ in full, radiant splendor as never before. The Lamb was now a Lion!

The Christ we read about in the Gospels, who emptied and humbled Himself when He came to earth and had no place to put His head, now reigns supreme in heaven, ablaze with supernatural glory and honor and power. *This* is the Christ whom we live for and serve. When we think of Him, *this* is the image we should have in our minds. Revelation 1:12-15 describes Him as the High Priest who offered Himself as the perfect and final sacrifice that secured our place in heaven. His hair, eyes, and feet are brilliant with His deity, holiness, and chastening authority that seeks to keep His church pure. He is the High Priest, King, Judge, and Lord of all.

We're told that "his voice was like the roar of many waters." This is the voice we will hear someday that, "with a cry of command," will call us to heaven in the rapture. His words will cause the dead in Christ to rise first, then we will be taken up (1 Thessalonians 4:16-17). It is His voice that will charge the dead to rise either to a resurrection of life or of judgment (John 5:28-29). No one will be able to resist His spoken commands.

Upon seeing Christ in all His majesty, John fell in reverent worship. Is that the attitude of your heart today and every day? When we think of Christ, may this be what comes to mind!

CHRIST, THE FOCAL POINT

*Write therefore the things that you have seen, those that are
and those that are to take place after this (Revelation 1:19).*

After Christ revealed Himself in blazing glory to the apostle John, He told His beloved disciple to take pen in hand and write the book of Revelation. John was to record "the things that you have seen" (the past), "those that are" (the present), and "those that are to take place after this" (the future).

This threefold outline provides us with a big-picture view of the entire book of Revelation. John was to document his vision of the glorified Christ (chapter 1), the words of praise and rebuke Christ had and continues to have for His churches (chapters 2–3), and Christ's actions in the future—specifically, during the end times and beyond (chapters 4–22).

What is stunning about this past, present, and future organization of Revelation is that from beginning to end, it keeps the spotlight on Christ. We see that the Savior who died on the cross is now very much alive. He who yielded His authority to die on our behalf now wields all authority. He who had been judged by men is now the supreme judge over all mankind.

In Revelation 2–3, we see Christ moving among His people, calling them to pursue holiness and abstain from sin. His chastening activity continues today and reminds us that we are His ambassadors, tasked with proclaiming the hope of eternal life to a dying world.

When the rapture occurs, the church age will end. Then He who is worthy of all glory and honor and power will unleash a rapid series of judgments upon the world. At the end of this time of wrath, He will return in triumph as King of kings and Lord of lords.

In the same way that Christ is the focal point of all the Bible and the entire book of Revelation, may He be the focal point of all that we do in our lives.

A CHURCH THAT SHINES
IN A DARK WORLD

These things says He who…walks in the midst of the
seven golden lampstands (Revelation 2:1 NKJV).

Christ is zealous about the spiritual health of His church. That is why, in Revelation 2:1, we read that He walks among the lampstands, or His churches. In Revelation chapters 2 and 3, we see Christ scrutinizing seven churches and alerting them to the ways they are being faithful or unfaithful. Exercising His authority over the church, Jesus directs and admonishes the believers in these seven churches with words also meant for all believers through the ages, including us.

As lampstands, churches are to stand out as lights in the world. All of us within the church are to contribute to that light by putting Christ on display through our words and actions. If unbelievers cannot see the evidence of Christ in us, then there is no light emanating from us.

A church that has become like the world has lost its light, and therefore, its ability to attract unbelievers. It's when we live holy and blameless lives that it is possible for those who live in darkness to see and be drawn to the light only God can give.

Is your faith evident? Can people see the difference Jesus makes in you? Do you engage with others in a way that you "let your light shine before others, so that they may see your good works and give glory to your Father who is in heaven"? (Matthew 5:16).

Ephesians 5:25-26 reveals there is a connection between Christ's love for us and His desire for us to be pure: "Christ loved the church and gave himself up for her, that he might sanctify her." He wants a church that is "holy and without blemish" (verse 27). Why? Only when we are a proper expression of Christ can we have any influence for Him.

Christ is walking among the lampstands even now. How bright is your light?

ENDURANCE

*I know you are enduring patiently and bearing up for my name's
sake, and you have not grown weary (Revelation 2:3).*

In the face of persistent trials and evil, the believers in Ephesus had
not grown weary. They had remained faithful and uncomplaining. In
response, our Lord praised them for their loyalty.

As we draw closer to the last days, we can expect difficulties and
wickedness to worsen. Satan will do all he can to wear us down. And
when we are worn out, it's easier to give in to temptation and compromise. Rather than counter the many pressures against us, we're inclined
to go with the flow so life won't be so difficult.

What motivated and enabled the believers in Ephesus to endure?
We find the answer in Jesus' commendation to them: They were "bearing up for [His] name's sake." They were driven by the desire to bring
honor to Christ's name and reputation. They recognized the importance of doing what was right and standing firm so that Jesus' reputation would not be damaged.

When we are eager to represent our Lord well, we will be energized
to stay strong and keep going. When our longing is to exalt Christ, we
are less likely to succumb to thoughts of giving up.

We find confirmation of this in 1 Corinthians 10:31, where we are
exhorted, "Whether you eat or drink, or whatever you do, do all to the
glory of God." Living with a dedicated concern for God's glory in every
way possible will have a powerful effect on our attitudes and actions.

If your desire is to endure and not grow weary, be earnest about
bringing honor to Christ. Your motivation to lift up the Lord will fill
you with the inner strength you need for pressing onward.

BACKING UP OUR LOYALTY WITH LOVE

*I have this against you, that you have abandoned the love you
had at first. Remember therefore from where you have fallen;
repent, and do the works you did at first (Revelation 2:4-5).*

The good news for the believers in Ephesus was that they received
strong marks for their faithfulness to Christ. But the bad news was
they had also "abandoned the love" they had formerly shown for their
Savior. Their fiery passion for Christ had diminished, making their service to Him cold and mechanical. This rebuke serves as a sober reminder
of our need to ensure our loyalty is backed by love.

Shortly after the birth of the church in Ephesus, Paul encouraged
the new believers there to be "rooted and grounded in love" (Ephesians
3:17). Love is the seed that germinates into a fruitful relationship with
our Lord. Remember the greatest commandment? "You shall love the
Lord your God with all your heart and with all your soul and with all
your mind" (Matthew 22:37).

When our love for Christ wanes, our relationship with Him will suffer, and our obedience will become hollow. That is why it's so vital for
us to keep feeding the flames of love burning within our hearts. Forty
years after Paul urged the Ephesian believers to be rooted and grounded
in love, Christ examined them and diagnosed that their love was lacking.

Jesus, the Great Physician, tells us what to do when we sense our love
is weak: "Do the works you did at first." These "works" include relating
intimately with God. That happens when we spend time in His Word,
prayer, and worship. Restoring our passion begins with prioritizing our
relationship with God above all else. The depth of our faithfulness is
proportionate to the depth of our time spent relating to God and growing in our love for Him.

AN EXHORTATION TO EVERY BELIEVER

He who has an ear, let him hear what the Spirit
says to the churches (Revelation 2:7).

When our Lord repeats an exhortation, it's His way of saying, "Pay attention—this is important!" So you can imagine the significance of a statement that is repeated seven times. That's what happened when Christ spoke to the seven churches in Revelation 2–3. To every single church, He said, "He who has an ear, let him hear what the Spirit says."

Because the commendations and rebukes Jesus gave to those seven churches continue to apply to all believers today, we should take this repeated command seriously. Very simply, Jesus was saying, "Listen and obey."

This charge makes sense when we remember Christ's reason for writing the letters to the seven churches. Back in Revelation 1:12-16, John described Jesus as a chastening authority who walks among His churches with an earnest desire that they be pure. Ephesians 5:25-27 tells us that "Christ loved the church and gave himself up for her, that he might sanctify her...that she might be holy and without blemish." When Jesus examined the Christians in Revelation 2–3, He was concerned about what their lives communicated to a watching world. He wanted their faith to be visible and to cause unbelievers to have a right impression of God.

Is your faith visible? Are you "blameless and innocent...without blemish in the midst of a crooked and twisted generation, among whom you shine as lights"? (Philippians 2:15). Can others see Christ in you?

The answer will be yes if you "hear what the Spirit says." First Peter 1:21 tells us the Holy Spirit is the author of all Scripture. As you heed God's Word, it has a cleansing effect on your life, and your light will shine and your faith will be visible.

THE WONDERFUL END
RESULT OF PERSECUTION

*I know your tribulation and your poverty (but
you are rich) (Revelation 2:9).*

At the time Jesus wrote to the church in Smyrna, the believers there faced great persecution.

A key reason for this is because the city was a major center for the worship of the emperor of Rome. Out of faithfulness to Jesus their Lord, the Christians refused to say, "Caesar is Lord." Because this was a capital offense, punishments were severe. Many believers could not get jobs, which explains why they were in poverty. Others were imprisoned or executed.

Though these believers were poor and paid dearly for their allegiance to Christ, from a spiritual standpoint, they were rich. James 1:2-4 tells us the precious result of enduring persecution: "Count it all joy, my brothers, when you meet trials of various kinds, for you know that the testing of your faith produces steadfastness. And let steadfastness have its full effect, that you may be perfect and complete, lacking in nothing." In the same way that enormous pressure and high temperatures deep within the earth produce physical diamonds, the trials and tests faced by those who are faithful to Christ turns them into spiritual diamonds.

When Jesus said, "I know your tribulation," He spoke with deep compassion from personal experience. He had suffered the greatest and most unjust persecution ever. He knew how much these believers were suffering, and He knew they endured out of loyalty to Him.

When Jesus offered loving encouragement for facing trials, notice He didn't suggest how to avoid the pain caused by them. He didn't offer any escape routes. Instead, He said that as we endure, we grow spiritually.

Suffering produces a wonderful result in us—a stronger faith that makes us more complete. May we gladly face difficulties for the Lord, knowing they enrich us spiritually.

A WILLINGNESS TO
EMBRACE PERSECUTION

*Do not fear what you are about to suffer. Behold, the devil is about
to throw some of you into prison, that you may be tested...Be faithful
unto death, and I will give you the crown of life (Revelation 2:10).*

Jesus commended the believers in Smyrna for enduring persecution
for His sake. Then His next words gave them reason to pray harder
than ever for the strength to persevere. He warned that their suffering
was about to worsen. The furnace of affliction would soon burn more
intensely. He went so far as to lovingly urge them to remain faithful
even "unto death."

For many of today's Christians, any suggestion that they might be
persecuted for their faith would provoke alarm and fear. In a culture
that says, "God wants me to be happy," the idea of suffering for Christ
is foreign and unwelcome. Yet God never promised that life would be
free of pain. Rather, He assured us of His constant presence in every
trial we face.

The apostles set the right example when they were beaten for proclaiming the gospel. Their response was one of "rejoicing that they were
counted worthy to suffer dishonor for the name" (Acts 5:41). Peter wrote
that we are to "rejoice insofar as you share Christ's sufferings, that you
may also rejoice and be glad when his glory is revealed" (1 Peter 4:13).

The early Christians willingly embraced suffering, even to the point
of death. They knew their trials had a purifying effect that made them
spiritually stronger and a brighter testimony to a watching world. Are
we ready to embrace suffering as they did?

Any loss we face from persecution is temporary, and every gain we
receive is eternal. Jesus promises "the crown of life" to all who endure
tribulation—a reward that can never be taken away. That is why we can
say, with boldness, "In God I trust; I shall not be afraid. What can man
do to me?" (Psalm 56:11).

MAKING THE RIGHT CHOICES

I know where you dwell, where Satan's throne is. Yet you hold fast
my name, and you did not deny my faith (Revelation 2:13).

The church in Pergamum was at the crossroads. Jesus both praised and condemned this congregation. And the church's response would determine whether the people would take the path that led to God and spiritual purity, or the path to compromise and spiritual ruin.

The believers in Pergamum had the challenge of living "where Satan's throne is." Though we don't know exactly what "Satan's throne" refers to, the city was a hotbed of pagan and emperor worship. So pervasive were these cult influences that it was remarkable the Christians had, to a great extent, resisted them. That is why Jesus commended them.

All believers today constantly find themselves at the crossroads because we live in a culture that is so thoroughly saturated with ungodliness. The battle never ceases and is made difficult for two key reasons: (1) We are reluctant to live with a courageous faith because we don't want to invite persecution, and (2) in a misguided effort to attract unbelievers to Christ, we try to culturally blend in with them so they feel more comfortable with us.

It is vital that we don't succumb to either way of thinking. A believer who isn't careful to hold fast to Christ and the faith will, by default, end up on the path to compromise. We can respond in one of two ways to the pressures around us: We can fit in and conform, or we can stand out and be distinct. We can seek to please those around us, or we can seek to please God.

When we find ourselves at the crossroad of conforming or being distinct, we need to remember Galatians 1:10: "Am I now seeking the approval of man, or of God?...If I were still trying to please man, I would not be a servant of Christ." By framing our choices as decisions between pleasing God or people, we can more readily see how to best respond.

LOVING THE CHURCH
AS CHRIST LOVES IT

I have a few things against you: you have some there who hold the
teaching of Balaam...So also you have some who hold the teaching
of the Nicolaitans. Therefore repent (Revelation 2:14-16).

Jesus opened his letter to the believers at Pergamum by praising them
for holding fast His name and the faith. Their loyalty was remarkable
because of the city's many satanic and pagan influences. Yet the church
wasn't paying careful attention—some people within the congregation
were promoting false doctrines, including the teachings of Balaam and
of the Nicolaitans.

What this means is that compromise and immorality were being
tolerated. Wrong beliefs were finding their way into the church and
leading to ungodly behaviors. While not everyone went along with the
false teachings, apparently little or nothing was being done to keep the
church doctrinally pure. For this reason, Jesus commanded the believers to repent—to weed out the error that was causing harm. By failing
to do so, they shared in the false teachers' guilt.

Right doctrine is essential for right living. It is harder to stay faithful
when we permit wrong ways of thinking to infiltrate the church—no matter how harmless they seem. That's why Christ is so adamant about doctrinal purity. Even a seemingly minor error, when tolerated, will spread
and worsen—just like small cracks, left unattended, grow into big ones.

The apostle Paul urged Timothy, to "give attention to reading, to
exhortation, to doctrine" (1 Timothy 4:13 NKJV). To Titus he wrote,
"Speak the things which are proper for sound doctrine" (Titus 2:1 NKJV).
The reason right doctrine should be a high priority is it serves as an anti-
dote to wrong doctrine. Holding fast to what is right and true is what
enables us to stay pure.

For us to hold fast to Christ and the faith calls for fidelity to the truth
as well as intolerance for error. When we care about doctrinal purity, we
love the church as Jesus loves it.

THE PRICE OF COMPROMISE

*The words of the Son of God, who has eyes like a flame of fire, and whose
feet are like burnished bronze: I know your works, your love, and faith
and service...But I have this against you...that you tolerate that woman
Jezebel...teaching and seducing my servants (Revelation 2:18-20).*

As we read Christ's letter to the church at Thyatira, His tone is stern. He has few commendations and many criticisms. He opens with a reference to His "eyes like a flame of fire"—that is, His piercing gaze as a judge. This repeats the description given of our Lord in Revelation 1:12-16, where we see Him walking among His churches in chastening judgment. Evidently the church in Thyatira needed a sharp rebuke that would remind them of whom they served and why. Christ had died for them to "sanctify and cleanse" them, that they "should be holy and without blemish" (Ephesians 5:26-27).

While the believers in Thyatira exhibited works, love, faith, and service, these traits were overwhelmed by all that was wrong. Sadly, it wasn't persecution or evil influences from outside that pressured the church into compromise and sin. Rather, the people had allowed corruption to fester from within. Many had been seduced by an influential prophetess who promoted false teachings and sexual immorality.

When we fail to exercise discernment and accept erroneous teaching, we will pay a high price and the result will be erroneous living. That is why the apostle Paul admonished us to "keep...the pattern of sound teaching...Guard the good deposit that was entrusted to you" (2 Timothy 1:13-14 NIV). We are to guard God's precious truth with zeal, for it alone can point us in the right direction. When we are diligent to make Scripture our sole authority in all things, we protect ourselves from any influences that might lead us astray.

HE SEARCHES OUR MINDS AND HEARTS

All the churches will know that I am he who searches mind and heart,
and I will give to each of you according to your works (Revelation 2:23).

When Jesus chastised the believers in Thyatira for tolerating false teaching and immorality within their church, He did not hold back. He warned that judgment would be swift and sure upon the compromisers if they didn't repent. Typically, we think of judgment as an event that will take place in the distant future. But because Christ does not want sin to have a cancerous influence in His church, He may exercise more immediate discipline to purge the people of sin and restore purity.

It is as we see Christ at work cleansing us that we will know it is He "who searches mind and heart." Nothing can escape His penetrating gaze. He knows our every thought, intention, motive, and action. As King David wrote in Psalm 139, "LORD, you have searched me and known me!...You discern my thoughts from afar...and are acquainted with all my ways. Even before a word is on my tongue, behold, O LORD, you know it altogether" (verses 1-4).

Christ's all-knowing gaze into our minds and hearts can fill us with either a negative fear or a positive one. We will experience negative fear when we're trying to hide something from Him, and that should convict us to confess and repent. And we will know a positive fear when we view His omniscience as a motivator for keeping ourselves pure. When we have a clean conscience, our fear of the Lord is one of reverence and not trepidation.

Christ is a fair and righteous judge. He says, "I will give to each of you according to your works." To those living in wrong, that brings fear; to those living in holiness, that brings comfort. May we always desire to say, with genuine eagerness, "Search me, O God, and know my heart! Try me and know my thoughts!" (Psalm 139:23).

WHAT DOES JESUS SEE?

You have the reputation of being alive, but you are dead. Wake up, and strengthen what remains and is about to die, for I have not found your works complete in the sight of my God (Revelation 3:1-2).

As we make our way through Christ's letters to the seven churches in Revelation 2–3, we notice an abrupt change in our Lord's message to the church at Sardis. The first four churches received praises as well as rebukes. But for Sardis, Jesus had mostly condemnation.

On the surface, the people had "the reputation of being alive." But in reality, they were dead. Externally they looked good. But internally—and spiritually—there was no life and power. Remember Jesus' words to the Pharisees, the legalistic religious leaders of His day? "You are like whitewashed tombs, which outwardly appear beautiful, but within are full of dead people's bones and all uncleanness" (Matthew 23:27). This was the problem in Sardis.

There must have been a small number of true believers, for Jesus said, "Wake up, and strengthen what remains." The call to "wake up" means to be alert. Evidently complacency had set in. The few believers who were left blended in with the culture around them. Unless that changed, the remnant of embers among the ashes would soon die out.

What is the remedy when we as believers become stagnant? "Strengthen what remains."

We need to stay watchful. What is the state of our heart? Our relationship with Christ? Are we abiding in Him? Are we devoted to the Word, which keeps us spiritually rooted and alive in the gospel and the truth? Are we diligent about staying nourished in the basics of our faith?

When we evaluate how we are doing as Christians, our tendency is to focus on what people see of us externally. But the test we should apply is this: What does God see internally? May the life we show be real and from the heart!

WHY JESUS CARES ABOUT OUR PURITY

Yet you have still a few names in Sardis, people who
have not soiled their garments…they will walk with me
in white, for they are worthy (Revelation 3:4).

In Scripture, garments are often illustrative of a person's character. So when Jesus talks about someone who has "not soiled their garments," He is speaking of a person who is diligent to maintain godly character.

Whenever we dress in preparation to be around others, we are super conscious of whether our clothes are clean. Even a tiny stain annoys us— to the point we'll do all we can to remove it. And if we can't, we'll replace what we're wearing. Undoubtedly, when you're with others, you've had times when you've self-consciously tried to hide a spot of dirt on a garment. It's distracting, isn't it?

That helps us to understand how Christ feels when we've become spiritually soiled, yet we've let it slide because we assume the things of the heart aren't all that visible to others. But they are! Jesus' admonishment about believers "who have not soiled their garments" serves to remind us of how much He cares about our purity.

When we profess to walk with Christ yet our character falls short, unbelievers will notice. Our sullied garments distract from who Christ is. Our stains obscure His righteousness in us. When we tolerate soiled character within us, we present to the world a soiled representation of Christ.

What people see of us will affect their perception of Jesus. That is why He is so zealous about our character. He desires for others to see Him clearly through our lives.

WHAT IT TAKES TO BE FAITHFUL

*I have set before you an open door, which no one is able to
shut. I know that you have but little power, and yet you have
kept my word and not denied my name (Revelation 3:8).*

Christ's praises for the church in ancient Philadelphia should get our
attention. This was a faithful church—so much so that Jesus had
no criticisms for the believers. If we want to know what it takes to be
faithful, we find tremendous insight here.

The "open door" Christ speaks of refers to opportunities for service, which no one could hinder. We find similar language in 1 Corinthians 16:8-9, where Paul said, "I will stay in Ephesus...for a wide door
for effective work has opened for me, and there are many adversaries."
Though Paul faced opposition, he was able to spread the gospel and truth.

That these believers had "little power" was not a negative and seems
to indicate the church may have been small yet was dynamic. This brings
to mind Paul's joyful words, "For the sake of Christ, then, I am content with weaknesses, insults, hardships, persecutions, and calamities.
For when I am weak, then I am strong" (2 Corinthians 12:10). From
a worldly standpoint, though we may be feeble, our complete dependence on God makes us vessels through which He can do mighty works.

What does it take to be a believer through whom God can accomplish much? As Revelation 3:8 says, "You have kept my word and not
denied my name." We see here a love for the Lord's Word and a love
for the Lord Himself. These loves are what enable us to persevere and
be faithful. Standing firm in the Word and staying loyal to Christ are
the keys to unleashing the power God makes available to us. The result?
God will open doors of ministry.

Even when we have little to offer, when we are faithful, God can
do much.

TAKEN UP BEFORE THE TRIBULATION

Because you have kept my word about patient
endurance, I will keep you from the hour of trial that
is coming on the whole world (Revelation 3:10).

J esus' instructions to the seven churches in Revelation 2–3 are also
meant for all believers through all time. His praises and rebukes are
intended for us too. Even today, Jesus continues His ministry of encouraging and chastising us so that we are the church He longs for us to be.

So the incredible promise given in Revelation 3:10 is one for all
Christians: We who give evidence of true faith through "patient endurance" will be kept "from the hour of trial that is coming on the whole
world." This "coming...hour of trial" speaks of a future event. And the
fact it will engulf "the whole world" speaks of global judgment—this
is not limited to the region around the church in Philadelphia. All this
fits what Scripture tells us about the seven-year tribulation—it is still
future, it will be severe, and it will be global. That this promise is given
in Revelation 3 to believers in the church age fits with the truth that
the rapture precedes the tribulation, which is later described in Revelation chapters 6–19 and is intended for unbelievers.

Jesus said He will keep us "from" this trial. The Greek preposition
used here, *ek*, best translates to "out of," and refers to separation. That
makes Revelation 3:10 a promise that we will be *removed*—that is, raptured—before the tribulation. This is in harmony with other passages
that say we will be delivered from the wrath to come (1 Thessalonians
1:10; 5:9-10).

Jesus' words "I will keep you" is a resolute promise. *This will happen.*
"Keep you" speaks of protection—of being put in a safe place while this
trial occurs. Before all hell breaks loose on earth, we will be taken up to
heaven to be with our Lord (1 Thessalonians 4:17). No wonder the rapture is called "our blessed hope"! (Titus 2:13).

HALFHEARTED CHRISTIANITY

I know your works...Would that you were either cold or hot!
So, because you are lukewarm, and neither hot nor cold, I
will spit you out of my mouth (Revelation 3:15-16).

Christ had no positive words for the church at Laodicea. With all-knowing discernment, He diagnosed its spiritual condition as neither cold nor hot. The people weren't spiritually dead, but neither did they display any spiritual life or zeal. They were lukewarm, marked by half-heartedness and apathy. In verse 17, Jesus stated the result: "You say, I am rich, I have prospered, and I need nothing, not realizing that you are wretched, pitiable, poor, blind, and naked."

What an indictment! The people couldn't see how destitute they were. They thought they were doing well, but the opposite was true. They lacked any fervency for Christ and His Word, exhibiting no commitment, no convictions. While Jesus does not condemn them for false teachings or serious sins, we can safely conclude that compromise filled the church because Jesus commanded the people to "be zealous and repent" (verse 19). There was enough sin and worldliness in their lives that it eclipsed their witness for Christ. With their mouths they identified with Him, but their actions gave no evidence that they belonged to Him. That He was ready to spit them out of His mouth tells us spiritual indifference is intolerable to Him.

The danger of halfhearted Christianity is that it leads us to believe we're doing well when we're not. It's easy for many little compromises to get in the way of our one big commitment—our devotion to Christ—such that we become unacceptable and useless to Him. When we sense our spiritual temperature diminishing, it's time for us to rekindle the flames of our devotion to Him. And there's no better way to do that than to love the Lord with all our being (Matthew 22:37).

CHRIST DISCIPLINES
THOSE WHOM HE LOVES

Those whom I love, I reprove and discipline, so be
zealous and repent (Revelation 3:19).

What should we conclude about a person who professes to be a Christian but shows no evidence of it? There are two possibilities: Either he is a believer who, for the time being, is living in a way that makes him indistinguishable from unbelievers, or he is an apostate—a counterfeit who once claimed Christ as Savior but later abandons the faith. This reveals he was never truly converted and was "not of us," as 1 John 2:19 says.

The church at Laodicea likely had both indistinguishable believers and pretenders. And it's to the first group that our Lord says, "Those whom I love, I reprove and discipline." Christ has no reason to rebuke apostates because they have thoroughly rejected Him. But He has every reason to discipline His own when they need correction. Second Timothy 2:13 says Christ remains faithful to us even when we are unfaithful.

When we are showing no signs of spiritual life and zeal, we can expect the Lord's chastisement and correction. And while "all discipline seems painful rather than pleasant…later it yields the peaceful fruit of righteousness" (Hebrews 12:11). When Christ reproves us, it's because He loves us too much to let us fester in fruitless living. The intended result of His discipline is that we return to a state of spiritual productivity and living righteously for Him.

We are not called to a halfhearted or casual Christianity. Christ made this clear when He said, "If anyone would come after me, let him deny himself and take up his cross and follow me." After Paul wrote of Christ's great sacrifice on our behalf in Romans 1–11, he then said in Romans 12:1, "I appeal to you, therefore…by the mercies of God, to present your bodies as a living sacrifice." Real faith and love for Christ are made evident by denial and sacrifice.

HE WHO HAS AN EAR

He who has an ear, let him hear what the Spirit says to the churches
(Revelation 2:7, 11, 17, 29; 3:6, 13, 22).

At the end of all seven letters to the churches in Revelation 2–3, Christ gave this urgent plea: "He who has an ear to hear, let him hear what the Spirit says to the churches." The fact Jesus repeated this statement in every letter tells us it is important. And if we look carefully, we see an interesting pattern: When Christ says this, He transitions from speaking to a whole church to speaking to an individual believer—that is, "he who has an ear." Note also that the word "churches" is plural. This tells us Christ wants *all* believers to heed what He wrote to *all* the churches. Every instruction in every letter is meant for every one of us.

"Let him hear what the Spirit says" is a call to obedience. We're to pay attention to our Lord's praises and rebukes to the seven churches, and act on them. These letters provide us with divine guidance for living as Christ wants us to live. And these instructions originated from the Holy Spirit, who inspired all of what is written in Scripture (2 Peter 1:21).

Every church is made up of individuals, which means it's up to each of us to be difference-makers who contribute to what a church ought to be. Christ's urging for the church to be pure requires each believer to commit to personal holiness. A congregation filled with weak Christians cannot become a strong church. It's only as every believer pursues spiritual maturity—and encourages others to do so—that a healthy church becomes possible.

While the seven letters were written to churches, all of them end with a call for us to take personal responsibility and heed Christ's words. The letters are meant just as much for us as they were for the churches they were written to. "He who has an ear, let him hear" is Christ turning to you and saying, "If you love me, you will keep my commandments" (John 14:15).

WHO ARE THE OVERCOMERS?

The one who overcomes…
(Revelation 2:7, 11, 17, 26; 3:5, 12, 21 NASB).

Every letter to the seven churches ends with one or more promises from God to "the one who overcomes." At first glance, to describe a believer as an overcomer—or a conqueror—seems to imply that some Christians will be more special than others in eternity. Will only strong believers who finish well be recognized as overcomers?

Two clues in Scripture help to answer that question. First, in 1 John 5:4-5, we read, "*Everyone* who has been born of God overcomes the world. And this is the victory that has overcome the world—our faith. Who is it that overcomes the world except the one who believes that Jesus is the Son of God?" Three times in the space of two verses, we're told that true faith in Christ as Savior and Lord is what makes us an overcomer!

Second, as we look at the gifts God lists for overcomers in Revelation 2–3, we discover they are benefits available to *all* believers. For example, in Revelation 2:7, Christ promised the overcomers in Ephesus that they will someday eat from the tree of life. When we read about this tree in the New Jerusalem in Revelation 22, no indication is given that some will have access to it while others won't. Because the tree of life represents eternal life, and because every believer possesses God's gift of eternal life, all will have the right to eat from this tree.

If you are a believer, you are an overcomer. Isn't that a thrilling title to have? And yet we are humbled when we realize it's not because of anything we've done, but because of what Christ has done for us. We are overcomers because He is *the* Overcomer. His victory over sin and death makes our victory possible as well. It is for this reason that, for all eternity, we will bow at His feet and sing, "Crown Him with many crowns!"

VIEWING THE FUTURE
FROM GOD'S THRONE ROOM

After this I looked, and behold, a door standing open in
heaven! And the first voice…said, "Come up here, and I will
show you what must take place after this" (Revelation 4:1).

The apostle John wrote Revelation chapters 1–3 while on earth. Then as we turn to Revelation 4, he is called up to heaven. He is told, "Come up here, and I will show you what must take place after this." In an instant, John found himself in God's throne room.

The transition in Revelation 4:1 is significant—it begins a new vision and a new section of the book. In chapters 2–3, we see Christ walking among His churches on the earth, giving instructions to them. Then in chapters 4–22, we are given a panoramic view of the future—the tribulation, second coming, millennial kingdom, and eternity—from the vantage point of heaven.

What's striking is that as the tribulation unfolds on earth all through chapters 4–18, nowhere do we see any mention of the church. This is consistent with the New Testament teaching that the church is not appointed to face God's wrath (1 Thessalonians 1:10; 5:9). Revelation 4:1, then, gives us a picture of what will happen at the rapture. Verse 2 tells us John was "in the Spirit" while in heaven, so he wasn't *physically* raptured. But the fact the tribulation will not occur until *after* all Christians are taken up to heaven communicates a parallel between John being taken up "in the Spirit" and the future, physical rapture of all believers.

What's amazing about this change of scene from earth to heaven is that through John's pen, we become guests in God's throne room itself, a truly spectacular setting. This allows us to see earth's final days from God's perspective. We are given a behind-the-scenes view of the Lord exercising His authority and carrying out His will upon a rebellious planet. For this reason, we are better able to understand the justness of all that God will do during the tribulation.

THE THRONE ROOM OF GOD

Behold, a throne stood in heaven, with one
seated on the throne (Revelation 4:2).

The apostle John had to have been utterly speechless. In a vision, he stood in God's throne room. Here before him was the creator, sustainer, and ruler of the universe in all His brilliant glory. Surrounding the throne were four living creatures and 24 elders who displayed the most fervent, most reverent, and most perfect of worship and praise to the Lord that John had ever seen. The colors and sounds and sights were simultaneously mysterious and enthralling. John does the best he can to describe the scene, but much of what he sees is beyond words. At the center of it all is the "one seated on the throne," surrounded by lightning and thunder.

Very few others have entered this most holy of places. Isaiah had a vision in which he "saw the Lord sitting upon a throne, high and lifted up" (Isaiah 6:1-7), Instantly, he was filled with reverent fear. Words eluded Ezekiel as he tried to describe his vision, needing to use the words "appearance," "like," and "likeness" (Ezekiel 1:26-28). During his vision, Daniel was privileged to see the preincarnate Jesus, "the Son of Man," enter the presence of "the Ancient of Days" (Daniel 7:13-14). And Paul was forbidden to share what he saw (2 Corinthians 12:3-4).

The few glimpses that Scripture provides into God's throne room— along with the responses of those privileged to see it—give us a hint of how truly unsearchable and transcendent God is. The splendor and worship surrounding Him proclaim the greatness of His majesty and holiness. The force of His wisdom and power and righteousness is overwhelming.

Our Almighty God is above all and beyond all. He rules from His throne with absolute and supreme authority. From that throne will come firm and final judgment for all who reject Him, as well as free and forever grace for all who receive Him. Whenever we come before God, may we remember who it is that sits on the throne, and posture our hearts accordingly.

WHAT MAKES HEAVEN *HEAVEN*?

Behold, a throne stood in heaven, with one
seated on the throne (Revelation 4:2).

Heaven. Much has been written about it, and we who have received Christ as Savior and Lord are intensely curious about our future home. We want to know what awaits us there, and what we will do. So we eagerly study all of what Scripture says about heaven. But as we do so, let's not forget why heaven will be so special.

What is it that will make heaven *heaven*? What will make it so spectacular and fulfilling? God's presence! *He* will be the reason we experience endless blessings and joy. In heaven, we will dwell with the very one who created us, loves us, gives us purpose, and takes pleasure in us. You can remove the angels and massive pearl gates, and heaven will still be heaven because God is there. But remove God, and suddenly, heaven will no longer be heaven.

Here's another way of looking at it: What made Eden paradise for Adam and Eve? God's presence. Imagine how traumatic of a change took place when they sinned. Beforehand, God walked with them. Afterward, they were separated from the maker and giver of life. Apart from God, all they could know was the opposite—darkness and death.

Ultimately, the difference between the world we live in now and the world to come is God's presence. A world separated from God is also separated from the life and blessings that only He can give. Just as God's presence is what will make heaven *heaven*, the lack of His presence is what will make hell *hell*.

Heaven will bless us far more than we can ever imagine. And it won't be because of *what* is there, but *who* is there. The God who created us, gave us life, and intended for us to enjoy His presence forevermore will be with us. In heaven, we will be where God intended for us to be all along—with Him. That is why our future home will be so glorious, so exhilarating, so fulfilling.

A HIGH VIEW OF GOD

Day and night they never cease to say,
"Holy, holy, holy, is the Lord God Almighty...!" (Revelation 4:8).

For as long as we are on this earth, our thoughts and view of God will never be as high as they could be. His transcendence and perfection are far greater than we could ever imagine. In our finite humanity, we are unable to fully comprehend God's infinite divinity.

As the apostle John welcomes us to the brilliant splendor of God's throne room, he turns our attention to the four living creatures around the throne. Together, they worship God day and night, proclaiming, "Holy, holy, holy." In Scripture, God's holiness is the only attribute repeated in a threefold manner. That's because His holiness isn't just one aspect of His character but is the sum of all that He is. God's love is holy, His grace is holy, His justice is holy, His power is holy, and more. It's no wonder we are told that God is "majestic in holiness" (Exodus 15:11).

For us to see God extolled for His holiness in Revelation 4 is timely because He is about to pour out His wrath against an unholy world. The tribulation is about to begin, and the words "Holy, holy, holy" resonate all the more powerfully as they are sung in anticipation that God's righteous fury is about to be unleashed.

The four creatures not only exalt God's holiness, but also His power. He is "the Lord God Almighty." God is so strong, so sovereign, so unassailable that nothing can oppose Him. As God exercises judgment, He will accomplish His will.

Because God is infinitely holy and powerful, He is infinitely worthy. This is why it is so appropriate that in His throne room, He is praised unceasingly. As we walk through each moment of each day, may we always be mindful of God's holiness and power so that we cannot help but be inspired to keep growing toward a higher view of Him.

CASTING OUR CROWNS AT GOD'S FEET

The twenty-four elders...cast their crowns before the throne,
saying, "Worthy are you, our Lord and God, to receive
glory and honor and power (Revelation 4:10-11).

In God's throne room are 24 elders engaged in constantly worshiping God. Their white garments and their crowns suggest they represent redeemed believers from throughout the church age—believers who were raptured and resurrected before the start of the tribulation and given their crowns, or heavenly rewards. We don't see any Old Testament saints represented in heaven just yet, for their resurrection won't occur until *after* the tribulation (Daniel 12:1-3).

This is the first of six times in Revelation that John tells us the elders fall before God in reverent worship. As they do so, we see them "cast their crowns before the throne." These crowns are the rewards given to them based on their service to the Lord while on earth.

This casting of crowns at God's feet makes for a powerful scene. We find it portrayed in the popular hymn "Holy, Holy, Holy," which proclaims how "all the saints adore thee, casting down their golden crowns around the glassy sea." When we are in heaven, we will recognize our rewards were made possible only because of God's grace and Christ's sacrifice on the cross. In response, we will place our crowns before the Lord.

Our primary occupation in heaven will be the reverent worship of God. As we recognize that we are undeserving of all that He has given to us, we will eagerly give Him all the credit for redeeming us, giving us every good gift from above, and preserving in heaven an inheritance that is ours. Even now, worship ought to be the posture of our hearts as we wait for heaven. The more intentional we are about expressing our gratitude and praise, the more heavenly minded we will become as we finish out our time here on earth.

THE LAMB TAKES BACK PLANET EARTH

Who is worthy to open the scroll and break its seals? (Revelation 5:2).

I t's hard to imagine anyone weeping with profound sadness while in heaven. Yet that's what happened to the apostle John while in God's throne room: "I saw a mighty angel proclaiming with a loud voice, 'Who is worthy to open the scroll and break its seals?' And no one in heaven or on earth or under the earth was able to open the scroll or look into it, and I began to weep loudly because no one was found worthy" (Revelation 5:2-4).

The word "weep" is the same one used when Jesus sorrowed over Jerusalem (Luke 19:41), and Peter wept bitterly after betraying Christ (Luke 22:62). John's grief was intense!

What was this scroll with the seven seals? In ancient Roman times, sealed scrolls were often legal records of an inheritance or a title deed—they indicated a right of possession. Reading ahead, we see that as the seals are broken, judgments are poured out on the earth. By the time all the judgments end, Christ returns to earth to claim it for Himself—for His kingdom.

When no one was found worthy to take the scroll, John wept because he knew that, under the curse of sin, Satan was "the ruler of this world" (John 12:31). Note that when Satan tempted Jesus in the wilderness, he offered the kingdoms of this world to the Lord in exchange for worship (Matthew 4:8-9). Though the devil does not own the earth, he has temporary domain over it. John could not bear the thought that this arrangement would continue without end!

Thankfully, because the Lamb is worthy, He will take the scroll. At the cross, He paid the price that broke sin's grip on this planet and confirmed Him as the true possessor of it.

The time is coming when Christ will bring the plan of redemption full circle. He is setting the stage to claim all that is rightfully His. He who secured the victory that redeems us will go on to redeem the earth. What was lost by the first Adam will be regained by the last Adam!

CHRIST EXALTED HIGH ABOVE ALL

Behold, the Lion of the tribe of Judah, the Root of David, has conquered,
so that he can open the scroll and its seven seals (Revelation 5:5).

No human, no angel, no creature was qualified to open the scroll with the seven seals—Christ alone was worthy. When one of the elders in God's throne room announced this to John, he did so in a way that calls attention to two great prophecies about Christ and His supreme authority. As this elder explains *who* alone is worthy, he makes clear *why* this one is worthy.

The title "the Lion of the tribe of Judah" comes from one of the earliest prophecies in the Bible about the Messiah as King. Genesis 49:9-10 said that "the scepter shall not depart from Judah." Israel's future and final king would descend from the tribe of Judah. The fact the "scepter shall not depart" means His reign will continue forever. This Lion will judge and rule with fierce strength and power.

The title "the Root of David" appears in Isaiah 11:1, 10, where we learn the Messiah will descend from David. This was true from both His earthly father's and mother's genealogical lines. Isaiah 9:7 tells us that "of the increase of his government and of peace there will be no end, on the throne of David and over his kingdom."

The elder further told John that this Lion and Root of David "has conquered." Christ alone was able to overcome what no one else could: the world (John 16:33), sin (Romans 8:33), death (Hebrews 2:14-15), and the powers of hell (Colossians 2:15).

In the space of very few words, the elder extolled the Lamb's eminence. The Lord Jesus Christ is no mere king among kings, but the eternal King above all kings. He is no ordinary overcomer, but the almighty Overcomer who alone was able to conquer what no one else could. For these reasons, He is uniquely worthy, the most supreme authority, exalted high above all!

FOREVER THE LAMB OF GOD

Between the throne and the four living creatures and among the elders
I saw a Lamb standing, as though it had been slain (Revelation 5:6).

Right from the start, the book of Revelation depicts Christ in blazing glory and power (Revelation 1:12-20). All through the rest of the book, His authority to bring wrath, judgment, and punishment are on full display.

Yet Revelation also mentions Jesus as the Lamb nearly 30 times. By comparison, He is called "the Lamb of God" only twice in the Gospel of John (1:29, 36). This may be surprising because typically, we think of Jesus as the Lamb who offered Himself as a sacrifice *before* the cross, and as the Lion who reigns victoriously *after* the cross.

Why the many descriptions of Jesus as the Lamb in Revelation?

For the book of Revelation to truly be a revelation of Jesus Christ, we must see Him in His fullness—He is both Lamb and Lion, Savior and Judge, Servant and King.

In Revelation 5:9, when the creatures and elders in God's throne room sing to Jesus, they proclaim, "Worthy are you to take the scroll and to open its seals, for you were slain, and by your blood you ransomed people for God." Note why Jesus is worthy: because He was slain. Then "many angels" will join the chorus, saying loudly, "Worthy is the Lamb who was slain" (verse 12). What Jesus did as the Lamb will cause all of heaven to roar with endless worship and praise.

When it comes to the salvation story, because Jesus first came as the Lamb, He is now able to return as the Lion. In His first advent, He went to the cross to rescue us. In His second advent, He will sit on His throne to reign over us.

During the tribulation, Christ will show Himself as both Lamb and Lion. As the Lamb, He will continue to call people to salvation—up till the very moment of His return as the Lion.

MAKING WORSHIP A WAY OF LIFE

To the Lamb be blessing and honor and glory and
might forever and ever! (Revelation 5:13).

After Jesus takes the scroll that indicates His rightful possession of the earth, the reaction is stunning. The creatures and elders around God's throne sing, "Worthy are you to take the scroll." Next, countless angels chime in: "Worthy is the Lamb who was slain, to receive power and wealth and wisdom and might and honor and glory and blessing!" (Revelation 5:9, 12).

Then comes the crescendo as "every creature in heaven and on earth and under the earth and in the sea, and all that is in them" pours forth their praise, saying, "To him who sits on the throne and to the Lamb be blessing and honor and glory and might forever and ever!" (verse 13).

Imagine being in John's sandals and witnessing an outpouring of worship that bursts forth from "*every* creature in heaven and on earth"— from all the universe!

From this scene, we can gain insight into what true worship is all about.

Worship is far more than lifting our voices in praise and song on Sundays. It goes much deeper—it requires that our heart have a reverent posture before the Lord. It involves a mindful, deliberate acknowledgment of His greatness and worthiness. For this to happen, we must recognize and recount all that is true about the Lord as revealed to us in Scripture. Because our Lord is unsearchable and inexhaustible, we will never be able to reach an end point in our worship—it will continue forever!

True and wholehearted worship maintains a heart posture and mindset of revering, loving, honoring, and exalting the Lord. It never tires of coming before Him and extolling Him. Worship sets our hearts and minds on God, and there's no better place for them to be. "From the rising of the sun to its setting, the name of the LORD is to be praised!" (Psalm 113:3).

THE PURPOSES FOR THE TRIBULATION

I watched when the Lamb opened one of the seven seals (Revelation 6:1).

The tearing open of the first seal on the scroll marks the beginning of a long succession of judgments to be unleashed upon a rebellious world. Once the tribulation begins, there will be no going back. Planet Earth will enter its darkest, most cataclysmic period ever. As time goes on, God's wrath will escalate and intensify. Nothing the world has faced up to this time will compare. Jeremiah 30:7 declares, "Alas! That day is so great there is none like it."

As we read about the horrors of the tribulation, we must be careful not to wrongly view God as lashing out in blind rage. We can know with certainty that no person will be unjustly punished. Psalm 96:13 says God "will judge the world in righteousness." His judgments will be fair and precise. Also, many will come to salvation during this time. As God makes Himself known, people will seek salvation in Him.

God has specific purposes for the tribulation, including these four:

1. For Jesus to reclaim what rightfully belongs to Him (Revelation 5:7; 6:1).

2. To discipline the Jewish people and awaken them to their need for the Messiah. Two-thirds will perish and die, but one-third will come to salvation (Zechariah 13:8-9).

3. To punish the unrepentant wicked (Revelation 16:9, 11, 21).

4. To convict many of their sin and draw them to salvation (Revelation 7:9-14).

Because God is all-knowing, He alone is able to accurately judge every person. His wrath does not function apart from any of His other attributes. When God exercises judgment, He does so in a holy, righteous, and loving manner. He is never unfair or unjust. And because God is unchanging, His wrath will always be expressed consistently. We can trust that the wrath God pours out during the tribulation period will be perfect and just in every way possible.

THE BIG PICTURE

...the seven seals...(Revelation 6:1).

As we survey the wrath God will pour out upon the earth during the tribulation, it's easy to be overwhelmed by all the chaos. From a big-picture standpoint, here is what will happen:

As Christ breaks the seven seals on the scroll one by one, a series of judgments will occur. The opening of the first six seals will bring six distinct judgments. When the seventh seal is broken, that will unleash the seven trumpet judgments. The seventh trumpet then brings the seven bowl judgments. Ultimately, all the judgments are instigated by the breaking of the seals.

Notice that it is the Lamb who initiates the tribulation events meant to bring an end to sin once and for all. Not until He breaks the seals do the judgments come. His permission for the wicked to carry out their deeds is also made clear by the language used all through Revelation. Consider the four horsemen of the apocalypse: The crown worn by the rider of the white horse "was *given* to him" (Revelation 6:2). The rider of the red horse "was *given* a great sword" (verse 4). The rider of the pale horse was "*given* authority over a fourth of the earth" (verse 8).

This affirms a powerful truth that runs all through Scripture: God is not the author of sin, nor is He responsible for people's actions. But He sovereignly permits and redirects the sinful works of people so that ultimately, His purposes are achieved. The greatest example of this in all the Bible is the crucifixion. It was wicked humanity that condemned a righteous Messiah to death on the cross. But it was God who ordained for this to happen and who used the evil that led to the cross to make salvation from sin possible (Acts 2:22-23).

History will end with seven years of unimaginable wrath. Yet that will be followed by 1,000 years (then an eternity!) of peace. God, in His mercy, will bring the tribulation to a swift end. And the blessings we experience in Christ's kingdom and heaven will never cease.

THE PERFECT HARMONY
OF BIBLE PROPHECIES

I watched when the Lamb opened...the seven seals (Revelation 6:1).

Some say God will begin pouring out His judgments during the first half of the tribulation, while others say the first half will be peaceful, and the wrath will occur during the second half.

Matthew 24 provides clues that resolve that debate. There, Jesus tells us that at the exact midpoint of the tribulation, the antichrist will enter the temple in Jerusalem and declare that he is God (verse 15). If that happens at the midpoint and the rest of Matthew 24 is about the *second* half of the tribulation, wouldn't it make sense for verses 4-14 to describe the *first* half?

Sure enough, we find these striking parallels between Jesus' words in Matthew 24:4-14 and the seal judgments in Revelation 6, when Jesus initiates the outpouring of God's wrath:

	Matthew 24	*Revelation 6*
False Christs	Verses 5, 11	Verse 2 (first seal, white horse)
Wars	Verses 6-7	Verses 3-4 (second seal, red horse)
Famines	Verse 7	Verses 5-8 (third and fourth seals, pale and black horses)
Earthquakes	Verse 7	Verse 12 (sixth seal)
Persecution	Verse 9	Verses 9-11 (fifth seal)

These parallels reveal that Jesus gave all the disciples—including John—a preview of the seal judgments in Matthew 24. Then 65 years later, John saw those same judgments played out in Revelation 6. Can you imagine the goosebumps he felt when he saw Matthew 24 come to life?

At first glance, the events of the tribulation may appear chaotic, but they aren't. God has planned everything in advance, with precision. Though we won't always understand how various prophecies in the Bible fit together, we can be confident that all the prophetic scriptures are in perfect harmony with one another—revealing God to be orderly and precise in all that He does.

WHO IS THE RIDER
ON THE WHITE HORSE?

I looked, and behold, a white horse! And its rider had a
bow, and a crown was given to him, and he came out
conquering and to conquer (Revelation 6:2).

The identities and actions of the four horsemen of the apocalypse
have fascinated Bible readers through the ages. Entire books have
been written about them, and it is the rider of the white horse who gets
a disproportionate amount of attention.

At first glance, because the horse is white and the rider wears a crown,
some have thought this is Christ, and that the conquering refers to the
spread of the gospel. After all, white represents holiness, and in Revelation 19, Christ returns to earth on a white horse.

But this identification raises three problems: First, Christ is opening
the seals, so He cannot be the rider. This horseman carries a bow, but in
Revelation 19, Christ bears a sword. And the crown on the white horseman is described with the Greek word *stephanos*—a temporary crown
won in athletic competitions. Christ wears *diademas*, or many crowns,
of a kingly nature.

These disparities make it clear the rider isn't Christ. Also, the other
three horsemen are not individuals, but represent the forces of war, famine, and death. The white horseman is likely a force as well. He has a
bow yet lacks arrows, which indicates a nonviolent conquest carried
out with promises of peace. But because the next horseman will "take
peace from the earth" (Revelation 6:4) and bring global war, the peace
brought by the first horseman is false. Similarly, the antichrist will promise peace and sign a treaty with Israel—yet will betray Israel by breaking that peace. Like the white horseman, the antichrist is an imposter
who will deceive many.

The white horseman will win over the people of earth with a false
peace. But after this deception occurs, all hell will break out—literally.
In contrast, when Jesus comes, the peace He brings will be real and last
forever. This makes it clear the white horseman is not Christ.

A CRY FOR JUSTICE

*They cried out with a loud voice, "O Sovereign Lord, holy and
true, how long before you will judge and avenge our blood
on those who dwell on the earth?" (Revelation 6:10).*

When the fifth seal is opened, under a heavenly altar we see "the
souls of those...slain for the word of God and for the witness
they had borne" (Revelation 6:9). Who are these souls?

Remember that before the tribulation, all church-age believers—both
dead and alive—will be raptured to heaven and given glorified bodies (1 Corinthians 15:51-53). We'll already be with Christ in our heavenly bodies. So the souls in Revelation 6:9-10, which lack bodies, must
be believers who are killed after the rapture and during the tribulation.

After the judgments of the first four seals have passed, there will
already be many believers in heaven who have died for their faith. The
souls of these tribulation martyrs—whose bloodied bodies remain on
the earth—are crying out to God for justice. When will He avenge their
blood against the evildoers who killed them?

"They were...told to rest a little longer, until the number of their fellow servants and their brothers should be complete" (verse 11). While
the news that vengeance wouldn't be immediate may have disappointed
them, we can imagine they rejoiced with the announcement that their
numbers were not yet "complete." God was still at work drawing more
people to salvation!

While God punishes the wicked during the tribulation, the antichrist will persecute the righteous. And while God will lovingly delay
vengeance on behalf of the tribulation martyrs so that more can become
saved, the antichrist's vengeance will be hateful and swift. We may wish
God would execute final judgment right now, but He waits with good
reason—others are destined to salvation, and God will not end history
until their numbers are complete.

NO MORE ATHEISTS

Hide us from the face of him who is seated
on the throne (Revelation 6:16).

When the sixth seal is opened, catastrophic destruction will convulse the entire earth and affect the nearby heavenly bodies as never before. Many natural disasters will strike simultaneously. A great earthquake will shake the planet, the sun will be blackened, the moon will become like blood, the stars will fall, the sky will vanish, and mountains and islands will tremble and collapse (Revelation 6:12-14).

So great will the devastation be that the eyes of all the wicked will be opened with a new awareness. We are told that "everyone [will hide] themselves in the caves and among the rocks of the mountains, calling to the mountains and rocks, 'Fall on us and hide us from the face of him who is seated on the throne, and from the wrath of the Lamb'" (verses 15-16).

Everyone will know the source of this calamity—Almighty God who sits on the throne, and the Lamb who judges as a Lion. There simply will be no other explanation. They will know that ultimately, God will prevail—they will cry out, "Who can stand?" (verse 17).

During the tribulation, a point will come when there will be no more atheists. God will make it clear to all that He is the source of the havoc that is tearing apart the earth. But the wicked will reject God so thoroughly that they will be like those described in Romans 1:21: "Although they knew God, they did not honor him as God or give thanks to him." Instead, "their foolish hearts were darkened."

The greatest tragedy of the tribulation will not be the judgments and devastations. Rather, it will be that unbelievers who come face to face with the reality of God's existence and the truth that their sin is the reason for His wrath will still refuse God. Instead of welcoming His love and light, in hatred, they will hide in darkness. They will choose misery over mercy, death over life.

THE GREATEST MISSIONARY FORCE EVER

I heard the number of the sealed, 144,000, sealed from
every tribe of the sons of Israel (Revelation 7:4).

Revelation 6 ends with the defiant masses of the world pleading for mountains and rocks to fall upon and kill them because the great day of God's wrath has come. In desperation, they cry out, "Who can stand?"

In Revelation 7, God answers that very question, pointing to large numbers of Jews and Gentiles He will save during the tribulation. It is these people who will stand and survive.

First, we're introduced to the 144,000 Jewish witnesses who will be given a seal of protection that will preserve them to the end of the tribulation (verses 1-8). They will spread the gospel worldwide, and no one will be able to kill them. God will appoint 12,000 from each tribe of Israel, and we can be certain they truly are Jews (and not the church, as some claim) because never in the Bible are the people of Israel or the 12 tribes identified with Gentiles or the church.

God's original purpose for setting apart Israel in the Old Testament was for the people to be His witnesses to the nations. They failed. After Christ's death and resurrection, the church was given that task. But when the church is removed from earth at the rapture, God will turn back to the Jews and miraculously choose 144,000 to proclaim the gospel. Remember when God chose and converted Paul to become an apostle (Acts 9:3-19)? This will be Paul times 144,000!

Then in the rest of Revelation 7, we see the tribulation martyrs. Though killed on earth, they will stand forever in heaven because they chose salvation in Christ—unlike the unrepentant.

During the tribulation—when evil and darkness are at their worst— God's beloved labor of redeeming people will not diminish. Though the forces of hell are at their fiercest, the forces of heaven will be stronger. A great missionary corps will reap an incredible soul harvest.

SILENCE IN HEAVEN

*When the Lamb opened the seventh seal, there was silence
in heaven for about half an hour (Revelation 8:1).*

When the sixth seal on the scroll is broken, the devastation that takes place on earth is so unprecedented, so overwhelming, and so terrifying that finally, all who have denied God will be forced to recognize He is behind what is happening. There will no longer be any atheists.

And from this point onward, the world's nightmare will get much worse.

From the moment the apostle John first arrived in heaven, he has been surrounded by a constant stream of sights and sounds. He has heard choruses of worship and praise from the heavenly host, thunderous peals of judgment raining down upon the world, and countless multitudes of tribulation saints crying out with loud voices. But when the seventh seal is broken, all the noise and activity come to a sudden halt. Heaven goes completely silent.

After the seventh seal is broken and the scroll unrolled, all of heaven could see what was to come next. They could read the grim details of the seven trumpet and seven bowl judgments that would telescope out of the seventh seal. While we are not told what caused the silence, we can safely guess that heaven was hushed with a holy grief over the gravity of the calamites about to descend upon the earth. From here onward, God's wrath would magnify in severity.

To be on the wrong side of God's judgment is frightening. It is because sin is so deadly and unrelenting that God must deal with it so harshly. So greatly does He detest how sin separated Him from His creation that He will completely purge it. God's wrath is His righteous, holy, and necessary response to the terminal cancer of unrighteousness. And though believers will never face His wrath because Christ has already done that for us, God's anger toward sin should cause us to realize the seriousness of giving it any foothold in our own lives.

THE ROLES OF
ANGELS IN THE END TIMES

*I saw the seven angels who stand before God, and seven
trumpets were given to them (Revelation 8:2).*

B y the time we reach the seven trumpet judgments, a clear pattern is
emerging: Angels are a prominent part of the book of Revelation.
They are mentioned 67 times, more frequently than in any other book
of the New Testament. Most notably, they have important roles in the
execution of God's judgments all through the tribulation.

As the trumpet judgments are about to begin, we see seven angels
standing at attention before God. Each one is given a trumpet that will
unleash specific judgments. Looking ahead to Revelation 16, every one
of the seven bowl judgments is administered by angels as well.

Elsewhere in Revelation, there are angels who will proclaim the eternal gospel to all the earth (Revelation 14:6), announce the fall of Babylon (verse 8), and warn of wrath upon those who worship the antichrist
and receive his mark (verse 9). Angels are involved in the slaughter of
God's enemies (verses 14-20) and will be part of the heavenly armies
at Christ's second coming (Revelation 19:14; see also Matthew 25:31).

Jesus taught that at the end of the age, angels will "gather out of his
kingdom all causes of sin and all law-breakers" (Matthew 13:41). They
will "separate the evil from the righteous and throw them into the fiery
furnace" (verses 49-50). They will accompany Christ at His return, when
"he will repay each person according to what he has done" (Matthew 16:27).

Angels are God's holy and obedient servants. They gladly fulfill the
tasks He assigns to them and are dedicated to carrying out His will.
Their service is done with humility and diligence, making them a wonderful example for us to imitate. Their devotion to worshipping God
without ceasing should inspire us as well, reminding us that He should
be our greatest joy.

HOW PEOPLE WILL RESPOND
TO GOD'S JUDGMENT

The first angel blew his trumpet...and a third of
the earth was burned up (Revelation 8:7).

There are some who suggest that part of the devastation that results from the trumpet and bowl judgments appears to describe the effects of nuclear conflagrations. They say that the burning up of the earth, the darkening of the heavenly bodies, and the poisoning of waters may be indicators of nuclear warfare and fallout. While it is possible that nations will use nuclear weapons during the tribulation, a careful look at the language that describes the trumpet and bowl judgments shows that the destruction they cause comes from God and heaven.

Note that hail and fire are "thrown upon the earth" and a fiery meteor is "thrown into the sea" (Revelation 8:7-8), pointing to origins apart from the planet. We're told "a great star fell from heaven" (verse 10). Only God is capable of directly striking the heavenly bodies (verse 12). Some of the darkened skies can be explained by the smoke that is released when locusts are let out of "the bottomless pit" (Revelation 9:2-11). Another star falls from heaven in Revelation 9:1, and all the bowl judgments clearly originate from heaven (Revelation 16).

The people who suffer from these judgments will point to God as the source. Some will be "terrified" to the point they give "glory to the God of heaven" (Revelation 11:13). This tells us the judgments will have their intended effect and cause people to repent. But others will not do that—instead, they will curse God (16:9, 11, 21). They will blame Him for their agony.

The plagues that strike earth during the trumpet and bowl judgments are amazingly similar to those God sent upon the Egyptians in Exodus. There will be no doubt they are of divine and miraculous origin; they will force every soul to concede God is real and sovereign. Faced with this ultimatum, people will make one of two choices: glorify God, or curse Him.

NO MORE DELAY

The angel whom I saw...raised his right hand to heaven and
swore...that there would be no more delay (Revelation 10:5-6).

Revelation 10 introduces us to "another mighty angel coming down from heaven" (verse 1). Some Bible scholars identify him as Jesus, and others say he is a powerful angel with great authority. There are good and trusted voices on both sides of this debate. But a major clue that favors this being an angel is that he's described as "another" angel (Greek *allos* = "of the same kind," rather than *heteros*, "of a different kind"). He is similar to other angels mentioned earlier in Revelation. Christ could never be described as "of the same kind" as any other being, for He is unique. The angels are created beings, and Christ is the uncreated and only Son of God.

Other aspects of Revelation 10 have generated discussion as well, but of vital importance is the angel's oath "that there would be no more delay." He states this before the seventh trumpet is blown, which will release the final set of judgments—the seven bowls. What does "no more delay" refer to? When the seventh trumpet sounds, voices in heaven proclaim, "The kingdom of the world has become the kingdom of our Lord and of his Christ" (Revelation 11:15). A transfer of ownership is about to take place—Christ is on the verge of returning to claim the earth!

The mighty angel's promise of "no more delay" is an answer to the tribulation martyrs' cry, "How long before you will judge and avenge our blood?" (Revelation 6:10). It is also an answer to the prayers of Christians of all eras who have longed for Christ's second coming.

For 2,000 years, believers have prayed, "Your kingdom come, your will be done, on earth as it is in heaven" (Matthew 6:10). Out of mercy, God has waited so the lost can turn to Him; this calls for understanding and patience from us. But soon, an angel will say, "Enough! No more delay." And at last, our prayer "Your kingdom come" will be fulfilled literally here on earth.

EVERY BELIEVER A WITNESS

I will grant authority to my two witnesses, and they
will prophesy for 1,260 days (Revelation 11:3).

The two witnesses are all-stars in the cast of characters in the book of Revelation. Many readers find their powers fascinating and are curious about their identity. Much speculation has gone into who they are, but if God wanted us to know, He would have named them. There's plenty more for us to learn about the two witnesses that doesn't require guesswork and is instructive for us. Setting aside *who* they might be, let's look at *what* they do, and *how.*

They are witnesses. Their sole mission will be to proclaim God to a watching world. Israel will be at center stage during the end times, meaning all eyes will be on the nation. A temple will stand in Jerusalem again (Revelation 11:1), and the two witnesses will carry out their ministry at ground zero. They'll be so prominent, so bold, the world cannot ignore them.

They will wear sackcloth. Their clothing symbolizes mourning (see Genesis 37:34).

They will prophesy for 1,260 days. Their ministry will continue through the whole first half of the tribulation (3.5 years). They will proclaim the gospel loud and clear that entire time.

They will have divine authority and power. "If anyone would harm them, fire pours from their mouth and consumes their foes" (Revelation 11:5). The fact no one can kill them, combined with their ability to do miracles like droughts and plagues, will confirm they are true prophets of God and not among the demonic counterfeits who will deceive many during that time.

In every age, God appoints witnesses who testify of Him—the prophets, the disciples, and all believers. During the tribulation, the gospel will be proclaimed far and wide through the two witnesses, the 144,000, and more, so anyone who rejects God will have no excuse. If you're a believer, you're a witness. Are you letting God use you as a spokesperson wherever you are?

AN UNHOLY CHRISTMAS

When they have finished their testimony, the beast...
will make war on them (Revelation 11:7).

The two witnesses will be the most hated people on earth.

They will begin their ministry at the start of the tribulation. Because all believers will have been raptured, everyone left behind will have rejected God, choosing instead to love sin and darkness. The two witnesses will have a hostile audience—one that extends worldwide, possibly because of high tech and social media. Their messages and miracles will draw global attention. They will be despised because of their convicting words about sin and the need for repentance. Because no one can kill them, their ministry will continue unhindered for 1,260 days.

That will change at the midpoint of the tribulation. "When they have finished their testimony, the beast...will make war on them and conquer them and kill them" (Revelation 11:7). The word "finished" is the same word Jesus used when He declared "It is finished" at the cross (John 19:30). The witnesses will not die before they complete their ministry.

The wicked will be so thrilled by the antichrist's victory that they'll "make merry and exchange presents, because these two prophets had been a torment" (Revelation 11:10). They will celebrate a demonic Christmas. But three-and-a-half days later, the witnesses will rise and be taken to heaven, bringing "great fear" on those who see this happen (verse 12). The entire world will see this powerful evidence that these were truly prophets of God.

The dark, wicked, and perverted nature of sin will be on full display during the end times. Gift-giving that was done in honor of Christ will be twisted to honor the antichrist. Instead of celebrating good's triumph over evil, people will rejoice when evil triumphs over good. Should we ever wonder if the judgments of the tribulation are too severe, this tells us the answer is no.

GOD AS OUR PROTECTOR

The woman fled into the wilderness, where she has
a place prepared by God (Revelation 12:6).

Revelation 12 begins with a short yet grand retelling of history from the beginning of Israel all the way to the end times: A pregnant woman, who is Israel, will eventually give birth to a male child, the Messiah. The dragon, or Satan, desires to destroy Israel to prevent this from happening.

But the Savior who is to "rule all the nations with a rod of iron" is born, achieves victory at the cross, and is then "caught up to God and to his throne" (verse 5). Later, the woman—or Israel—will flee "into the wilderness, where she has a place prepared by God, in which she is to be nourished for 1,260 days" (verse 6). The woman's flight represents Israel seeking safety after the antichrist declares himself to be God and begins persecution of the Jews, which will happen at the midpoint of the tribulation (Matthew 24:15-21). The 1,260 days in hiding from the dragon-inspired antichrist is a clue this will occur during the second half of the tribulation.

In this panoramic overview of Satan's attempts to defeat God's plans for Israel, the Messiah, and the salvation of mankind, we see a key trait of God on display: He is a protector. He protected Israel so the Messiah could be born, He ensured Jesus made it to the cross to pay the penalty for our sins, and He will protect a remnant of Israel once again during the tribulation.

Scripture describes God as our fortress, strength, rock, shield, refuge, hiding place, shelter, and stronghold. This is why we can say with the psalmist, "Even though I walk through the valley of the shadow of death, I will fear no evil, for you are with me" (Psalm 23:4). No matter how fierce Satan's attacks, we have no reason to be afraid. Israel's recent rebirth as a nation and Christ's victory at the cross are spectacular affirmations of God's supernatural ability to preserve His own. Because you are one of His children, He protects you too.

SATAN'S STRATEGY TO DIVIDE GOD AND US

The accuser of our brothers has been thrown down, who accuses
them day and night before our God (Revelation 12:10).

S atan hates God. Through the ages, the devil has done everything he can to prevent God's prophetic plans from being fulfilled. That's because God's success means Satan's failure.

As God's plans have unfolded, Satan has found it necessary to change his strategies. Unable to prevent Israel from giving birth to the Messiah, Satan did all he could to prevent Jesus from going to the cross and rising from the grave. Having failed that, now Satan is eager to prevent Christ's return and forthcoming judgment, for that will spell the end for him.

So great is Satan's hatred for God that he never rests—he seeks every opportunity to hurt God by hurting God's people. This explains anti-semitism against the Jews, and it explains persecution against Christians. It also explains Satan's constant attempts to use every means he can to strain our relationship with God.

One of Satan's tactics for driving a wedge between us and the Lord is that he "accuses [us] day and night before our God" (Revelation 12:10). When we sin, he tells God that we are unworthy of His love and mercy. At the same time, Satan uses our sin to guilt us into feeling unforgive-able and unable to approach God. His goals are to turn God away from us and turn us away from God. Satan knows that ultimately, his defeat will be permanent. But anytime he can sow division between us and God, that gives him the satisfaction of a temporary victory.

When Satan accuses us, he lies. He condemns those who have no condemnation (Romans 8:1), and he calls unrighteous those who have been given Christ's righteousness (2 Corinthians 5:21). Don't listen to the accuser, but to our "advocate with the Father, Jesus Christ" (1 John 2:1). He has saved us completely and is faithful to always intercede for us! (Hebrews 7:25).

SATAN'S DOOM IS SURE

He knows his time is short! (Revelation 12:12).

As we've turned the pages of the book of Revelation, drawing closer to the final chapters, we've seen key indicators that the end is near.

One interesting clue appears in Revelation 5:6, where the apostle John said he "saw a Lamb standing." As Christ prepares to take the seven-sealed scroll into His hands, He is standing rather than sitting. This is significant, for in Luke 22:69, Jesus told the chief priests and scribes, "From now on the Son of Man shall be seated at the right hand of the power of God." Christ would sit after He finished His role as our high priest. Hebrews 1:3 said of Jesus, "After making purification for sins, he sat down at the right hand of the Majesty on high."

The apostle Peter reported that after Christ ascended to heaven, God told the Son, "Sit at my right hand, until I make your enemies your footstool" (Acts 2:34-35). This tells us Christ will remain seated until it's time to defeat His enemies.[16] So for Christ to stand in Revelation 5:6 is a sign He is getting ready to unleash judgment upon the people of earth.

Next, in Revelation 10:6, a mighty angel declares there will be "no more delay." God had long said He would bring an end to sin and evil, and it was now time to fulfill that promise.

Here in Revelation 12, after war breaks out between the heavenly angels and Satan's demonic angels, the latter will be "thrown down to the earth" (verse 9). No longer will Satan be able to accuse us before God. This striking down of Satan alerts us that the end is near. In response, he will exhibit "great wrath, because he knows that his time is short!" (verse 12).

As believers, we can take comfort in the truth that when the future looks bleak, when evil appears to have the upper hand, when darkness and depravity overwhelm us, time is running out for Satan—and his doom is sure.

NO MATCH FOR GOD

I saw a beast…and to it the dragon gave his power and
his throne and great authority (Revelation 13:1-2).

*B*east is a fitting moniker for the antichrist because he will be the most brutal, most monstrous, most powerful dictator the world has ever known. He will be arrogant and blasphemous (Daniel 11:36; Revelation 13:5), lawless and destructive (2 Thessalonians 2:3), wicked and deceptive (verses 10-11). He will possess a fierce hatred for Jews and Christians (Matthew 24:15-21; Revelation 13:7) and will ruthlessly kill every person who refuses to worship him (Revelation 13:15).

Because the prefix *anti* can mean "opposed to, instead of, against," the term *antichrist* can mean "opposed to Christ," "instead of Christ," and "against Christ." The beast will be the opposite of Christ in every way—total darkness versus total light, pure evil versus pure righteousness. The reason the antichrist will be the most atrocious ruler ever is that his power will come directly from Satan, and Satan will share his throne with him. Because Satan is the god of this world (2 Corinthians 4:4), this means the beast will possess extraordinary authority.

Yet no matter how strong Satan and the antichrist will be, God is stronger. God's power is absolute, Satan's is not. God is uncreated and transcendent; Satan is a created being with limitations. Though Satan managed to convince Adam and Eve to rebel against God and thus put all of creation under the curse of sin and death, God has broken the power of the curse.

God and Satan are not equals. God is infinitely preeminent. This truth is evident from Genesis to Revelation. God always has been and always will be the victor in the outcome of every encounter between them. Satan has never been able to overcome even the tiniest aspects of God's plans and actions up to this day, and he will never be able to do so—ever.

THE FALSE PROPHET

*I saw another beast rising... [it] makes the earth and its
inhabitants worship the first beast (Revelation 13:11-12).*

Through the ages, Satan has done everything he can to spread spiritual blindness and deception, and he has carried out this work through false prophets. During the end times, he will work through what turns out to be earth's foremost and final false prophet: the second beast.

The first beast, the antichrist, will rise to power as a political and military leader. Through charm and clout, he will become ruler over all. The second beast will come alongside the first to make him a religious leader as well, forcing everyone to worship the antichrist as God.

The false prophet will possess "all the authority of the first beast in its presence" (Revelation 13:12). He will set up a global religious system that requires all the earth to worship the one-world ruler. He will perform great and convincing miracles that deceive many (verse 13). He will require that an image of the antichrist be built, and he will be "allowed to give breath [Greek *pneuma*] to the image of the beast" (verse 15), making it appear alive. Note that he will only give *breath* to the image, not *life* (Greek *bios*), which only God can do. And he will administer the mark of the beast, establishing the antichrist as the ultimate totalitarian.

Satan, the antichrist, and the false prophet will work together to form a counterfeit and unholy trinity that seeks to usurp the holy Trinity of God the Father, the Son, and the Holy Spirit. Their global kingdom, built on deception and lies, will appear invincible. But their false might will come to a swift end when Christ, who possesses true might, returns to earth. In an instant, Christ will slay His enemies. Then He will throw the two beasts into the lake of fire and bind Satan for 1,000 years in a bottomless pit. "Not a trace" of the antichrist's kingdom will remain, and the one true God "will set up a kingdom that shall never be destroyed" (Daniel 2:35, 44).

THE MARK OF THE BEAST

[The false prophet] causes all...to be marked (Revelation 13:16).

One of the more popular topics in Bible prophecy is the mark of the beast. Interestingly, the Bible doesn't say much about it. Because people are so curious about this mark, they have many questions about its significance and meaning. Unfortunately, this lack of details has led some people to offer all kinds of harmful speculations that have led to confusion about the mark.

Here is what Scripture tells us for certain:

- The mark will be mandatory—all will be forced to take it (Revelation 13:16).

- It will be placed "*on* the right hand or the forehead" (verse 16). It will be "on" the surface, not hidden. Its primary intent is to confirm a person's allegiance to the antichrist.

- Those who refuse the mark will not be able to buy or sell (verse 17). This will be the ultimate form of social control, making it impossible for anyone without the mark to survive.

- Those who refuse the mark will be put to death (Revelation 20:4).

- To take the mark will be to swear loyalty to the antichrist and to be subject to God's wrath (Revelation 14:9-10; 16:2).

- Based on the chronology of Revelation, we know that the false prophet's command for people to take the mark will not happen until the second half of the tribulation. The mark won't exist before the rapture, nor during the first half of the tribulation.

The fact the mark of the beast will not arise until after we are taken up to heaven in the rapture gives us the wonderful assurance that we, as believers, will never accidentally accept the mark. During the tribulation, anyone who takes the mark will do so knowingly, fully aware that they are pledging allegiance to the antichrist and rejecting God. There will be nothing hidden or secret about the mark because it will be clearly visible on those who will bear it.

SECURE IN GOD'S HANDS

On Mount Zion stood the Lamb, and with
him 144,000 (Revelation 14:1).

Revelation 14 brings us to an interlude that jumps ahead in time and gives us a preview of the end of the tribulation. Here, we encounter the 144,000 Jewish witnesses again. We first met them in Revelation 7, when they were sealed and promised protection from their enemies. True to His word, God preserved them, and every single one of them has survived through the tribulation.

We see the 144,000 standing on Mount Zion, or the Temple Mount, with the Lamb. It appears the Jewish witnesses will be there to greet Christ at His second coming. They will have front-row seats to His glorious return, and deservedly so, for they will have sacrificed greatly in their service to the Lord. They will be eager to finally meet the one whom they proclaimed!

The 144,000 are described as "firstfruits for God and the Lamb." In the Old Testament, the firstfruits of a harvest were offered to God (Deuteronomy 26:1-11) and made available for His use (18:3-5). Because God chose these witnesses at the beginning of the tribulation, they can be viewed as the firstfruits of the believers who endure the seven years of wrath and enter the millennial kingdom. Or, they may represent the firstfruits of all the Jews who will be saved during the tribulation (see Zechariah 12:10; Romans 11:25-26).

God's power to preserve the 144,000 should encourage us. Though we aren't protected from death as they will be, we are sealed with the Spirit, which guarantees our eternal destiny (Ephesians 1:13-14). As Jesus said, no one can snatch us out of His hand (John 10:28).

"If God is for us, who can be against us?" (Romans 8:31). What a triumphant declaration! Because God is sovereign and omnipotent, no one can derail His plans for us and promises to us. Because no one is greater than God, it is not possible for anyone to overrule what He has ordained for us. Every Christian's future is absolutely and entirely secure in God's hands.

PATIENT TO THE VERY END

*I saw another angel flying directly overhead, with an eternal
gospel to proclaim to those who dwell on earth, to every nation
and tribe and language and people (Revelation 14:6).*

In Revelation 14, the apostle John fast-forwards us to the end of the
tribulation. We are given a preview of the 144,000 witnesses on Mount
Zion, where they will greet Christ upon His return. And in the air, we
see angels circling the earth. These angels bear messages that will reach
"every nation and tribe and language and people."

The first angel will proclaim "an eternal gospel," urging people to
"fear God and give him glory, because the hour of his judgment has
come" (Revelation 14:7).

The second angel will follow and cry out, "Fallen, fallen is Babylon
the great" (verse 8). This looks ahead to Revelation 17 and 18, which
describe the total destruction of Babylon prior to Christ's return. Babylon will be the political, economic, and religious center of the antichrist's kingdom. This angel's warning will alert the world that final
judgment is at hand.

The third angel will say with a loud voice, "If anyone worships the
beast and its image and receives a mark on his forehead or on his hand,
he also will drink the wine of God's wrath" (Revelation 14:9-10). At the
same time, he will exhort believers to remain faithful (verse 12).

Between the 144,000 witnesses and the angels who circle the earth,
God will plead for people everywhere to choose His grace over His
wrath. He will go to extraordinary lengths to make His patience and
mercy known all the way to the very final moments of human history.

Even when judgment is near, God still exhibits great patience, desir-
ing that people become saved. That is why His warnings of wrath are
accompanied by offers of mercy. When people end up facing God's judgment, it is because they rejected His patience and mercy.

LOOKING BEYOND FINAL JUDGMENT

I saw another sign in heaven, great and amazing, seven
angels with seven plagues, which are the last, for with
them the wrath of God is finished (Revelation 15:1).

Revelation chapter 15 pulls back the curtain on the grand finale of the book of Revelation. Seven angels are standing at attention, ready to dispense the bowl judgments, which are the closing act. They will usher in the most frightening, most horrifying, most devastating period of time the world has ever known. God's wrath is about to hit peak intensity in response to the peak depravity on earth.

As this scene unfolds, the apostle John sees, around God's throne, "those who had conquered the beast and its image and the number of its name" (verse 2). These are believers who refused to take the mark of the beast and died for their faith during the tribulation. The antichrist killed them—and here, they are said to have "conquered the beast." The antichrist's victory over them will be temporary, and their victory over him will be permanent.

As the worst of God's judgments are about to come, we see the tribulation saints singing! They will exalt God because the last of His wrath is about to be poured out. They will rejoice because the antichrist will soon be crushed, their deaths will be avenged, sin's reign of terror on earth will finally end, justice and truth will prevail, and God will rule over all.

It is sobering to ponder the severity of God's judgment and wrath during the end times. But the fact it will be final—yes, *final!*—is reason for rejoicing. Christ's return will extinguish sin and darkness and begin a new day that will never end. The wonders that await us are so great that they should fill our hearts with praise even while it is still night. When we live in anticipation of the joys of tomorrow, they will supply us with joy for today.

"IT IS DONE!"

The seventh angel poured out his bowl into the air, and a loud voice came out of the temple, from the throne, saying, "It is done!" (Revelation 16:17).

Seven seals, seven trumpets, and six bowls. By this time, the cumulative effects of all these judgments will have left earth and its people reeling. The seventh bowl judgment, the final outpouring of God's wrath, will bring the most catastrophic devastation of all, altering the planet's geography. After flashes of lighting and thunder will come "a great earthquake such as there had never been since man was on earth, so great was that earthquake" (Revelation 16:18).

This will cause "the great city" to split into three parts and the cities of the nations to fall (verses 19-20). Some say the great city is Babylon, but Jerusalem makes more sense because in Scripture, it is always regarded as great compared to other cities in the world.[17] Also, we know from Zechariah 14:4-10 that a mighty earthquake will strike Jerusalem upon Christ's return.

The Revelation 16 earthquake will cause islands to disappear and mountains to crumble, and massive hailstones weighing about 100 pounds each will crush everything (verses 20-21). All of this will coincide with the end of Armageddon and Jesus' second coming.

Even after witnessing great signs and wonders that are clearly of divine origin, people will still curse God (verses 9, 11, 21). It is possible for people's hearts to be so hardened that no miracle from God will convince them. This is a testimony of the blinding power of sin.

Jesus' words "It is finished," spoken at the cross, are the most beautiful a seeking heart could ever hear, for they mean eternal salvation and a return to God are possible. But God's words "It is done!," spoken after the seventh bowl judgment, will be the most painful an unrepentant heart could ever hear, for they mean eternal condemnation and separation from God.

THE RISE AND FALL
OF RELIGIOUS BABYLON

Come, I will show you the judgment of the great prostitute
who is seated on many waters (Revelation 17:1).

Chronologically, Revelation 17 takes place during the first half of the tribulation. Here, we read about a false religious system that will rise in Babylon. Because every Old Testament reference to Babylon is literal, and the other cities named in Revelation are literal (with the exception of 11:8, which is clearly symbolic), we can view Babylon in Revelation 17 as a literal city.

The chapter opens by introducing us to "the great prostitute." In Scripture, prostitution often speaks metaphorically of false religion and unfaithfulness to God (Ezekiel 20:30). This harlot is "seated on many waters," meaning this religious system will involve many peoples and nations. The rest of the chapter tells us this apostate religion will…

- have a powerful, intoxicating influence (verse 2)
- control the antichrist for a time (verse 3)
- be corrupt (verse 4)
- persecute true believers and kill them (verse 6)
- be destroyed by the antichrist and the kings under his authority (verses 16-18)

At the midpoint of the tribulation, when the antichrist declares himself to be God, he will no longer need the false world religion. While the system will be destroyed, the city of Babylon won't. It will continue as the antichrist's commerce center (see Revelation 18).

When people reject God and truth, they open themselves to apostasy and deception. It is amazing how quickly spiritual harlotry can take root and spread. By the midpoint of the tribulation, a popular and intoxicating false religious system will evolve into global worship of the antichrist as God. When truth is abandoned, the descent into error is swift and steep.

THE FALL OF BABYLON

Fallen, fallen is Babylon the great! (Revelation 18:1).

The tribulation will end with a massive bang. Around the same time as or during the seventh bowl judgment, the mighty city of new Babylon will be destroyed, and the antichrist will carry out the campaign of Armageddon. It will be chaos in hyperdrive.

Babylon will be the economic centerpiece of the antichrist's global empire. The stature and prosperity of his capital will be so unparalleled that the question is asked, "What city was like the great city?" (verse 18). We are told that "the merchants of the earth [will] have grown rich from the power of her luxurious living" (verse 3). Not only will Babylon be the pinnacle of luxury and wealth on earth, but it will also be the pinnacle of sin and wickedness: "She has become a dwelling place for demons, a haunt for every unclean spirit" (verse 2). All the rulers of the earth will have "committed immorality with her," and evil will be so prevalent that "her sins are heaped high as heaven" (verses 3, 5).

As payback for Babylon's great wickedness, God will pour out an especially fierce judgment upon her: "Plagues will come in a single day, death and mourning and famine, and she will be burned up with fire; for mighty is the Lord God who has judged her" (verse 8). God's wrath will be so devastating that the city falls "in a single hour" (verse 10).

When Babylon falls, the world system dependent upon the city will collapse. This disaster will contribute to the antichrist's fury as he readies the world's armies for Armageddon.

From Eden to the end of the tribulation, Scripture is clear: God must and will punish sin. His righteousness and holiness obligate Him to do so. God takes sin seriously because it is contrary to Him in every way. As God's children, we should take sin seriously too. Our gratitude for the high price God paid to free us from sin should cause us to hate sin as He does.

SATAN'S LAST STAND AGAINST THE JEWS

They assembled them at the place...called Armageddon (Revelation 16:16).

Through the antichrist, Armageddon will be Satan's last stand against the Jewish people. With fierce hatred, he'll try to wipe them out. Armageddon will not be a battle, but a campaign with eight phases:

1. Demonic forces and the antichrist will gather "the kings of the whole world, to assemble them for battle...at the place... called Armageddon" (Revelation 16:14, 16).

2. While these forces are getting prepared, God will bring judgment against Babylon through a military coalition (Jeremiah 50:13-14, 23, 25, 40; Revelation 18).

3. The swift destruction of Babylon will enrage the antichrist, who will then lead the world's armies to go south and attack Jerusalem (Zechariah 12:1-3; 14:2).

4. After demolishing Jerusalem, the antichrist will pursue the remnant of Jews who earlier fled to Bozrah and went into hiding (Matthew 24:15-21; Revelation 12:6, 14).

5. As the remnant is threatened, a spiritual awakening will occur. The Jews will cry out for their Messiah to save them (Zechariah 12:10; Romans 11:25-26).

6. Christ will first go to Bozrah to protect the remnant (Isaiah 34:1-7).

7. Then the Lord will slay the antichrist and his armies (Revelation 14:19-20; 19:11-16).

8. Finally, Christ will stand triumphant on the Mount of Olives, which will split (Zechariah 14:3-4; Revelation 16:17-21).

When the armies of heaven and earth clash, Christ's victory will be instant and Satan's annihilation complete. With the perfect fulfillment of every single prophecy about Christ's second coming, we will witness one of the mightiest displays of God's majestic sovereignty ever.

FROM CROSS TO CROWNS

Salvation and glory and power belong to our God (Revelation 19:1).

At His first coming, Jesus came quietly as a baby wearing swaddling clothes. He was born to parents of lowly stature, surrounded by animals and pastures. Very few were aware of His arrival. He was of humble circumstances, grew up in obscurity, and during His ministry, had no place to lay His head.

Jesus came not to be served, but to serve. He came in peace to bring the good news of salvation. He came to die for His enemies, suffering greatly while He was nailed to a cross. As Philippians 2:7-8 says, He "emptied himself, by taking the form of a servant, being born in the likeness of men...he humbled himself by becoming obedient to the point of death, even death on a cross." *This was Jesus as Savior.*

At His second coming, Jesus will come triumphantly on the clouds, with His power and majesty on full display. Every eye will see Him. He will wear many crowns and be followed by countless numbers of heavenly hosts and glorified believers.

When Christ comes as King of kings and Lord of lords, He will do so in war to pour out judgment on His enemies. He will then rule from David's throne and receive worship from the peoples of every nation. As Philippians 2:9-10 says, "God has highly exalted him and bestowed on him the name that is above every name, so that at the name of Jesus every knee should bow, in heaven and on earth and under the earth." *This is Jesus as Sovereign.*

God's perfect plan called for Christ's first and second comings to have distinct purposes. As Savior, He came to make it possible for us to return to Him. As Sovereign, He will come to establish His kingdom, in which we will dwell with Him forever. Through both comings, Jesus makes clear just how greatly He loves us.

FAITHFUL AND TRUE

Behold, a white horse! The one sitting on it is
called Faithful and True (Revelation 19:11).

If there is any one title that Jesus has proven Himself worthy of, it is *Faithful and True*. Clearly, He has proven Himself worthy of *every* title and name ascribed to Him in Scripture. But in terms of what He has done and continues to do on our behalf, this title should be especially dear to us.

He is Faithful. Jesus is entirely trustworthy. He does what He says He will do; He fulfills His every role and promise. While on earth, He was faithful to do the Father's will, which included going to the cross, as dreadful as that was. He was faithful to His disciples even when they weren't faithful to Him. For us, He is a faithful shepherd who cares for every one of His sheep. He says, "I am with you always, to the end of the age" (Matthew 28:20). He is our constant intercessor, and He assures that our salvation is eternally secure. He will keep His promise to come and take us to Himself, that where He is, we will be also (John 14:3). We can trust that He will keep every promise about our eternal destiny and heavenly inheritance.

There is no one who is more faithful.

He is True. The meaning of "True" here is rich. Jesus is inherently true, He is the truth, and everything He speaks is true. He came into the world "to bear witness to the truth" (John 18:37)—to proclaim what is true about God, man, sin, salvation, and more. Christ is true in the sense that He is the standard of truth, and He is reliable.

There is no one who is more true.

In the times when you find yourself in need of guidance or help, turn to the one whose name is Faithful and True. He who is trustworthy and truthful has promised to walk alongside and care for you. You will find no better hands in which to be upheld and stay secure.

AT LAST, THE SECOND COMING!

In righteousness he judges and makes war (Revelation 19:11).

The moment that every prophet and writer of Scripture, every Old and New Testament saint, and every one of the heavenly hosts has longed for has finally arrived. Every person and being who has witnessed and experienced the wretched effects of sin and yearned for justice to be done and for righteousness to be restored has waited for this. The most eagerly anticipated event of all time, the second coming of Christ, is finally about to take place. The door of heaven has opened, and ready to descend to earth in all His might and splendor and fury is the Lord Jesus Christ.

Ever since Eden, God has directed all human history to this pivotal point. Revelation 19:11-16 portrays Christ as the almighty judge whose wrath cannot be evaded and whose authority is all-encompassing. With righteous anger He will charge into battle against massive, hostile armies led by Satan and the antichrist. All who took part in the rapture will descend with Him, "arrayed in fine linen, white and pure...following him on white horses" (verse 14).

From our Lord's mouth will come a sharp sword. By the power of His words alone, He will slay all His enemies. The carnage will be brutal. The antichrist and false prophet will be cast into the lake of fire, and Satan bound in an abyss. Then the King of kings and Lord of lords will ascend His throne in Jerusalem and establish His kingdom rule over all the earth.

It is impossible to overstate how spectacular and thrilling Christ's second coming will be. The transition from curse to blessing, darkness to light, lawlessness to righteousness, suffering to glory will bring about an extraordinary transformation. With Christ in His rightful place as King, heaven will truly come to earth. Our awareness of what our Lord's return will mean to us, to fellow believers, and to this world should stir within us an always-growing anticipation and love for Him. May our hearts be filled with excitement even now!

KING OF KINGS AND LORD OF LORDS

On his robe and on his thigh he has a name written, King
of kings and Lord of lords (Revelation 19:16).

As the King of kings and Lord of lords, Christ is supreme over all kings and lords. What makes Him so supreme? His absolute and divine perfection.

In contrast, the kings and rulers of this world are imperfect. That's because they are humans incapacitated by sin. Because of their fallen and finite condition, they are destined to make mistakes and disappoint us. As mortal beings, they rise and fall; they come and go. Inevitably their power comes to an end, so they cannot guarantee what the future holds. The best of what human leaders can offer is temporary and flawed. As a result, their subjects live in a state of instability and uncertainty.

The absolute perfection manifest by the King of kings and Lord of lords applies to every single one of His attributes. He possesses perfect holiness, perfect power, perfect knowledge, perfect wisdom, perfect love, perfect grace, perfect mercy, perfect faithfulness, perfect justice, and more. He is perfectly glorious, infinite, transcendent, and eternal.

In every way, our Lord is supreme. His counsel and rule will stand. His kingdom will endure forever. And He will provide His subjects with their every need and fulfill them with every blessing imaginable.

The Lord Jesus Christ is infinitely worthy of the title King of kings and Lord of lords. In eternity, we will never tire of praising and acknowledging His preeminence. We will never fully search out the height or depth or breadth of His greatness and majesty.

In the moment we place our faith and trust in Christ, we become the subjects of an eternally perfect King and are destined for His eternally perfect kingdom. Wonder of wonders!

CHRIST'S 1,000-YEAR KINGDOM ON EARTH

They will reign with him for a thousand years (Revelation 20:6).

No human kingdom has ever lasted. Every single one has collapsed or will. One reason is that Satan is "the ruler of this world" (John 14:30). He will always stir up strife—and wars—between people. Another reason is that all people are sinners, and among their behaviors are "enmity, strife, jealousy, fits of anger, rivalries, dissensions, [and] divisions" (Galatians 5:20). Not until the Prince of Peace comes to set up His earthly kingdom—which, at the start, will be inhabited only by Jewish and Gentile believers—will there be true peace and a kingdom that lasts.

Six times in the opening of Revelation 20, we are told this kingdom will last for 1,000 years. The Greek term for "a thousand" is *chilioi*, which became *millennium* when the Bible was translated into Latin. This is why Christ's 1,000-year reign is called the millennial kingdom.

The believers on earth who manage to survive the tribulation will enter this kingdom in their unglorified bodies. This means they will be able to have children who populate this kingdom (Isaiah 65:23). In contrast, raptured believers, as well as the Old Testament saints who are raised up at the beginning of the millennium (Daniel 12:1-2), will enter with glorified bodies and not have children. They will reign with Christ (Luke 22:30; Revelation 5:10; 20:4). Israel will be restored, a millennial temple will be built, and Christ will reign from David's throne.

The paradise lost in Eden will be restored in the millennial kingdom. It is this kingdom we look forward to when we pray, "Your kingdom come." It is this kingdom the prophet Isaiah had in view when he said the government would be on Christ's shoulders, and "of the increase of his government and of peace there will be no end" (Isaiah 9:6-7).

The millennial kingdom will prove that only Christ can create heaven on earth. Only He can replace this world's endless cycles of human failure with blessings that will never cease.

ISRAEL'S RETURN TO GLORY

You shall be my people, and I will be your God (Ezekiel 36:28).

The Old Testament prophets who warned rebellious Israel of coming judgment also spoke of a future day when God would fully restore Israel. They gave prophecies about Israel's return to glory—prophecies that looked ahead to the millennial kingdom. They said a time would come when Israel is "the head and not the tail" of all the nations (Deuteronomy 28:13).

All through the Old Testament, God promised to make Israel a great nation again. He will fulfill that promise during the millennial kingdom (see Isaiah 2:2-4; 65:18-23; Jeremiah 31:31-37; Ezekiel 34:25-29). In that day, the world will recognize the Holy Land belongs to Israel. No longer will the nations battle Israel, nor will antisemitism exist. Instead, people everywhere will revere the Jewish people. The prophet Zechariah said that during this time, "Ten men from the nations of every tongue shall take hold of the robe of a Jew, saying, 'Let us go with you, for we have heard that God is with you'" (Zechariah 8:23).

The Messiah will rule the entire world from the temple in Jerusalem (Ezekiel 43:7). And the Jewish people will prosper and dwell in peace. God promises to them, "You shall be my people, and I will be your God" (Ezekiel 36:28).

During the millennium, God will put on display His power to transform the fallen human heart. To Israel, He promised, "A new heart also will I give you, and a new spirit will I put within you" (Ezekiel 36:26). By grace, God will change Gentile hearts as well: "Many peoples and strong nations shall come to seek the LORD" (Zechariah 8:22).

It is God's amazing grace that will bring about Israel's return to glory and the world's eagerness to worship Him during the millennial kingdom. He will bring about all the wonders we experience during that incredible age, and to Him must go all the credit, praise, and adoration.

LIFE DURING THE MILLENNIAL KINGDOM

In you all the families of the earth shall be blessed (Genesis 12:3).

When God promised Abraham that He would make Israel a great nation, He also said that through Israel, "all the families of the earth shall be blessed" (Genesis 12:3). Primarily, this prophecy pointed to the blessing that would come when the Savior, who would be born through Israel, would make salvation possible at the cross. But this prophecy also points to the blessings the entire world will experience when Jesus rules during the millennial kingdom. Christ will reign as the ideal King, and He will provide for us an ideal kingdom:

- There will be no more war (Isaiah 2:4).

- People who are still in their mortal bodies will live very long lives (Isaiah 65:20).

- Illnesses and disease will not exist (Isaiah 33:24).

- Deserts will bloom (Isaiah 30:23-24; 35:1).

- The lamb and the lion will live in harmony (Isaiah 11:6-7).

- Christ's government will bring peace, justice, and righteousness (Isaiah 9:6-7).

When God called Israel as His chosen nation, His ultimate purpose was to fill the earth with blessings. Through Israel would be born a Messiah who, at His first coming, would bring the blessing of salvation. Then at His second coming, Christ will bring many more blessings that will be experienced by all who live in His kingdom ruled by perfect wisdom, love, and power.

The millennial kingdom will be a very different world from the one we live in now. As a perfect King, Christ will run a perfect government. We who are glorified will rule alongside our Lord and minister with Him to the unglorified. We will have more blessings than we can count—with the greatest one being the privilege of serving the King of kings and Lord of lords Himself.

WHAT IS THE PURPOSE OF
THE MILLENNIAL KINGDOM?

The LORD will be king over all the earth (Zechariah 14:9).

As we explore what the Bible says about the millennial kingdom, we cannot help but wonder: What is the point of Christ's 1,000-year kingdom on earth? After the second coming, why doesn't God just take all of us directly to heaven and eternity? Here are the reasons:

To fulfill God's agenda for all of history. Christ's rule on earth is the final step in God's plans to bless the world through Israel (Genesis 12:1-3; 17:6), place a forever ruler on David's throne (2 Samuel 7:16), and redeem a people and kingdom for Himself (Revelation 5:9-16).

To give Jesus what is rightfully His. After Jesus breaks the seven seals on the scroll, He will have dominion over all the earth (Psalm 2:7-8; Hebrews 1:1-2).

To fulfill God's promise that David's throne will endure forever (2 Samuel 7:10-17).

To fulfill the entirety of God's land promise to Israel. Israel has never had full possession of the land God gave to them (see the borders described in Genesis 15:18 and Numbers 34:7-9). This land was to belong to Abraham and his descendants "forever" (Genesis 13:14-15).

To fulfill God's promise to restore Israel and make her great (Isaiah 62:1-12).

To reward believers for their faithful service (Matthew 16:27; 25:14-30).

To prove that even in ideal conditions, fallen people will still rebel against God. At the end of the millennium, Satan will be released from the abyss and gather many people for one last rebellion. Even people who live under a perfect King in an ideal kingdom will reject God if they haven't had the change of heart that comes from saving faith in Christ (Revelation 20:7-9).

Through the millennium, God will fulfill many prophetic promises. In the times when we don't fully understand God's plans, we can rest in the truth that they are always perfect, rejoice that they will achieve His wise purposes, and know that they will be carried out to completion.

ONE MORE INSURRECTION

When the thousand years are ended, Satan…will come out to deceive the nations…to gather them for battle (Revelation 20:7-8).

All through history, Satan has fiercely hated Christ. Before the cross, he repeatedly attempted to destroy the Jewish people and prevent the cross from happening. Since the cross, he has tried to wipe out the Jews and prevent Israel from becoming a nation again, in the deluded hope that somehow, he might prevent Christ's return. And even after his 1,000-year imprisonment during Christ's earthly kingdom, he will once again attempt an insurrection against the Lord.

When Satan is released, he will "deceive the nations," and his followers will number "like the sand of the sea" (Revelation 20:7-8). Where will he find all these rebels?

We know from 1 Thessalonians 4:16-17 that all living Christians on the earth will be raptured *before* the tribulation. We also know from Revelation 20:4 that believers who are killed *during* the tribulation will be resurrected at Christ's return. But there will also be believers on earth who survive to the end of the tribulation. They won't be resurrected. Instead, they will enter Christ's millennial kingdom in their unglorified bodies. This means they'll be able to have children. It is these children—and their descendants—who will repopulate the earth. Those who reject Christ's authority will join sides with Satan for this final revolt. The attack will fail. Fire will come down from heaven and consume them all (verse 9).

Why will God allow this? By permitting Satan's final revolt, God will show that apart from saving faith in Christ, no person can achieve righteousness. Everyone who is born during the millennium will be a sinner by nature who needs a Savior—even though they appear to be good and live in an ideal environment. This rebellion will unveil the true state of people's hearts and will prove the necessity of receiving Christ as Savior for the heart to truly change.

FINAL JUDGMENT FOR UNBELIEVERS

*I saw the dead, great and small, standing before
the throne (Revelation 20:12).*

One of the most tragic scenes in the Bible appears in Revelation 20:11-15. Here, at the end of the millennial kingdom, we see a massive gathering of every unbeliever who has ever lived: "I saw the dead, great and small, standing before the throne…And the dead were judged by what was written in the books, according to what they had done."

Because all Old and New Testament saints will have already been resurrected, we know every person standing before the great white throne will be an unbeliever. Face to face with Christ the Judge, they will be stricken with dread. They will know the fate that awaits them. Every deed ever committed by them will have been recorded "in the books." Nothing will remain secret—not a single thought or motive. "Great and small" will be here; no one will evade scrutiny. Nor will anyone be able to change their mind. As Hebrews 9:27 says, "It is appointed for man to die once, and after that comes judgment."

The verdict given at the great white throne judgment will be final: "If anyone's name was not found written in the book of life, he was thrown into the lake of fire." Matthew 25:46 says they will "go away into eternal punishment." The word "eternal" used along with "punishment" is the same word used to speak of eternal life in that same verse. They will be in hell forever.

In the Bible, Jesus talked about hell more than anyone else. He warned it is a real place of eternal torment and outer darkness, separated from all else by an impassible chasm. He was direct with people about hell because of how greatly He sorrowed over the lost. Are we willing to be forthright as well? That's what true compassion does—it is willing to speak on the uncomfortable topic of hell so that people see their need for a Savior.

FROM TIME INTO ETERNITY

Then I saw a new heaven and a new earth (Revelation 21:1).

In Revelation 21:1, an incredible transition takes place in John's vision of what is to come: We are taken across the threshold from time into eternity.

Our introduction to eternity will be an exhilarating experience unlike any we've ever known. Imagine trying to process all that is new and different because we've gone from a finite existence into an infinite one. Having been locked into the realm of time all our lives, even during the millennial kingdom, our first steps into eternity are sure to be an explosion of thrilling discoveries and sensations.

The joys of this new experience will be all the more heightened by the fact the old earth and heaven are no more, and God has brought about a new earth and heaven. For the first time ever, we will experience true paradise. At last, what was lost in Eden will have been regained. What we've only read about in the first two chapters of Genesis will become reality for us forever!

Not only will Satan have been entirely and eternally banished, but every last trace of sin as well. Every iota of what made our earthly existence frustrating and painful will be gone.

While the millennial kingdom will have been heavenly, the fact it will include mortals who can still choose to sin means there will be aspects of imperfection around us even as our perfect Lord rules over the earth. But in eternity, there will be no imperfections. Perfection will be absolute.

Only an infinitely transcendent and almighty God could make eternity all that it will be. Anytime we ponder the wonders of eternity, we are sure to be inspired toward a higher view of God. He is truly greater than we will ever be able to fathom or express!

OUR NEW HOME

I saw the holy city, new Jerusalem, coming down
out of heaven from God (Revelation 21:2).

A long with the new heaven and earth, God will give us a new home—the new Jerusalem, a holy city that will come down from heaven. This will be a *real* city that we inhabit in our glorified bodies, a *holy* city in which there is no sin, and a *new* city that comes from God Himself. This brings to mind Jesus' words in John 14:2, where He said He was leaving earth "to prepare a place" for us in heaven. We are very much on Christ's mind as He readies a future dwelling for His bride, the church.

The new Jerusalem will be spectacular, "having the glory of God, its radiance like a most rare jewel" (Revelation 21:11). Its qualities will reflect all that God is. His character will be visibly on display in its features. The city will be ablaze with His light, having "no need of sun or moon to shine on it, for the glory of God gives it light" (verse 23). It will be massive as well, with dimensions measuring about 1,500 miles by 1,500 miles by 1,500 miles.

Adding to the splendor of our new home will be high walls that include 12 gates inscribed with the names of the 12 tribes, and 12 foundations inscribed with the names of the apostles. Angels will stand at the gates, and each gate will be a single pearl.

The best part of all? "Behold, the dwelling place of God is with man. He will dwell with them, and they will be his people, and God himself will be with them as their God" (verse 3). We will live in God's very presence!

In the new Jerusalem, we will enjoy direct and ongoing fellowship with God. Never again will our hearts ache from the separation caused by sin. Prayers voicing endless needs will be replaced by praises voicing endless adoration. In God's presence, we'll be very much at home.

EVERY TEAR GONE

He will wipe away every tear from their eyes, and death shall be
no more, neither shall there be mourning, nor crying, nor pain
anymore, for the former things have passed away (Revelation 21:4).

One way we can grow in our appreciation for our new home is to recognize all that will be missing from it. Because we live in a fallen world, we cannot avoid grief, pain, trials, and loss. These are our constant companions—never welcome, and always wearying.

Sin is the reason all of us struggle with the works of the flesh, including "sexual immorality, impurity, sensuality, idolatry, sorcery, enmity, strife, jealousy, fits of anger, rivalries, dissensions, divisions, envy, drunkenness, orgies, and things like these" (Galatians 5:19-21). None of these will enter the new Jerusalem. Instead, all we will ever know is "love, joy, peace, patience, kindness, goodness, faithfulness, gentleness, self-control" (verses 22-23).

With the curse also came decay, illness, and death. These enemies are the reason we are frequently acquainted with pain, grief, and sorrow, all of which can end up fostering anger, despair, loneliness, and more. Sin contaminates everything, leaving no part of our lives untouched. But sin and its repercussions will no longer exist in the new heaven and new earth.

In eternity, there will be no need for legal systems, law enforcement, militaries, or medical care. Courts, prisons, weapons, hospitals, and cemeteries will be no more.

When we arrive in our heavenly home, God will "wipe away every tear" from our eyes (Revelation 21:4). The singular phrase "*every* tear" speaks of God's deep compassion for specific and personal hurts. No tear will go unwiped; every reason for grief and sorrow will vanish. Not a single effect of sin will follow us into eternity, making heaven truly heaven.

WHAT ABOUT LOVED ONES WHO DON'T MAKE IT TO HEAVEN?

He will wipe away every tear from their eyes...neither
shall there be mourning (Revelation 21:4).

Will we remember loved ones who don't make it to heaven? This is one of the more difficult questions that Christians grapple with about eternity. When they read about how there will be no crying nor mourning in heaven, they wonder: *Does the wiping away of our tears also mean the wiping away of our memories? Will we forget our loved ones who ended up in hell?*

Revelation 21:4 simply tells us that sin and its effects—which cause us agony and pain—will not follow us into heaven. It doesn't comment on what will happen to our memories. Though Scripture doesn't give us a clear-cut answer, here's what we do know: In Luke 16, when the rich man died and went to Hades, he remembered his brothers who were still alive on earth. Other Bible passages indicate we will know and recognize one another in heaven (2 Samuel 12:22-23; Matthew 8:11; 17:1-3; 1 Thessalonians 4:13-18). In Revelation 5:11-12, the fact all of heaven praises Christ as "the lamb who was slain" seems to indicate that when we're in heaven, we will remember what we were saved from. For us to remember Him as the Lamb of God who died for our sins may mean we'll remember the past to some extent. How much, we don't know.

As we struggle with whether we will remember loved ones who don't make it to heaven, we can find comfort in these four truths: God loves the lost more than we do (2 Peter 3:9); we can trust His character—there is no one more just and loving and righteous than He; because we are imperfect, we don't have the perfect perspective that He does; and those who end up in hell will know they belong there. If we do remember lost loved ones who don't make it to heaven, we can rest assured that will not diminish in any way the joys and blessings we experience in heaven. That is what God promises us when He says there will be no more tears in eternity.

LIFE ABUNDANT

*The angel showed me the river of the water of life...also, on
either side of the river, the tree of life (Revelation 22:1-2).*

B ecause of sin, death casts a foreboding shadow on the horizon of
every person's life. It cannot be avoided. In eternity, however, we
will dwell with the giver and sustainer of life, and two prominent features of our new home will be the water of life and the tree of life. Our
entire existence will be defined by life.

The water of life will flow unceasingly from God's throne. While we
have good reason to believe this will be a literal river, this water may
also symbolize God's perpetual provision of spiritual life and blessing to
every one of us. That the river flows continuously is fitting, for in eternity, we will enjoy life everlasting.

The tree of life will line the banks of the river, and bear fruit at all
times. There will be no dormant season, no time at which life pauses
even momentarily. The trees' 12 kinds of fruit are an indicator of the
amazing variety of produce God will supply to us.

Both the constant flow of the river and the ongoing fruitfulness of
the trees represent the bountiful provisions we will experience in eternity.
Presently while we are on earth, we are already able to experience God's
generosity in many ways. Second Corinthians 9:8 says it well: "God is
able to make *all* grace abound to you, so that having *all* sufficiency in
all things at *all* times, you may abound in *every* good work."

Jesus came to earth so that we "may have life and have it abundantly"
(John 10:10). Presently, we are already enjoying spiritual and eternal life.
Someday, our physical bodies will be raised up and transformed as well.
And when we enter eternity, we will experience abundant life in all its
fullness forever.

"I AM COMING SOON"

Behold, I am coming soon (Revelation 22:7).

I n the final chapter of the book of Revelation, Jesus repeats the following prophecy three times:

- "Behold, I am coming soon" (verse 7).
- "Behold, I am coming soon" (verse 12).
- "Surely I am coming soon" (verse 20).

Christ prefaced all three statements with "Behold" and "Surely." This was an important announcement, and He wanted to both encourage and exhort us. He wanted to assure us He truly *will* come. And He wanted us to be ready, for He could come at any time.

Even though these words were spoken nearly 2,000 years ago, we shouldn't wonder if perhaps Jesus might not come after all. When the Lord delays, it is because He "is patient...not wishing that any should perish, but that all should reach repentance" (2 Peter 3:9). Also, the Messiah's "soon" is different than our "soon."

Jesus repeated this prophecy to alert us His coming is imminent. It can happen at any time, for there are no prophecies that need to be fulfilled before the rapture. Also, He wanted believers in every era to be ready. Paul urged the believers of his day to be "waiting for the blessed hope, the appearing of the glory of our great God and Savior Christ Jesus" (Titus 2:13). John urged his readers, "Abide in Him, so that when He appears we may have confidence" (1 John 2:28). Just as the early believers lived in anticipation of the rapture, so should we.

In the final chapter of the Bible, our Lord had good reason for His threefold repetition of "I am coming soon." These are His closing words in His revelation of Himself to us. He has promised He will return, and He wants us to be ready. The fact He could rapture us at any time should serve as a powerful motivator for us to live with a constant sense of expectancy.

CHRIST'S GRACE WILL
CARRY YOU TO ETERNITY

The grace of the Lord Jesus be with all (Revelation 22:21).

The book of Revelation begins and ends with wishes of grace for its readers. Though the book describes the pouring out of God's wrath during the tribulation, we never want to lose sight of the truth that, above all, Jesus is a Lord of grace. He came to save the lost. Christ's grace is evident in all the prophecies about Him from Genesis to Revelation. We see His grace expressed in the first messianic prophecy ever given, in Genesis 3:15, on that dark day when sin entered the world. Immediately, the first couple was given the promise of a Savior who would crush Satan and make it possible for them to return to God. As we continue onward in God's Word, we learn these wonderful truths about our Lord's never-ending grace:

His grace is available to everyone. The extent of our Lord's grace is especially evident in Genesis 12:3, which tells us that through Abraham's descendants "all the families of the earth shall be blessed." From the people of Israel would come a Savior whose grace would be offered to all the world.

His grace is given to us freely. Isaiah 55:1 says, "Come, everyone who thirsts, come to the waters; and he who has no money, come, buy and eat! Come, buy wine and milk without money and without price." The gift of eternal life is free to those who ask for it (Romans 6:23).

His grace is more than sufficient. When Paul prayed to God in a time of great need, the Lord said, "My grace is sufficient for you" (2 Corinthians 12:9). God's grace is higher, deeper, and greater than anything we will ever face. It is impossible for us to exhaust His grace.

His grace is eternal. The grace you experience at salvation is just the beginning. Christ's grace will sustain and carry you to eternity. As Psalm 23:6 says, "Surely goodness and mercy shall follow me all the days of my life, and I shall dwell in the house of the LORD forever."

COME, LORD JESUS!

Amen. Come, Lord Jesus! (Revelation 22:20).

How glorious and appropriate it is that Jesus' last words in the Bible are, "Surely I am coming soon" (Revelation 22:20). He clearly wants us to remember that He has promised to come! And we know He is looking forward to calling us home someday in the rapture because of the tremendous affection He conveyed when He said, "If I go and prepare a place for you, I will come again and will take you to myself, that where I am you may be also" (John 14:3). The Old Testament ended sadly with a curse, and the New Testament ends triumphantly with a promise of blessing. Christ has said that He will return, that He will establish His kingdom, and that we will dwell with Him for all of eternity.

Three times in Revelation 22, Jesus said He is coming soon. After His third declaration, the apostle John was so excited that he wrote, "Amen. Come, Lord Jesus!" His eagerness leaps off the page, and it is a contagious enthusiasm meant to inspire all who read the Bible's final words.

The word "Amen" means "so be it." When we say, "Amen" alongside John, we are agreeing with His response to Jesus' promise "I am coming soon." John couldn't hold back. So ecstatic was he that he exclaimed, "Amen—may it be so!" John was thrilled by Christ's promise to come again, and we should be too.

Every prophecy about Christ's second coming is a call for us to look to the future with anticipation. All through the Bible, God has included reminders for us that this temporary and sin-infested world will be replaced by a glorious and eternal home. As believers, we have been and will be raised with Christ, so we should seek the things that are above. With every day that goes by, may we become increasingly excited and joyful because His return is one day nearer.

NOTES

1. Kenneth S. Wuest, *The New Testament: An Expanded Translation* (Grand Rapids: Wm. B. Erdmans, 1994), Ephesians 5:16-21.

2. *The Complete Works of Thomas Brookes,* Vol. VI (Edinburgh: James Nichol, 1867), 382-383.

3. At first glance, Daniel 12:2 appears to teach a simultaneous resurrection of the righteous and unrighteous, which does not accord with other passages that teach separate resurrections for believers and unbelievers. However, the literal text of Daniel 12:2 is not advocating a simultaneous resurrection. For an excellent explanation of this, which is supported by John Walvoord and Hebrew scholars S.P. Tregelles, Nathaniel West, and S.R. Driver, see John F. Walvoord, "Contemporary Interpretative Problems: The Resurrection of Israel," *John F. Walvoord,* https://walvoord.com/article/109. See the section titled "The Resurrection of Israel in Daniel."

4. Thomas D. Ice, "Modern Israel's Right to the Land," *Scholar's Crossing* (Lynchburg, VA: Liberty University, May 2009), 2.

5. John Phillips wrote, "This psalm contains thirty-three distinct prophecies which were fulfilled at Calvary." *Exploring the Psalms: Volume One Psalms 1-88* (Neptune, NJ: Loizeaux Brothers, 1988), 169.

6. John MacArthur, *The MacArthur Study Bible* (Nashville, TN: Thomas Nelson, 1997), 783, note for Psalm 45:10-15.

7. See Matthew 27:34, 48; Mark 15:23, 36; Luke 23:36; John 19:29; Romans 11:9-10.

8. Because God is all-knowing, He does not forget our sins, but He does choose to not remember them anymore (Isaiah 43:25; Hebrews 8:12).

9. Isaac Watts, "When I Survey the Wondrous Cross," 1707.

10. For a more detailed explanation about how we know the identity of the nations in Ezekiel 38:2-6, see pages 270-273 in my book *Foreshadows* (Eugene, OR: Harvest House, 2022).

11. Scripture says the antichrist will *not* be revealed until after "the restrainer," the Holy Spirit, is taken out of the way (2 Thessalonians 2:6-8). That will happen when all Christians, who are indwelt by the Spirit, have been removed through the rapture, described in 1 Thessalonians 4:15-17. Once the Spirit is gone via the rapture, the antichrist's identity will become known.

12. To see the helpful calculations provided by scholars, see Tim LaHaye and Thomas Ice, *Charting the End Times* (Eugene, OR: Harvest House, 2001, 2021), 89 and *The Bible Knowledge Commentary: Old Testament*, eds. John F. Walvoord and Roy B. Zuck, gen. eds. (Colorado Springs, CO: David C. Cook, 1985), 1363.

13. C.H. Spurgeon, "God with Us," Metropolitan Tabernacle, December 26, 1875.

14. Some Bible commentators say there are seven parables, and others say eight.

15. Jesus' message about the end times is also recorded in Mark 13 and Luke 21.

16. One notable exception is when Stephen is put to death and sees Jesus "standing" at the right hand of God (Acts 7:55). We're not told why Christ stands, but among the reasons suggested is that (1) He was welcoming the church's first martyr, (2) He was standing as a witness in a heavenly court to make a plea on Stephen's behalf, or (3) He was getting ready to exercise judgment. This last option is in harmony with the reason Jesus stands in Revelation 5:6.

17. See, for example, Revelation 11:8, which clearly calls Jerusalem "the great city," which "symbolically is called Sodom and Egypt" because of the people's rebellion against God.

PRIMARY SCRIPTURE INDEX

*The passages listed below are the primary passage for each devotion in this book,
and do not include the passages that appear within the text of each devotion.*

MORE BIBLE PROPHECY RESOURCES
BY STEVE MILLER

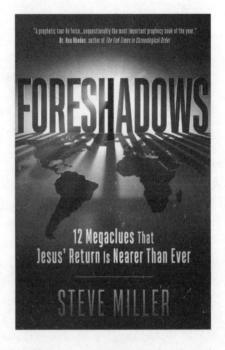

To learn more about Steve's book
Foreshadows: 12 Megaclues That Jesus' Return Is Nearer Than Ever,
or to follow Steve at the *Foreshadows Report* podcast,
go to stevemillerresources.com